Assessment in Music Education

Martin Fautley

MUSIC DEPARTMENT

OXFORD
UNIVERSITY PRESS

OXFORD
UNIVERSITY PRESS

Great Clarendon Street, Oxford OX2 6DP, England

198 Madison Avenue, New York, NY 10016, USA

Oxford University Press is a department of the University of Oxford.
If furthers the University's aim of excellence in research, scholarship,
and education by publishing worldwide in

Oxford New York

Auckland Cape Town Hong Kong Karachi
Kuala Lumpur Madrid Melbourne Mexico City
Nairobi New Delhi Shanghai Taipei Toronto

With offices in

Argentina Austria Brazil Chile Czech Republic France Greece
Guatemala Hungary Italy Japan Poland Portugal Singapore
South Korea Switzerland Thailand Turkey Ukraine Vietnam

Oxford is a registered trade mark of Oxford University Press in the
UK and in certain other countries

Chapters 1–17 © Martin Fautley 2010

Foreword © Mary James 2010

Martin Fautley and Mary James have asserted their right under the
Copyright, Designs and Patents Act, 1988, to be identified as Authors
of this Work

Database right Oxford University Press (maker)

First published 2010

British Library Cataloguing-in-Publication Data
Data available

Library of Congress Cataloging-in-Publication Data
Fautley, Martin.
    Assessment in music education / Martin Fautley.
        p. cm. — (Oxford music education series)
    ISBN 978-0-19-336289-5 (pbk.)
    1. School music—Instruction and study. 2. Music—Instruction and
study. 3. Effective teaching. 4. Grading and marking (Students) I. Title.
    MT1.F36 2010
    780.71 — dc22   2009041076

10 9 8 7 6 5 4 3

Typeset by RefineCatch Limited, Bungay, Suffolk
Printed in Great Britain by Ashford Colour Press Ltd

Foreword

The high stakes now attached to assessment in schools has made it one of the most hotly debated issues in education. In the face of political pressures for accountability based on ever more tightly prescribed quantitative measures, educators struggle to reassert the primacy of the principle that assessment should serve the interests of learners and learning. Part of the problem is that teachers are sometimes ill equipped to offer better alternatives to the frameworks handed down by government agencies. One reason is that while there is plenty of advice on general assessment principles, procedures and issues, and strong literatures on teaching in subject domains, these two areas are rarely brought together except in the traditional core academic subjects of science, mathematics, and national language. Yet it is precisely this articulation between assessment and the subject that creates the greatest challenges for practice.

In this book, Martin Fautley does a huge service for teachers, teacher educators, advisers, researchers, and indeed policy makers, who puzzle about what valid, reliable, manageable, and effective assessment should look like in music education. In order to do this he considers, but moves beyond, the usual assessment themes concerning purpose, quality, and form, to engage deeply with the nature of knowledge in music education, and especially the question of what makes it *musical* and how this can be evidenced. He deals in detail with the three key elements of the music curriculum—performing, composing, and listening—and explores the implications for assessment of knowing that, knowing how, knowing as acquaintance, and knowing values. He tackles head-on the especially tricky issue of progression and argues that rather than passively accept a single model of step-wise linear progression, teachers should use their intimate and sustained experience of pupils' learning to propose possible alternative models that better reflect reality.

While being deeply informed by current research and scholarship, Martin Fautley is also well aware of the practical constraints on busy music teachers who often have responsibilities beyond the classroom. For this reason his suggestions and examples of the way teachers can lightly integrate assessment into classroom practice, which also involves making music and learning music, will be particularly welcomed. And his jokes will be enjoyed.

Mary James, Associate Director of Research
University of Cambridge Faculty of Education

Acknowledgements

I am grateful to a number of people for their help—witting or unwitting—with the writing of this book, far more, in fact, than can be named here. I would, however, especially like to thank Mary James for getting me to ask better questions, and Ian Cross, for getting me to ask bigger questions! My colleagues in music education at Birmingham City University, Janet Hoskyns, Helen Coll, Ted Bunting, and Ian Axtell, have been very helpful in letting me get on with writing, and assisting me with some thorny problems. I am grateful to Janet for affording me thinking space, to Helen for her insights into musical thinking, to Ted for his deep understanding of improvisation, and to Ian for his useful 'But what about…' questions. Some of their ideas I have unashamedly stolen—sorry, but thanks! (Any inaccuracies, however, are entirely my own.) Also at BCU, I would like to thank Simon Spencer, for his patience and understanding, and Richard Hatcher, for his unerring ability to get straight to the heart of a problem when I was going 'all round the houses'. Thanks also to Philip Croydon and the team at OUP, for their unwavering help in the preparation of this book.

An important acknowledgement to make is to my pupils and students over the years, who have frequently asked me difficult questions, especially 'Why…?'. Music teachers too, whenever I visit schools, in particular those who are aggrieved with the state of assessment in music education—thank you for being cross, and sharing your cross-ness with me!

I wish to record a big 'thank you' to my family, who have allowed me to quietly disappear to get on with writing, through weekends and holidays, with a tolerant understanding.

Finally, I wish to thank the late Janet Mills, the series editor, who saw the early stages of this book before her untimely death. Almost the last converstion we had involved her asking me to put more jokes in. I have tried, Janet, but I'm not sure I've always succeeded!

About the author

Martin Fautley began his career as a music teacher, teaching in secondary schools in the Midlands (UK). He taught a broad spectrum of pupils, was director of a number of successful school musical ensembles, and ran a music centre, where he was in daily contact with instrumental learning. Following an in-service MA in education, he then returned to full-time study at Cambridge University, where his doctoral research into group composing, and the role that teacher assessment can play in developing it, bridged the education and music faculties. In 2007 Martin became Reader in Music Education at Birmingham City University, where he has written and published widely on matters concerning creativity and assessment (including, with J. Savage, *Assessment for Learning and Teaching in Secondary Schools,* 2008). He continues to undertake research into these key areas of education, and is a regular presenter at conferences.

Contents

List of abbreviations

A2	Advanced level 2
ABRSM	Associated Board of the Royal Schools of Music
AfL	assessment for learning
APP	assessing pupils' progress
ARG	Assessment Reform Group
AS	Advanced Supplementary
GCSE	General Certificate of Secondary Education
IEPs	individual education plans
KS	Key Stage
MAEA	music education as aesthetic education
MANA	Music Advisers' National Association
MI	multiple intelligences
MMCP	Manhattanville Music Curriculum Programme
NAME	National Assocation of Music Educators
NC	National Curriculum
PGs	primitive gestures
PLTS	personal learning and thinking skills
SEAL	social and emotional aspects of learning
TGAT	Task Group on Assessment and Testing
WCIVT	whole class instrumental and vocal tuition
ZPD	zone of proximal development

Chapter 1

Introduction to assessment in music education

Assessment is a key topic in education today. As a part of the debate concerning assessment and its role, those involved in the teaching and learning of music are having to address a wide variety of issues. Assessment in its broadest sense touches all areas of music education, yet the implications of more recent understandings of its role in teaching and learning have still to be felt in some quarters. There is a long tradition of assessment within music education, and in many ways, '. . . music has been the most assessed of disciplines, both in the school context and beyond' (Philpott 2007: 210). However, it could be argued that it is only a specific aspect of music which has traditionally been assessed, namely performance, and that within this only a limited range of instrumental skills have been looked at. For this reason it is safe to say that practices which may have been historically appropriate are now being questioned, and at the same time newer ideas and techniques are finding their way into the daily activities of classroom music and instrumental teachers. Views concerning assessment in music education are hotly debated. These range from those who say assessment is impossible, and should not even be attempted, to those who want to establish an encyclopaedic series of competencies which need to be measured. In between these extremes are many varying shades of opinion, including those who say that it is only the personal response which matters, and those who affirm that technical issues are the only assessable thing.

It is against this constantly changing and complex background that this book was conceived. Its purpose is to investigate assessment from a variety of perspectives concerned with learning and teaching in music. During the course of this book a number of topics of interest to classroom teachers, peripatetic instrumental teachers, studio music teachers, trainee teachers, researchers, legislators, pupils, parents, and many others, will be investigated, discussed, analysed, and commented upon.

We know that for many involved in the teaching and learning of music, assessment is thought of as problematic. 'Whether it is in teaching or research communities there always seems to be considerable unease about the how and why of musical assessment. Formative or summative, process or product, quantitative or qualitative, teacher or pupil based, the apparent opposites represent a picture of uncertainty' (Savage 2002: 38). And, as Keith Swanwick observes, '. . . why is it that assessment in education and especially in the arts appears to be problematic? It is when we find ourselves moving away from informal assessment that things start to get tricky. For assessment ranges from making instantaneous choices in our daily life to the relative formality of analytical reporting' (Swanwick 1999: 71).

It is the proliferation of what Savage refers to as 'apparent opposites' which causes problems for music education practitioners, rightly concerned as they are with developing the musical learning of their own pupils. To try to get beneath the surface of this problem, let us begin by thinking about what variety of constructs, concepts, and activities are encompassed by the terminology *assessment*.

What is assessment?

The word 'assessment' carries with it a number of different shades of meaning. There is some debate as to the origin of the word itself. The Oxford English Dictionary traces it from the Latin *ad sedere*—to sit beside—where it was originally a term used in jurisprudence for one who advised a judge, often with relation to fines or levies. Turning to education, most meanings of assessment are along the lines of '. . . to judge the extent of students' learning' (Freeman & Lewis 1998: 9). 'To judge' involves making an informed evaluation of a situation, and this is an action which places one person literally in judgement over another. It is this complex relationship which forms the heart of many of the discussions in this book.

There is a common, but erroneous, belief that assessment is synonymous with marking and grading. Allied to this notion, another error is to believe that only formalized tests or testing regimes count as assessment. There are many reasons why formal assessments take place, ranging from external certification of achievement, via the imperative of teachers having to provide schools with assessment data, to teachers using the results of in-class tests to develop learning programmes. These formal assessments represent specific moments in time during the teaching and learning process. One of the issues at stake here is that teachers in general, and music teachers in particular, have long viewed assessment as being a process external to their teaching. A potential cause for confusion which arises from viewing assessment as involving only marking and grading is that the meaning of the word 'assessment' becomes unnecessarily restricted, so that only external assessments assume any importance. This 'folk view' of assessment needs unpicking somewhat in order to try to undo its pervasive influence.

A folk view of assessment

The folk view of assessment is that it happens separately from a course of teaching or instruction, and represents a series of fixed points which demarcate the progression of a learner. This view of teaching, learning, and assessment can be represented diagrammatically as in Fig. 1.1.

In this way of thinking about assessment, it can be seen to *only* happen separated from teaching. This can be characterized as being the way that graded examinations in instrumental music have traditionally taken place. It is also the way in which, in the UK at least, some aspects of General Certificate of Secondary Education (GCSE), Advanced Supplementary (AS), Advanced (A2), and other externally organized examinations occur. A feature of a number of these forms of examination is that the assessment is not only separated from teaching, but also that it is undertaken by an unknown third party who has had little or no contact with teacher or learner either beforehand, or afterwards. This way of assessing learning in music detaches assessment from teaching, the learner from the learned, and the teacher from the taught. What it does is to prioritize such that the only thing that counts is performance at the appointed hour of the assessment itself. The learning process that has been gone through is subsumed within the presentation of that which has been learned.

Thinking of assessment as happening separately from teaching in the way represented in Fig. 1.1 can create problems for both teacher and pupils. Indeed, many view this way of thinking about assessment as needing attention: '. . . assessment and instruction are often conceived as curiously separate in both time and purpose' (Graue 1993: 291). This notion of formal assessment being 'curiously separate' is one which downplays other aspects of assessment, and has itself come to be challenged by many current views, and is discussed in more detail in later sections of this book.

A wider view of assessment

In comparison with the folk view of assessment, involving only formalized assessment routines, a contemporary counter viewpoint states that informal

Fig. 1.1 Teaching and assessment

assessments take place all the time, and form a constant background against which any teaching and learning encounter takes place. Viewed from this perspective, assessment becomes an essential and integral component of every lesson. Teachers make judgements all the time concerning what to do next, what topics to include, which pieces of music to perform, what starting points for composing are appropriate, and which pieces to listen to. As the lesson progresses the teacher also makes judgements as to how fast or slow certain aspects need to be worked, whether all, most, or some of the pupils have understood the learning objectives, whether certain specific pupils need more help with some aspects of the lesson, whether other specific pupils have thoroughly grasped the topic already and are ready to move on. All of these judgements are assessments. However, it is the case that all too often these informal judgements are not recognized by practitioners as being assessments: it seems that for many only formalized testing is important enough to carry the weight of this terminology. The important area of assessment for learning, with its focus on improving the learning process, is but one example that proves this narrow view is not the case.

The folk view of assessment carries with it the commonly heard phraseology employed by teachers 'I will be carrying out an assessment next lesson'. A side-effect of this folk view is to unintentionally downgrade teachers' judgements when compared with external 'curiously separate' assessments, yet it is the teacher's judgements which are essential to making progress in music. This downgrading can be seen to create a false dichotomy, as during the course of every lesson the teacher will be carrying out hundreds of informal assessment judgements necessary for her to help her pupils to progress, and for the lesson to proceed. The assessment judgements of teachers *do* matter, they are important to the successful development of every child in learning music, and, as a number of recent initiatives observe, every child matters.

Viewed from this altered stance, it becomes impossible to separate assessment from teaching. Indeed, as Swanwick observes '. . . to teach is to assess' (Swanwick 1988: 149). Considered in this way, assessment becomes an integral part of teaching and learning, perceptions shift '. . . so that it is used to help students learn and to improve instruction rather than being used only to rank students or to certify the end products of learning' (Shepard 2000: 31). This shift in perspective has the effect of moving assessment from its 'curiously separate' location as external to teaching, and has placed it as an integral component of the teaching process. This shift can be represented diagrammatically by redrawing Fig. 1.1 to include assessment within teaching, as in Fig. 1.2.

This altered perspective, where assessment is integral to teaching and learning, runs like an *idée fixe* through many of the subsequent sections of this book.

Fig. 1.2 Assessment within teaching

Assessment, recording, and reporting

Assessment, recording, and reporting, sometimes referred to as AR&R, are three different links in the chain of assessment events. It is important not to confuse these terminologies, as assessments do not solely exist in the recording of their marks. *Assessment* refers to the first link, the process of gathering evidence about something, and this includes a wide range of information gathering techniques: '. . . the term "assessment" refers to all those activities undertaken by teachers, and by their students in assessing themselves, which provide information to be used as feedback to modify the teaching and learning activities in which they are engaged' (Black & Wiliam 1998b). The term *recording* refers to the second link in the chain, the way in which information from assessments is notated, stored, and saved for future retrieval. The commonest form this takes is still the teacher's mark book, but there are, as we shall discuss in later sections, other alternatives for this. *Reporting* is a third link in the chain, and refers to the ways in which information gathered from assessments is promulgated. This can be in grades given to pupils, school reports, examination mark sheets, or many other more or less official forms of documentation. It is worthwhile to note that for some internal purposes, where only teacher and pupils are aware of comments, marks, and grades, that it might not occur formally at all.

Endnote

There are many aspects appertaining to Assessment as it occurs in teachers' daily practice. As well as those of formalized testing, and the more infrequent external assessment regimes, there are also the judgements made, and decisions taken during the course of every lesson. Investigating teaching and learning from the perspective of assessment requires thinking about what assessment is, and what is contained in a lesson or learning encounter in music. In order to begin to address this, the next chapter focuses on the terminologies which are employed when discussing assessment, and explores ways in which they can be of value to the music teacher.

Chapter 2

Clarifying terminologies: uses and purposes of assessment

Introduction

As we saw in Chapter 1, the role of assessment in music education is a contested area. The very word 'assessment' carries with it a great deal of baggage, and has different meanings for different people. This means that there are many understandings of what assessment is, and of what it should be. For the music teacher there are inevitably links to examinations and tests, and of considering the teaching of pupils to be akin to an obstacle race, with hurdles to jump over, and hoops to jump through. In order to begin to think about what assessment is, and what it could be, this chapter considers a number of aspects of assessment, introduces terminologies that will be employed throughout this book, outlines uses and purposes of assessment as applied to music education, and provides some suggestions for teachers to think about when working with their pupils.

Uses and purposes of assessment

The terminologies 'uses' and 'purposes' can be considered as being quite close in everyday English. In discussions concerning assessment, however, they have quite specific meanings, and it is appropriate to distinguish between them. In the UK, the Task Group on Assessment and Testing (TGAT) was formed in 1987 to look into the way in which the then new idea of a National Curriculum could be assessed. The Task Group produced a report (TGAT 1988) which placed a number of assessment terminologies into the wider public domain. In this report, TGAT described what they saw as being four *purposes* for assessment. These were:

- Summative: for the recording of the overall achievement of the student in a systematic way.

- Formative: so that the positive achievements of a pupil may be recognized and discussed and the appropriate next steps may be planned.

- Evaluative: by means of which some aspects of the work of a school, a local authority, or other discrete part of the education service can be assessed and/or reported upon.
- Diagnostic: through which learning difficulties may be scrutinized and classified so that appropriate remedial help and guidance can be provided. (From TGAT 1988, paragraph 23)

Each of these terminologies will be considered individually in more detail below. It is important to note that this list of purposes is not a taxonomy of assessment typologies, but a way to think about and label these things in a straightforward fashion.

Summative assessment

The purpose of summative assessment is to provide information which can be used to certify pupil achievement in some way:

... in the case of summative assessment there are various ways in which the information about student achievement at a certain time is used. These uses include: internal school tracking of students' progress; informing parents, students and the students' next teacher of what has been achieved; certification or accreditation of learning by an external body; and selection for employment or higher education. (Harlen 2005a: 208)

Music teachers will be very familiar with many aspects of summative assessment. The graded examinations of the Associated Board of the Royal Schools of Music (ABRSM) being examples of a common form of summative assessment, used to certify achievement at eight distinct grades. Another common experience is that of public examinations, such as the General Certificate of Secondary Education (GCSE), or Advanced Supplementary (AS) and A2 examinations. These are often referred to as 'high-stakes' assessments, as they are ones which can have a significant effect on the future of the pupil concerned. Summative assessment also occurs when the class teacher listens to a group of pupils perform pieces of music they have been rehearsing, and gives them, say, a mark out of ten for how well they did. In the UK, National Curriculum assessment (QCA 2007) involves allocation of one of nine levels (eight levels, and 'exceptional performance') for the overall achievement of a pupil, statutorily at the end of a key stage, and, increasingly, at other times too.

Harlen & James defined the characteristics of summative assessment like this:

- It takes place at certain intervals when achievement has to be reported
- It relates to progression in learning against public criteria
- The results for different pupils may be combined for various purposes because they are based on the same criteria

- It requires methods which are as reliable as possible without endangering validity
- It requires some quality assurance procedures
- It should be based on evidence from the full range of performance relevant to the criteria being used. (Harlen & James 1997: 373)

Summative assessment is concerned with measurement and certification of pupil achievement, and is essentially something which is 'done to' the students. There are times when summative assessment can appear all too easily to fall into the category of 'curiously separate' from instruction, but, as we shall see in later sections of this book, this need not always be the case.

Formative assessment

Formative assessment has also become known as *assessment for learning*, and although there are those who would argue that there are subtle differences between the two, in this book the terms will be used interchangeably throughout. Formative assessment happens where the purpose of assessment is to elicit information which will be of use to the pupil and the teacher in deciding what ought to be done next in order to develop learning. What this means is that, '. . . in order to serve a formative function, an assessment must yield evidence that, with appropriate construct-referenced interpretations, indicates the existence of a gap between actual and desired levels of performance, and suggests actions that are in fact successful in closing the gap' (Wiliam & Black 1996: 543). This is a long way from the 'curiously separate' notion of assessment and instruction described in Chapter 1. Unlike summative assessment, which is 'done to' pupils, formative assessment is 'done with' them: 'Both teachers and learners tend to prefer formative to summative assessment yet it has been the summative variety that has generally been imposed on schools by government agencies' (Fox 2005: 239).

Music teachers have long been using formative assessment as a key element of their work with pupils. Indeed, in the original guidance for teachers of all subjects it was a music lesson which was chosen to exemplify good formative assessment practice (DfES 2002, 2004a). To listen to a group of pupils working at a composing task and to suggest ways in which they could develop their work is to undertake formative assessment. Similarly reflecting on a lesson, and deciding that the pupils need more time to perform their pieces next lesson is to undertake formative assessment. Neither of these examples require written documentation of any sort, nor do they involve giving a grade to the pupils. In formative assessment the emphasis is on making judgements which will aid the pupils in their future learning requirements. The aim of helping pupils with their learning is to bring about a situation where the pupils make progress in moving from one stage to another, where understanding is effected, and where knowledge is obtained:

Formative assessment is that process of appraising, judging or evaluating students' work or performance and using this to shape and improve their competence. In everyday classroom terms this means teachers using their judgements of children's knowledge or understanding to feed back into the teaching process and to determine for individual children whether to re-explain the task/concept, to give further practise on it, or move on the next stage. (Tunstall & Gipps 1996: 389)

This notion of teachers using the results of their judgements to feed back into the teaching and learning process is an important component of formative assessment practice. What it also means is that 'knowing about pupils' existing ideas and skills, and recognising the point reached in development and the necessary next steps to take . . .' (Harlen & James 1997: 369) is fundamental to formative assessment, and is a key one for music teachers. However, it is not enough for the teacher simply to have identified what they feel the next steps needed are; they also need to share these with the pupils. This sharing process is referred to as 'feedback'.

Feedback

The notion of feedback is an important one in formative assessment. It involves a dialogue between teacher and pupils concerning what the pupils are doing at present, and what they need to do next. As the Assessment Reform Group (ARG) put it: 'Learners need information and guidance in order to plan the next steps in their learning. Teachers should: pinpoint the learner's strengths and advise on how to develop them; be clear and constructive about any weaknesses and how they might be addressed; provide opportunities for learners to improve upon their work' (Assessment Reform Group 2002).

In the process of music learning, this involves the teacher being involved in a series of stages along the learning route. Figure 2.1 depicts a graphical representation of this.

What Fig. 2.1 shows is a learning episode along the top, for example a group composing task at KS3. As the teacher moves from group to group in the classroom, she has a discussion with each group of pupils. This discussion centres on the work the group are doing at the moment, and what they might do to develop or improve their work in the future. This discussion gives feedback to the group, and they are able to use this information to develop their learning in the next stage of the work. In Fig. 2.1 each of these learning episodes is given a number. The diagram shows four such episodes in this example, but of

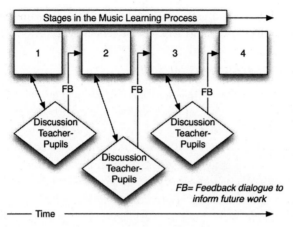

Fig. 2.1 Feedback in practical music learning

course the actual number will depend upon the circumstances for each teacher, class, and group.

The feedback given by the teacher influences the work which the pupils do in the next part of their work, which means that the feedback is focused on future improvement. It is for this reason that a number of commentators have renamed feedback to *feedforward*, as its intentionality is based upon forward development. Whichever term is used, the principle, and, more importantly, the effect should be the same. There are many facets to developing feedback in formative assessment in the classroom, and more specific details will be discussed in ensuing chapters with regard to various aspects and components of music education. However, the use of appropriate feedback in music education is important (Murphy 2007), and to be encouraged.

Diagnostic assessment

The purpose of diagnostic assessment is to diagnose issues with a pupil's learning which might affect the propensity for learning of that pupil. In music lessons this type of assessment is frequently to be found with relation to performative aspects of music practice. For example, a teacher notices that one of her pupils is having problems playing the keyboard, and makes the diagnosis that it would help the child if they were to use a more regularized and logical fingering technique.

It might be argued that with custom and practice over time the four terminologies of assessment purposes outlined by the TGAT report have mellowed into three, and that diagnostic purposes for assessment have, by and large, been subsumed within the notion of formative assessment. After this short description of diagnostic assessment it will be treated in this way, as a component of formative assessment, for the remainder of this book.

Evaluative assessment

The purpose of evaluative assessment was originally to evaluate the performance of a whole school. This information was first available to people working in the school, or in the wider context of a local authority. An increasingly common trait is for this sort of assessment information to be found in published league tables. More recently, evaluative assessment has also been used to investigate the efficacy of individual education programmes. In the English National Curriculum music often fared poorly in this respect, with comparatively low numbers of pupils achieving average performance at age 14 when ending their Key Stage 3 studies. There are many complex reasons for this, including a lack of validity and reliability of unmoderated teacher assessments, and the possible misunderstanding of the National Curriculum level statements themselves. We shall revisit this aspect of assessment in later chapters of this book.

Discussion concerning purposes of assessment

It is important to note that these differing purposes of assessment need not be distinct in practice from each other:

It is sometimes difficult to avoid referring to these as if they were different forms or types of assessment. They are not. They are discussed separately only because they have different purposes; indeed the same information, gathered in the same way, would be called formative if it were used to help learning and teaching, or summative if it were not so utilized but only employed for recording and reporting. While there is a single clear use if assessment is to serve a formative purpose, in the case of summative assessment there are various ways in which the information about student achievement at a certain time is used. (Harlen 2005a: 208)

What this means for the music teacher is that there is some overlapping of utility between the two commonest purposes for assessment, formative and summative. Indeed, there is an increasing tendency for schools to use the information gathered from summative assessments for formative purposes too. This is commonly referred to in educational parlance as *the formative use of summative assessment.*

Assessment at different times

Sometimes assessments are categorized by when they take place, rather than as being formative or summative, and the terms 'day-to-day' and 'periodic' assessment are used. This categorization by mode of employment works well when all parties understand what is being discussed, but there is a potential problem that 'day-to-day' assessment could be lots of mini-summative assessments, which are then used to fulfil both a formative and summative purpose, including the formative use of summative assessment. It is also possible that day-to-day assessment can be truly formative, in which case it can manifest itself in a totally different fashion. For the music teacher, it is important to distinguish assessment from testing, and so the timing of assessment activities will be treated as a separate matter in this book.

Having described different purposes of assessment, it should be clear that it is the uses to which information arising from them is put that are of serious concern to the music teacher.

Assessment data

The term *assessment data* is used to describe such information. For many music teachers the phrase tends to conjure up images of statistics and spreadsheets, but this need not be the case. Assessment data can be statistical, but can also exist simply as prose, written or spoken, and as things which have arisen during the course of a conversation. It can be helpful to think of assessment data as being on a continuum from *tangible* to *intangible*. Tangible assessment data being that which exists in a physical, often written format, whereas intangible assessment data often exists solely as spoken comments. In between these two extremes will be information recorded in differing degrees of complexity This is not to privilege one over the other, simply to note that they both exist for different reasons. Music teachers will use both ends of this continuum at different times, and move between them for differing aspects of classroom assessment.

Plotting tangible-intangible as one axis, and then marrying this with a formative-summative axis provides a useful way of thinking about the different types of assessment data which arise on a daily basis in the classroom. Figure 2.2 shows an example of such a plotting, with exemplar material provided for each quadrant.

The quadrant from the lower left of this chart, intangible summative data, is the least likely form to be found in schools today, although it does still exist where, for example, teachers ask pupils to perform, record a mark or grade, and do not tell the pupils what they got. The examples given of the other forms of assessment data are appropriate at different stages during the teaching and learning of music. Again, these will be referred to in more detail later.

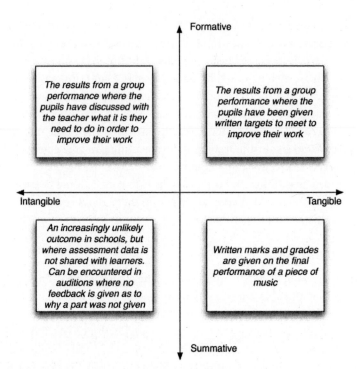

Fig. 2.2 Intangible–tangible and formative–summative continua

Marking and grading

Marking and grading are activities which have clear links with assessment. Indeed, for a number of music teachers the terminologies seem to be synonymous, as Asmus notes 'for many teachers, assessment simply means grading' (Asmus 1999: 19). However, the processes of marking and grading are distinct ones which have very specific meanings for teachers in general, and music teachers in particular. *Marking* refers to the process of going through a piece of work and commenting on specific aspects of it. *Grading* refers to the part of the assessment process where a specific grade is afforded to a piece of work. A potential problem is that conflating assessment, marking, and grading in the minds of practitioners might have the unintentional effect of de-legitimizing some aspects of the assessment process, in particular formative assessment.

Criterion referencing

Marking work often involves assessment against a set of criteria. This type of assessment is usually termed *criterion-referenced*, and means that there exist a set of themes, topics, skills, or concepts that a pupil needs to evidence in order to achieve a satisfactory standard. If the pupil meets the requirements, then they are deemed to have passed. 100% success rates are not problematic here. If all meet the standards required, then all pass. Where problems can arise, however, is with regard to the initial formulation and writing of assessment criteria, as 'writing good criteria that do not trivialise what is being assessed is difficult. As written criteria look authoritative and then tend to be treated as the right criteria, if they have not been well-conceived, clearly this causes all kinds of problems' (Freeman & Lewis 1998: 20).

In music we can see that creation of a good set of assessment criteria might well prove problematic. Take the case of a group of students undertaking a composing task involving ostinato in a KS3 lesson. In order to establish what the assessment criteria are, it is necessary to have a view of the deconstructed process which is being examined, and a *staged* sequence of descriptors which can be used has to be produced. These descriptors can allow for human interpretation, and judgement, but they need to exist in a usable form, and reliability and validity need to be established. In the example in question the important assessment criteria are likely to relate to the use of a repeating pattern of some sort in the music. This can be as simple as a binary yes/no marking system—yes it has an ostinato, tick box; no it does not have an ostinato, do not tick box. This might satisfy the immediacy of a busy class-room teacher, but is it really telling the teacher or the pupils anything meaningful about the *quality* of the ostinato? Example 2: in A level harmony, the use of a passing 6/4, involving the outer parts moving in contrary motion, and correct inner part voice-leading in the Ia/b-Vc-Ib/a movement can be taught and learned in an atomistic fashion, and yet the teacher will want the pupil to be able to employ this in a musical phrase, so what other criteria will they wish to employ? Example 3: The criteria employed for written answers in a text-based format are likely to be different from the criteria employed for practical music making, and having a clear view of what it is that is being assessed is, as we shall see, important for the validity of assessment. These three examples are but a brief selection amongst many, and in Chapter 9 a more detailed discussion of appropriate criteria for assessment in a number of key areas of musical learning are discussed.

Grading work follows on from marking, and it is here that assessment criteria will give rise to a grade. This can be in a number of formats: a mark out of ten, a letter grade from A to E, possibly shaded by the use of a + or − sign, a National Curriculum level, or some other system. The way that grades are arrived at should involve a careful consideration of the varying applicability of different assessment criteria, employed along some form of meaningful scale. Yet all too often music teachers can be observed making context-free judgements. In one KS3 lesson where pupils had been practising and performing the theme tune from 'Titanic' (already some years old during the lesson in question) the following exchange was noted:

Teacher: 'That performance was a little shaky, I'll give you a level 2'
Pupil: 'Oh miss, I think I tried quite hard'
Teacher: 'Yes, but it wasn't accurate'
Pupil: 'No, but I have done it better when I was practising'
Teacher: 'That's not the point'

There was no sharing of criteria, no dissection of the grading given, and no reference to any form of external legitimization of the grading process. When asked after the lesson what the 'level 2' meant, the teacher replied that this was a National Curriculum level, which is, in itself, an idiosyncratic interpretation of National Curriculum assessment criteria. The sole arbiter of judgement here was the teacher, and giving a grade was not based upon any criteria other than the teachers' impression.

Norm referencing

Norm-referenced assessment is used to establish an ordering of students, comparing one with another, within a specified cohort. This means that some students are deemed 'better' than others in performance in the assessment, and that improvement in an individual pupil's score is achieved at the expense of others in the cohort. When a large number of students are involved, the performance in norm-referenced assessment leads to the bell-curve graph of normal frequency distribution.

The primary implication of the use of norm-referenced assessment is that performance can vary from one assessment situation to another, so students results will to some extent be determined by their peers. Thus an average student, scoring exactly at the mid-point of the test—not the curve—will do better in a poor cohort than in a good one.

The main reason for the employment of norm-referenced assessment is for selection from the cohort. It does not imply an absolute standard, it selects according to a variable standard depending on the group of pupils involved.

Norm referencing was common in the days of the 'O'-level examination in music, but is less so now. GCSE examinations are normally criterion based, but grade boundaries are moved slightly each year in order to regularize achievement levels year on year. There are anecdotal reports of some schools trying to ensure that end of key stage National Curriculum assessments show some form of normal frequency distribution, but this is not enshrined in legislation.

Ipsative assessment

Ipsative assessment occurs when the student self-references their achievements, comparing them with their previous ones. Thus a student wishing to improve the speed and accuracy with which they play scales on the piano will practise with a metronome, noting the increase in speed over time. 'This is a particularly appropriate form of assessment when students set their own learning objectives' (Freeman & Lewis 1998: 21). This can be a helpful mode of assessment in many aspects of music learning, as when pupils do set their own objectives, they can then be used as a basis for discussion. Ipsative assessment is commonly to be found in informal music learning too, with guitarists developing their facility at playing riffs, and drummers the speed at which they can do drum-rolls.

Uses of assessment

The two main purposes of assessment are formative and summative. Each of these figure in different ways in the uses which teachers make of the assessment data which arise from them. In other words it is the *uses* to which assessment data will be put that, by and large, determine which *purposes* are to be employed. What this means in practice is that *uses* of assessment can be thought of in terms of the data produced, and what the teacher does with this information. One implication of this is that when thinking about formative and summative assessment, 'these terms are therefore not descriptions of kinds of assessment, but rather of the use to which information arising from the assessments is put' (Weeden et al. 2002: 19). As we shall see, formative assessment in music education has very different uses from its summative cousin, and it is these uses which are likely to be of concern to the music teacher.

It is in the area of uses of assessment data that the music teacher has a wide range of available options. Indeed, it is the uses made of assessment that are likely to form an important aspect of classroom practice for many teachers. We know from the extensive work done by members of the Assessment Reform Group (*inter alia* Assessment Reform Group 1999, 2002; Black & Wiliam 1998a, 1998b; Black et al. 2003, 2004, 2006; J. Gardner 2006; Wiliam 2001) that considered and appropriate use of formative assessment strategies can make a real difference to raising standards in the classroom and beyond, its influence reaching into improving results in high-stakes testing. Formative assessment involves using assessment to help improve the future performance of the pupils. Figure 2.3 encapsulates this aspect of formative, as opposed to summative, assessment.

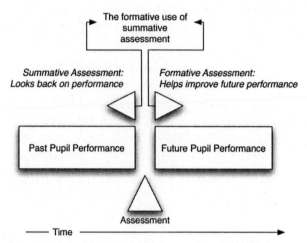

Fig. 2.3 Different stances of formative and summative assessment

There are a number of key features of formative assessment which music teachers can employ; in fact, many of these are things which have long formed a part of the regular practice of the profession. In order to deconstruct aspects of this, let us go back to first principles with regard to formative assessment. The ARG defined a number of principles of assessment for learning with regard to classroom practice. Their definition serves a useful starting point: 'Assessment for Learning is the process of seeking and interpreting evidence for use by learners and their teachers to decide where the learners are in their learning, where they need to go and how best to get there' (Assessment Reform Group 2002). What this means for the music teacher is that one of the prime aspects of their role is that of making judgements about what the pupils can do, and make decisions concerning what they need to do in order to get better. To operationalize this the music teacher needs to make a series of professional decisions, and share the thinking behind these with the pupils. This makes assessment for learning an integrated part of the teaching and learning process. In order for teachers to help pupils improve, they need to know what the pupils are capable of doing, and then build from there to discuss with the pupils what it is specifically that needs to be done in order to get better.

The formative use of summative assessment

Another aspect of summative assessment is also shown in Fig. 2.3, the formative use of summative assessment. This is where a summative assessment is carried out, and the data it produces is not just used for certification and summary purposes, but for informing future progress too. There is a need for clarity with regard to this, as there have been a number of cases of what might be called 'terminology slip', and understandings and misunderstandings of formative and summative purposes have become a little confused at times:

> because formative assessment has to be carried out by teachers, there is an assumption that all assessment by teachers is formative, adding to the blurring of the distinction between formative and summative purposes and to teachers changing their own on-going assessment into a series of 'mini' assessments each of which is essentially summative in character (Harlen & James 1997: 365).

This is an important distinction, and one which we can readily recognize in the music class. The subtle changeover from aspects of formative assessment, with teachers talking with pupils, and giving them regular, specific, and targeted feedback, has gradually been replaced *as a notion of assessment* with the use of tasks and tests which provide data then used to inform the future progress of the pupils. This does not mean that there has been a wholesale change in pedagogy, but that the idea of talking with pupils and helping them with their learning has been slowly replaced by the grading of a summative task or test. 'Such grading often masks a confusion, as it is described as formative (since it informs about progress and standards reached) when the function is really summative (a snapshot of where I am now)' (Stobart 2008: 159).

This is the centre of the confusion, music teachers, doubtless taking their lead from school assessment managers, are providing a series of snapshots, and using these as the basis of assessing what their pupils are able to do at that particular moment in time. What this means is that assessments are having to do what Boud (2000) refers to as 'double duty':

- 'They have to encompass formative assessment for learning and summative for certification
- They have to have a focus on the immediate task and on implications for equipping students for . . . [the] future' (Boud 2000: 160).

This 'double duty' of assessment is not, of itself, problematic, but music teachers do need to be clear in their own minds as to which assessment is taking priority, and what are the reasons for it being undertaken.

The importance of formative assessment in music education

There seems to be a widespread consensus teaching style for dealing with practical aspects of music making in the classroom at Key Stage 3, particularly composing, which seems to have evolved over time. This involves the teacher establishing group work as a normal methodology, and the pupils working together in small groups, often comprising four to six members, in order to complete a composing task or project. Whilst this groupwork is taking place, the role of the teacher is to circulate between groups giving feedback, in the fashion depicted in Fig. 2.1. This is formative assessment in action, and this is important to emphasize. Formative assessment involves, amongst other things, verbal interaction, sharing criteria, engaging in feedback dialogue with pupils, and pointing out areas for improvement or development in future work. None of these involve giving a grade at this stage. This way of working with formative assessment has been a strength of music teachers over time, and is one which classroom music teachers have historically used effectively in teaching and learning exchanges in the classroom. Indeed, as we mentioned earlier, in the UK, one of the early publications from the Government-sponsored Key Stage 3 strategy included a video recoding of a music teacher in a comprehensive school in Solihull teaching a group composing lesson to a year 7 class (DfES 2002). This video was used for training purposes for teachers of all subjects in the use of formative assessment, and what had been normal practice for music teachers seems to have come as something of a shock to teachers of other subjects, '. . . as one non-music teacher observed: Do you mean I have to have conversations with my pupils, I'm not used to doing that in my subject' (Fautley 2007: 3). This strength in using formative assessment may have been based in custom and practice, but was real nonetheless. It is important for this aspect of music teachers' formative assessment practice to be maintained and celebrated, after all the use of a music lesson in an important government initiative shows that this practice was perceived to be a strong one.

Although music teachers' historical use of formative assessment was a strength, it may have been an atheoretical one, but it is also worth observing that researchers and commentators on improving assessment practice in schools had been advocating its use. In a study reported on by Black and Wiliam, considerable gains in achievement were made by students where formative assessment techniques were employed routinely:

The research reported here shows conclusively that formative assessment does improve learning. The gains in achievement appear to be quite considerable, and as noted earlier, amongst the largest ever reported for educational interventions. As an illustration of just how big these gains are, an effect size of 0.7, if it could be achieved on a nationwide scale, would be equivalent to raising the mathematics attainment score of an 'average' country like England, New Zealand or the United States into the 'top five' after the Pacific rim countries of Singapore, Korea, Japan and Hong Kong . . . (Black & Wiliam 1998a: 61).

The techniques which they were discussing included many which would have seemed familiar to music teachers:

- it is embedded in a view of teaching and learning of which it is an essential part;
- it involves sharing learning goals with pupils;
- it aims to help pupils to know and to recognize the standards they are aiming for;
- it involves pupils in self-assessment;
- it provides feedback which leads to pupils recognizing their next steps and how to take them;
- it is underpinned by confidence that every student can improve;
- it involves both teacher and pupils reviewing and reflecting on assessment data. (Assessment Reform Group 1999: 7)

This does not mean that these practices were universal in the late 1990s, but many of the factors being discussed were not alien to widespread music class-room practice. A challenge for the future is, against a fast-changing back-ground of standards and accountability, maintaining that which is worthwhile in music education, without losing sight of the inherently *musical* nature of the subject matter.

Comment-only assessing

In some subjects, teachers have adopted a type of assessing known as 'comment only'. Here no grades are given, pupils are simply given advice on how to improve their learning and doing. For music teachers, well used to giving oral, rather than written feedback, this is a perfectly logical way of doing things. As music happens in time, an immediate oral response catches the moment, and enables progression comments to be delivered with immediacy. Indeed, Stobart (2008: 168) reports that comment-only feedback can lead to signifi-cant learning gains. Traditionally written work has assumed a lower impor-tance in generalist music classes, but here too comment-only assessment can be a useful way of interacting with pupils.

Summative grades

When we talk about a pupil being a Grade 5 pianist, music teachers have a rough idea as to what the competency of that player is likely to be. The termi-nology 'Grade 5' is being used here as a sort of shorthand as to the typical level of performance that this person evidences. Knowing this, we would be unlikely to book them to play the Grieg piano concerto, for example. So ingrained has this become, that even without the appropriate certification, pupils can be referred to in this fashion, and mutual understanding is taken for granted. Summative assessments of a more everyday sort also use this model. The grade or level awarded is a shorthand referent for a collection of competences which the person concerned evidences. Whilst this can be useful in everyday speech for summarizing attainment, it can be dangerous if the shorthand becomes a label for the pupil. It is also important to distinguish between what a pupil does and the person they are: 'Comments that focus on the work rather than the person are more constructive for both learning and motivation' (Assessment Reform Group 2002). Pupils are not level 4, but their work might be; pupils labelling themselves in inappropriate ways such as 'I'll be a nothing' (Reay & Wiliam 1999) are not helpful to self-esteem, and hence not conducive to the pupil making good progress either.

Endnote

From a discussion of uses and purposes of assessment, we now turn our attention to looking in more depth at what happens during assessment, particularly in terms of two key aspects, those of reliability and validity.

Chapter 3

Reliability and validity

Reliability and validity are important terminologies in discussions concerning assessment, and each has a specific meaning which we now explore. In addition there a number of aspects to the ways in which they are manifested in assessments in music which warrant investigation.

Reliability

Reliability in assessment term refers primarily to the consistency or otherwise of assessment results. Examples include:

- If a pupil undertook the same assessment on two subsequent days would that pupil obtain the same results?
- If a single assessment done by a single pupil is marked and graded by two different assessors will the results be the same? This aspect of reliability is known as 'inter-rater reliability'
- If the same assessor marked a single assessment on two different occasions would the pupil achieve the same results?
- If the same assessment was undertaken by two groups of pupils of more-or-less similar ability would both groups of pupils achieve the same results?

We can see from this that the aim for assessors and test producers is to try to make public examinations as reliable as possible. This we accept, but how likely is it?

Educational assessments are unreliable for a number of reasons. The individuals being tested are not consistent in their performance—people have 'good days' and 'bad days'—and, apart from multiple-choice tests, there is also some inconsistency in the ways that assessments are marked. But the most significant cause of unreliability is the actual choice of items for a particular test. If we have an annual assessment like the national curriculum tests or GCSE examinations, then, because the papers are not kept secret, new versions have to be prepared each year. The question is then are the tests interchangeable? The two tests might be assessing broadly the same thing, but one of the two tests might suit a particular candidate better than the other. We therefore have a situation where the scores that candidates get depend on how lucky they are . . . (Wiliam 2000a: 108)

We need to be aware that in any educational setting people are involved, both in undertaking the assessment, and in marking and grading it, and that people are not machines. Consequently, this itself is going to introduce another form of reliability problem. In musical terms we know that we can play the same piece many times over, and some times are better than others, or, as a Jazz musician might put it 'last night we were really smokin' ' whereas other nights are less aflame! Assessment under these circumstances will vary. We will consider in further depth some of these issues in Chapter 10 when we discuss the problems associated with assessing performance.

We need to be very aware too that some aspects of music education are amenable to assessment, others less so. Deciding whether a violin is in tune is a different order of assessment to judging the relative merits of diploma candidates' performances. The implication of this is that reliability '. . . is concerned with precision and accuracy. Some features, e.g. height, can be measured accurately, whilst others, e.g. musical ability, cannot' (Cohen et al. 2000: 117). This opens a whole new problem for music educators! Measuring height does seem straightforward, and we do at least begin by knowing what it means. Measuring 'musical ability' requires a different approach, as here, to begin with, we are likely to be less sure what it means, and, whatever definition we eventually settle on, we can be sure than it won't come up with an answer as simple as 1.85 metres! However, let us put aside the thorny problem of measuring musical ability, or even of asking what it might be, and turn to validity.

Validity

Validity refers to the notion of an assessment procedure actually assessing what it is trying to assess, and not inadvertently assessing something else. Building on the work of McCormick & James (1983), and James (1998), it is possible to extract seven categories of validity which are applicable in terms of assessment material with regard to music education:

1. Face validity, wherein something looks, on the face of it, as if it is able to measure what it purports to measure. This can be an issue in classroom assessments where what is intended to be assessed is some form of musical response, maybe listening and appraising, whereas what is actually being assessed is the pupil's use of English.

2. Content validity: This refers to an assessment covering all of the relevant subject matter, and not just isolated aspects. This can be an issue within music, and it is hard to find an assessment which covers performing, composing, listening, reviewing, and evaluating. What tends to happen is that teachers produce separate assessments for each area of content they wish to assess.

3. Criterion-related validity: This refers to whether or not the results from an assessment agree with a different criterion, for example the teacher's own judgements concerning ability. If, in a teacher's judgement, a pupil underperforms on an assessment, then it may be worth considering whether the issue was the assessment itself.

4. Predictive validity: This is where the validity of an assessment is determined by its ability to predict future attainment. Many classroom assessments are intended to be cumulative, in that they lead towards a final grade or National Curriculum level. A question of concern here is how valid is an assessment task at marrying up its results to final attainment?

5. Construct validity: '. . . requires a clear and accurate definition of the domain being assessed so that the assessments test the construct and not something else' (James 1998: 154). A simple definition of a construct in terms of music education is that it is a specific concept or skill. Thus in these terms we can view composing as a construct. The effect of this in validity terms is that in practice this becomes a more complex version of face validity, but one where there is a mismatch between different constructs. A common example of this is to be found in a Key Stage 3 music lesson, where the intention of what is to be assessed is a composing task, whereas what actually becomes assessed is the pupils' performance of their piece of music.

6. Internal validity: 'Basically it refers to the soundness of an explanation (i.e. whether what is interpreted as "cause" produces the "effect") . . .' (McCormick & James 1983: 174). For music teachers this can have implications as to whether the assessment is in agreement with itself, in other words is the effect directly attributable to the cause in question. Here the issue can relate to what prior knowledge a pupil brings with them to an assessment. If, as in one case observed recently, a pupil having private piano lessons plays a piece in class very well using just one hand on a keyboard, then it is difficult for the teacher to claim this is a result of her lessons. This is an example of a different cause producing the effect.

7. External validity: this is concerned with whether the results of an assessment are generalizable. For example, as we have seen, music teachers talk in shorthand of a Grade 5 violinist, and know what this means, and also know how this equates with a Grade 5 flautist. This is due to ABRSM having done a lot of work to ensure their assessments have as much external validity as possible.

Another form of validity, *consequential validity*, is also worthy of consideration. This is rather different to the list above in that it refers to the '. . . worth of assessments in terms of their social, personal and educational consequences' (James 1998: 155). This places this form of validity into a slightly different league to the others, as Shepard observes: 'As a short hand, consequential validity is now used by many to refer to the incorporation of testing consequences into validity investigations. Most measurement specialists acknowledge that issues of social justice and testing effects are useful ideas, but some dispute whether such issues should be addressed as part of test validity' (Shepard 1997: 5). Music teachers will be aware that many forms of assessment have social consequences, whether or not that affects their validity as assessments is what the notion of consequential validity endeavours to address.

All of these forms of validity will occur in varying amounts in any assessment undertaken in and beyond the classroom. The task for the music teacher when devising and administering any form of assessment is to ensure that there is some attention paid to issues of validity. However, what we need to bear in mind all the time when discussing assessment is that there will always be some form of inaccuracies inherent within it, or as Caroline Gipps succinctly puts it, 'Assessment is not an exact science, and we must stop presenting it as such' (Gipps 1994: 167). Trying to achieve a high level of validity and reliability is worthwhile, but as music educators we ought to be very wary of presenting results from our classrooms, studios, or rehearsal rooms as being scientific facts.

Dependability

Reliability is often held to be the prime requirement of assessments, so that they can be considered to be replicable across and between contexts. There is an argument which states that reliability is key, because if there are doubts about the replication of an assessment, then there must also be concerns that it is, in fact, measuring that which it purports to be measuring. However, there are problems with this view, as:

. . . this argument tends to lead to attempts to increase reliability which generally means closer and closer specification, and use of methods that have the least error. It results in gathering and using a restricted range of evidence, leading to a reduction in validity. On the other hand, if validity is increased by extending the range of the assessment to include outcomes such as higher level thinking skills, then reliability is likely to fall, since many of these aspects of attainment are not easily assessed. (Harlen 2005b: 247)

This raises a very pertinent discussion of a problem for music education, as, in efforts to increase reliability, it is all too easy to fall back upon things which are easily assessable, which, whilst probably reliable, are not necessarily valid in measuring aspects of *musical* learning. For example, can an evaluation of a diploma-level pianist's interpretation of a Beethoven piano be undertaken solely by assessing their fingering? This is fairly straightforward to assess, probably does not vary much between performances, and so is reliable, but, as an assessment of musical worth, its validity is questionable. Not dissimilar instances are regularly to be found in classroom and instrumental music lessons.

So far reliability and validity have been presented as independent constructs. However, there is also a relationship between the two, and they do need to be considered in terms of how they interact with each other. As Mary James observes, 'Broadly speaking, reliability is a property of the assessment procedures themselves, whereas validity is a property of the information they produce' (James 1998: 158). Because of this interaction between the two, the notion of *dependability* is often used. Wynne Harlen describes this as '. . . the extent to which reliability is optimised while ensuring validity' (Harlen 2007: 24). The issue at stake for music teachers is which of the two areas of reliability and validity take priority in considering dependability of assessments. Whilst striving for the highest possible property of each is clearly going to be the aim, nonetheless this does not mean that music teachers should rethink assessments root and branch. Formative assessment can have a high degree of validity, but, because it does not go beyond the students in question, can be low in reliability, but we know that formative assessment is key to making improvements in learning.

Endnote

As reliability and validity are important constructs in assessment, it is worthwhile for music teachers to consider how they will impinge upon the assessments that they do with their learners. Are the constructs being assessed the ones which are truly deemed worthwhile, or are they being assessed because they offer a simple way of so doing? The issue of validity is important, we would not want to assess a drummer by getting them to write an essay about drumming, for example. This takes us into the area which is addressed in the next chapter, that of how musical achievement is evidenced, and consequently assessed.

Chapter 4

Evidencing achievement

In Chapter 2 we saw how both formative and summative assessments will provide data. Many aspects of musical achievement are themselves the subject of assessment, from the child playing their first xylophone tune in the classroom, to the diploma performance examination. In this chapter we examine what the notion of evidencing achievement entails, ways in which achievement in various aspects of music education can be evidenced, and what sorts of assessment evidence might arise from different assessments.

Questions to ask of classroom learning

In order to know what pupils can do now, and could do in the future, we require information. For example, in choosing a topic for a unit of work, typical pieces of information a music teacher will need include the answers to questions like these:

1. What can the pupils already do?
2. Can they all do this?
3. If so, how well can they do it?
4. What about those who struggle?
5. What about those who find it easy?
6. How should I introduce this topic?
7. Have they enough prior knowledge already to do it?
8. Is the proposed learning sufficiently challenging?
9. Why is this topic worth doing, and not that one?
10. What resources will we need, and do we have them?

All of these are the sorts of questions a teacher will ask themselves as they start planning a unit of work. But the key question, as yet unasked, is this:

- How will I know the answers to these questions?

And it is this which is key to the assessment process. To answer this question requires *evidence*. To be really effective the list of questions above needs to be reframed in terms of evidentiary outcomes:

1. What evidence is there to show what the can pupils already do?
2. What evidence is there to say whether they can all do this?
3. If so, what evidence is there to show how well can they do it?
4. What evidence is there to tell me which (named) pupils will struggle?
5. What evidence is there to tell me which (named) pupils will find it easy?
6. What evidence do I already have to tell me how I should introduce this topic?
7. What evidence is there to show whether or not they have enough prior knowledge already to do it?
8. What evidence is there to tell me if the proposed learning is sufficiently challenging?
9. What evidence do I have as to why this topic is worth doing, and not that one?
10. What resources will we need, and do we have them? (Hopefully this is evidenced from the daily practice of the teacher, although for peripatetic teachers and visiting artists it is worth asking.)

Reframing the list of questions in this fashion shifts the emphasis from anecdotal responses, or the teacher's unsubstantiated feelings, to a requirement of evidence. Evidencing knowledge and attainment is clearly better than assuming things, and so for this reason many teachers are already using a variety of types of evidence as a way of ensuring that they know what their pupils know, and can do. The list above is essentially a series of formative assessment questions which the teacher can ask to help with planning and developing pupil learning in the classroom.

Evidence

Formative assessment is concerned with improving and developing achievement, and summative assessment with documenting it. Both of these, therefore, rely on the pupils evidencing what they are able to do, in order to be able to assess it. What this means is that the pupil has to be able to demonstrate, explain, show, discuss, or in some other fashion provide evidence for what they can do. The implications of this are that pupils need to be given opportunities to do this, a statement which may seem obvious, but in many cases needs planning and management. We cannot get inside people's heads, and so our only way of accessing achievement is to see it manifested in some form. This may be straightforward when the evidentiary requirements of the task are simple, e.g. playing a C major root position triad on the keyboard, but less so when the

task is more complex, for example evidencing a musical response to a composing stimulus. A danger here is that, under pressure to provide assessment data
for some external function, the teacher simply ignores worthwhile assessments
that have a problematic evidentiary requirement, and uses a simpler, less meaningful assessment, as it does at least provide data of some sort (this is an example
of McNamara's fallacy, which we look at later). Evidence of achievement is
important, but this needs to balanced with a view as to what *worthwhile* evidence consists of. At its most simplistic a group composition task could have the
requirement that it needs the following:

- An ostinato
- A crescendo
- A diminuendo
- A positive start
- A definite end

Assessment of these could be very simple. Each might be considered in terms
of a binary outcome, i.e. yes/no. The teacher has an assessment grid, as shown
in Table 4.1.

So, is this a good piece of music? Sadly that criterion is totally absent from
the assessment grid. Does this matter? The answer to that will depend on what
the assessment is being used for. As a simple ready-reckoner of things to be
included in a composing task, Table 4.1 is fine, and can then be used as a basis
for further discussions with the pupils about their music, and what it is they
are doing. If it is the basis for an end of unit summative assessment, then it
misses the finer nuances of a good piece of music, which can have the result
that:

... we may all too easily allow ourselves to be trapped by compromise, making
important what can most easily be evaluated rather than valuing what is important.
In which case, why do we bother with ... anything that relies upon the exercise
of imagination, creative response, and the expression of independent views
(Paynter 2002: 216)

Table 4.1 Checklist for musical features

Musical feature	Yes	No
An ostinato	✓	
A crescendo		✓
A diminuendo	✓	
A positive start	✓	
A definite end		✓

Table 4.2 Types of evidence

Musical evidence:	This will take the form of sounds
Written evidence:	This can either be expressed in written text, or some form of musical notation
Oral evidence:	Things which the pupils talk about
Pictorial evidence:	Where the pupils have drawn illustrations

In music there will be a number of types of assessment evidence. For normal purposes these can be divided into four types, as shown in Table 4.2.

Each of these has a part to play in developing an overall judgement about a pupil's profile, and each will be considered to be important at different times. There is no distinction drawn in this list between formative and summative purposes of assessment; the aim is simply to consider that range of evidences which the teacher will have to deal with. Neither is the table exclusive; there may well be other sources too, as the multi-attributed quotation that 'writing about music is like dancing about architecture' implies!

Musical evidence

Much as modern foreign linguists talk about education in the target language, then we can consider that in music education the target language will involve musical sounds. From this it follows that an important source of musical evidence will lie in the ability of the pupils to be able to produce sounds. This will patently be the case in instrumental music lessons, but it will also hold true for classroom music in many cases too.

Practical music examinations, such as those of ABRSM, are predicated on sequential musical evidencing of achievement in performance, and ABRSM has developed a wealth of expertise over the years in conducting such examinations. The bulk of evidence required from candidates involves them in playing prepared pieces on their instrument. This evidence is gathered in a high-stakes final summative assessment, and, as is often the case in high-stakes summative assessment, no account is taken of the candidate's musical journey before they arrive at the examination. This way of working is well-established, and has an associated pedagogy and methodological imperative we shall explore in later chapters. It is a clear example of a summative assessment in music where the assessment is focused on musical achievement evidenced directly in practical performance.

The types of knowledge that this way of evidencing achievement and understanding addresses are those of direct involvement with music. This shows a practical application of musical understanding and is evidenced directly in, and through, achievement. This is musical understanding, hopefully being demonstrated in a musical fashion, and will hold true for practical instrumental performance, as well as for compositions and improvisations.

Audio recording

If musical achievement is evidenced in the target language of musical utterances achieved in sound, then it seems that a logical way of capturing this is to use audio recording equipment. Modern technology means that capturing, recording, saving, and archiving audio is now very straightforward, and building up a picture of pupil development over time can be undertaken using quite modest technological resources. This is an invaluable way of evidencing achievement using primary sources, and is considered in more detail in Chapter 14.

Written evidence

Text

There may be times when the production of musical sounds alone may not of itself be sufficient to demonstrate understanding; or there are some summative assessment situations, written tests and examinations, for example, where practical performance is not appropriate, or required. There are also some forms of musical knowledge which are not amenable to practical evidencing, such as historical, analytical, theoretical, descriptive, musicological, some aspects of ethnomusicological, and those which can be categorized as being knowledge *about* music.

For assessment purposes written evidence of musical knowledge and understanding will take a number of forms, varying from high-stakes, such as terminal examinations for courses, to classroom descriptions and evaluations of work done. One aspect of written assessment material for musical purposes which needs to be monitored is ensuring its appropriate utilization. Thus whilst it may be entirely legitimate for A-level students to write about the rise of the madrigal in Renaissance Italy, it may be less purposeful for KS3 pupils to describe a composing project they have been doing in written form. This is an issue of validity, and it seems to be the case that sometimes music teachers seem afraid of the musical nature of musical evidence, and require it to be written down as words in order to feel it is valuable!

Notation

The sorts of written evidence we have been considering so far are those which can be rendered into words, and written down as text. Western art music has its own highly evolved form of recording information in staff notation, and this needs consideration in terms of how assessment can be used with regard to fostering its use. It is important at this stage to think about the learning which is entailed in the use of staff notation, as assessment can only be used to help foster it if the intention for its utilization is clear.

The use of staff notation in music education has become something of a 'hot potato', with claims and counter-claims for its place in the generalist music curriculum being regularly encountered. From an assessment perspective we need to separate out the issues, and consider what sort of knowledge is supported by the teaching and learning of staff notation, and how this type of knowledge can contribute to musical understanding.

In order to do this we need to think about why staff notation is used, and what its primary function is. Let us begin with musical thinking and compare it with 'normal' thinking. When thinking takes place in most people, it does so in the head, and, obviously, has close linkages with language. In most normal individuals, thinking does not take place in the form of a constant stream of written text which passes before the mind's eye, as it were. Instead, thinking happens using the older form of the spoken language: 'Unlike in the case of written language, the brain has had millions of years to evolve speech. The processes are deeply embedded and we are entirely unaware of them. The alphabetic system that has come to be the predominant writing system in the world's languages is parasitic on the ancient human speech system' (Blakemore & Frith 2008: 240). We know that illiterate individuals are capable of holding conversations, and retaining complex information, so the 'parasitic' form of the written word is an overlay upon this more primitive form of cognitive functioning. We also know that musical thinking began very early in the development of human beings:

The earliest unambiguously musical artefact identified to date is a bone pipe dated to around 36,000 BP found near Württemberg in southern Germany, which was uncovered in a context that associates it with modern Homo sapiens sapiens. The pipe predates almost all known visual art, and in any case a capacity for musicality (most likely vocal) would predate the construction of a sophisticated musical artefact such as a pipe, probably by a considerable period. Archaeology suggests that human musicality is ancient . . . (Cross 2003: 21)

It seems to be not unreasonable to assume that as the bone pipe predates visual art, that early man did not notate his compositions! For contemporary musical thinking, the implications of this are that the relationship of sound to symbol in music is likely to be similar to that of written to spoken language. Just as we do not usually think in written words, then most normal adults do not have a cognitive processing device which converts all heard music into staff notation in their heads. This is an important point with regards to under-standings of musicality, as it means that a knowledge of staff notation does not *enable* musical thinking, it simply codifies certain aspects of it.

For assessment purposes, then, we need to be clear as to what the place of staff notation is in teaching and learning. We know, for example, that learning to play a musical instrument in the western art tradition from printed music is a relatively recent innovation, dating from as recently as the mid-nineteenth century (McPherson & Gabrielsson 2002: 100). So even for classically trained instrumentalists, staff notation is not itself a way of thinking musically, it is at one stage removed from this, it is 'parasitic' on musical thinking. So hoping to inculcate musical thinking by teaching notation first, is, in many respects, to put the cart before the horse. Indeed, there can be dangers in teaching nota-tion separately from musical experience, '. . . notation should not be taught in isolation of perception because of the danger that children will be forced to make choices beyond their competence and will tend to do so in contradiction of their perception' (McPherson & Gabrielsson 2002: 105).

Janet Mills observed a similar thing happening in classroom practice: 'Thousands of students every year are confused by teachers' well-intentioned, but misplaced, attempts to teach them to read rhythms and pitches' (Mills 2005: 100). The implications of this are that we need to think about the pur-poses of any learning before we can begin to apply principles of assessment to it. Learning staff notation does have a place in music education and is speci-fied in the National Curriculum, but it is a symbolic reference system, not a thinking system. But this then begs the questions as to how staff notation can be taught, learned, and assessed according to the National Curriculum? To begin to answer this question we need to unpick the process of evidencing learning a little more. This will be done in the chapters which deal with the various aspects of composing, performing, and listening. For the moment it is important to note that musical *thinking* is the key feature we are trying to develop.

Oral evidence

Whilst we may well feel that written evidence is important in providing 'hard copy' for comparative and developmental purposes, we also need to attend to things pupils have to say. For many pupils, the requirement to write things down can be an inhibitor to expression. We have already discussed the diffi-culties associated with staff notation, and being able to notate their composi-tions need not be a means of demonstrating musical understanding. So talk is an important source of evidence for assessment purposes. We also need to be aware that '. . . we can know more than we can tell' (Polanyi 1966: 4), and so in assessing pupil responses orally teachers need to phrase questions carefully, and build on previous responses to tease out understandings. In the UK, and many other countries too, Bloom's taxonomy (Bloom 1956) has been used in training materials to develop teachers' thinking about questioning, and this forms a useful place to begin to think about developing oral responses.

Bloom's taxonomy

Bloom's taxonomy delineates thinking according to its level of complexity, with higher order thinking occupying a more privileged position than lower order thinking. Bloom's original taxonomy was produced back in 1956, and a revised version was produced almost fifty years later, in 2001. The original and revised versions are shown in Fig. 4.1. Higher order thinking skills occupy the top three layers of the pyramid, and lower order the bottom three.

There are a number of differences between the two. The revised version changes the nouns to verbs, which makes a difference in a consideration of the ways in which pupils undertake thinking. The revision also removes the category 'synthesis', moves 'evaluation' to second place, and creates a new top-level thinking skill of 'creating'. For music education this can be problematic as we want our pupils to be involved in creating and re-creating music from the very earliest teaching and learning encounters. However, in terms of developing thinking, the taxonomy and its revision does enable the teacher to think about the sorts of questions that will lead to oral responses which have the propensity to develop pupil thinking. We know, for example, that many of the questions asked by teachers concentrate on thinking at the bottom layer of the taxonomy: 'There is considerable evidence that the questioning strategies employed by teachers are often very narrow, are focused primarily on lower-order aspects of capability such as recall and automated skills . . .' (Wiliam 2000b: 10).

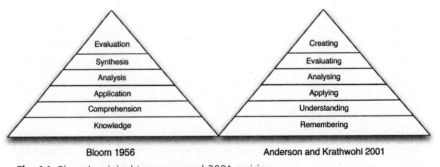

Bloom 1956   Anderson and Krathwohl 2001

Fig. 4.1 Bloom's original taxonomy and 2001 revision

Asking appropriate questions is therefore an important part of eliciting information from pupils. This is a key aspect of the teaching and learning process, and for formative assessment purposes it may well be the case that more does not mean better when it comes to questioning. 'Learning is enhanced when we ask fewer but better questions, and seek better answers . . . Adults help children learn by asking productive questions, and by encouraging children to ask their own questions' (DfES 2004b: 61).

Pictorial evidence

For many pupils, drawing a picture comes easier than writing text. This is not only true for younger pupils, but for many older ones too. Many music teachers have asked their pupils to produce a pictorial representation of their understandings of a piece of music. Sometimes this can be a useful way into developing discussions concerning what pupils have heard. Pictorial evidence can also be used as a form of notation which does not need to be developed in the same way that staff notation does. The principles behind graphic scores can be grasped relatively rapidly, and pupils can use them to produce an *aide-memoire* for their own composing.

Primary and secondary evidence for musical thinking

For assessment purposes the teacher needs to be clear about what the assessment they are undertaking is providing evidence for. Issues of validity matter here, in the sense that assessments should measure that which they purport to be measuring. This is made all the more difficult in music education because there are different types of musical thinking and musical knowledge that teachers wish pupils to engage with. What needs to happen is for the teacher to identify the primary aspects of musical thinking they are concerned with assessing, and then decide if this can be measured directly, or whether it has to be mediated through a secondary evidentiary basis. Thus a complex construct like musical ability does not have a single unitary outcome; we do not say that a pupil has a musical ability of 45%, for example, as this would be meaningless. However, a simpler construct like 'fingering' in an instrumental lesson can be assessed on a primary evidentiary basis, by the teacher observing the pupil. This is likely to result in an assessment which can be constructed using a small number of reference points, and ticking an appropriate box, as in Table 4.3.

This, however, does not tell us anything about the musicality of the performance, and so we need to beware of extrapolating too much from this information; this can be an all too simple trap into which to fall.

Table 4.3 Fingering assessment

Completely correct
Mostly correct
Partially correct
Totally incorrect

Misreading assessment evidence

In many secondary schools in the UK, classroom music lessons can be found which involve teaching what have become known as the 'musical elements'. In the 2007 version of the National Curriculum for England these were defined as including:

- pitch
- duration
- dynamics
- tempo
- timbre
- texture
- silence

These very specific terminologies describe attributes of music and are technical terms for its basic building blocks. However, what has become commonplace is for teachers to treat pupils' lack of familiarity with the specific terminologies as implying that there is a corresponding lack of the concept to which the terminology applies. This results in 11-year-old pupils being taught about pitch and rhythm, concepts they had probably firmly grasped by the age of 7:

> . . . a reasonably competent 7-year old should understand the basic metrical properties of his musical system and the appropriate scales, harmonies, cadences and groupings, even as he should be able, give some motifs, to combine them into a musical unit that is appropriate to his culture, but is not a complete copy of a work already known (H. Gardner 1973: 197).

What is happening in some cases is that teachers note that pupils do not readily invoke technical language regarding elements of music upon arrival at secondary school, and so teachers mistake a lack of evidence for understanding, with evidence of a lack of understanding. This is an important distinction, and, at its worse, gives rise to 'guess what I'm thinking' type questions from the teacher. None of us would deliberately ask such a question, where we have a fixed answer in our minds and 'fish around' for the answer, but this is what results from having a too fixed view. Janet Mills gives what she calls a 'gross example' of this:

The teacher took a large suspended cymbal and soft beater. First she hit the cymbal softly at the rim. Second, she hit the cymbal as hard as she dared. She asked the [11-year-old] pupils if they could tell her in what way the second sound differed from the first one. One pupil volunteered that the second sound was longer than the first sound. No, that was wrong. Another pupil ventured that the second sound was more metallic, and the first more wooden. No, that was wrong too. A third pupil suggested that the pitch of the second sound wavered, whereas that of the first sound was higher, and more constant in pitch. No, that was still not right. Eventually, a pupil pointed out that the second sound was louder than the first. When she evaluated this lesson at the end of the day, the teacher wrote that most of the class had not grasped the concept of loud-soft, and were consequently still working towards the achievement expected of [7-year olds in the National Curriculum]. (Mills 2005: 109)

This sort of interpretation seems ridiculous when considered in this fashion, but can be all too common. The reason behind the misinterpretation lies in the teacher not thinking through the complexities of possible alternative answers to the question which had been asked and therefore of having a 'guess what I'm thinking' model of answer in their head already, which precludes other legitimate answers from being acceptable. To take this further we can invoke an example from Saussure and semiotics, and say that this confusion arises amongst teachers because they have mistaken a sign, or signifier, for the thing for which the sign stands, the signified (Chandler 2002: 55). In this case, the signifier, National Curriculum music-specific vocabulary, is being mistaken for the thing for which it stands. So, referring to Mills' example above, the teacher assumed that the pupils lacked the concept of volume. This is a major error in this case, because, as the quotation from Gardner observed, a 'reasonably competent 7-year old' already has this concept. To extrapolate from this, the approach where the secondary school teacher assumes the pupils know nothing, and, in effect, starts again, is unlikely to have a positive effect on learner motivation. In assessment terms, this is an example of misreading assessment evidence, with a potentially detrimental effect upon learning.

Two-fold nature of classroom assessment practice

The sorts of assessment which will take place in music lessons will normally fall into one of two categories. These are the routine assessment judgements made by the teacher during the course of normal ongoing classroom work in music, and those which arise as a result of separate assessment tasks. These are *not* divided between formative and summative purposes, because it will depend to what use the information is put. This two-pronged way of assessing takes us to the heart of assessment during a lesson, either as a result of work undertaken assessed by the teacher whilst it is taking place, or as a result of a separate assessment event. Figure 4.2 shows a graphical representation of this.

This figure needs unpicking somewhat. The right-hand side of the diagram shows a number of different assessment tasks being undertaken. In a music class these happen over time, and often produce musical evidence. The left-hand side shows ongoing assessment happening, again over time, and again using evidence of achievement directly involving music. Both of these can feed into an assessment profile for each child that the teacher builds up. They will also provide evidence for the teacher's own lesson evaluations, either formal or informal, which can also provide evidence for a pupil assessment profile.

The differences between ongoing assessment and assessment tasks warrants closer investigation. Music teachers often talk of having 'an assessment lesson' as a discrete event, and as though assessment does not happen at any other time. The assessment lesson in music has evolved in a way which might be described as another sort of 'folk pedagogy', and typically involves groups of pupils taking in turns to perform their piece to the rest of the class and the teacher. In some cases the non-performing groups are given a type of peer-assessment sheet to complete as each group performs. Managed well, these

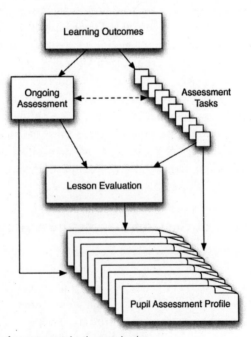

Fig. 4.2 Modes of assessment in the music class

lessons can be a useful source of peer commentary and open and frank exchange of views regarding the music. Managed not so well, these can become pointless form-filling exercises. 'Both self-appraisal . . . and pupil appraisal of music of their peers can become mundane and pointless exercises if the teacher does not have clear ideas about the ways in which these methods can enhance learning' (Adams 2000: 174). Sadly, all too often the assessment lesson can also become a major problem of class management, as for the majority of time most of the pupils will not be actively engaged in music making. As one teacher put it:

It's actually a very difficult lesson and for a lot of kids it's a waste of time, because they'll play their piece, and that's two minutes. So they're going to spend another forty eight minutes potentially sat around listening to other people's, and even if you give them a little form, and say okay here's the theme, smiley face, sad face, ambivalent face and I want a reason why for each performance, it's still an inherently, quite a dull lesson, even though you're listening to other people's performances and it's enjoyable and everything, I feel that for me and the way our students are here it's not the best use of time.

It seems that many teachers work like this for a number of reasons:

- It looks like proper assessment
- It matches up to other subjects
- It gives music a feeling of comparability
- It satisfies managerial demands to be 'doing' assessment
- It gives the pupils something to aim for
- It provides 'real' assessment data

But increasingly music teachers are abandoning the separate assessment lesson, and integrating ongoing assessment into the routine work of the classroom.

However teachers assess, it is important to bear in mind that assessment of attainment in music is not unproblematic. The types of evidence obtained relate closely to the types of knowledge being assessed, and it is to that area that the next chapter addresses itself.

Chapter 5

Learning and knowledge in classroom music

This chapter investigates and discusses issues concerned with learning and knowledge in music education. The reason for this is that in order to get to grips with assessment, it is important to have a view as to the types of learning which are going on, as otherwise assessment can only be based on broad general principles. In other words, there can be a '. . . difficulty of assessment in cases where a clear conceptualization of the learning has yet to be established' (James & Brown 2005: 9). We shall therefore be thinking about learning from a range of theoretical stances, and then allying these to assessment mechanisms which either derive from them, or seem particularly suited in terms of applicability.

Theoretical approaches to learning

There are many theories of learning in existence, and it would be impossible to undertake a review of all of them. However, for everyday music-learning purposes it is possible to classify learning theories into three broad families. These are behaviourist views, constructivist views, and socio-cultural or situated views (James 2006; Taetle & Cutietta 2002).

Behaviourist views

Behaviourism is concerned with observable human behaviours, and arose and became popular during the early to mid-twentieth century. Much of the early work on behaviourism arose from research into animal behaviours. One of the most famous of these is Pavlov's research into dogs, where he conditioned the animals to associate a sound with the presentation of food, ultimately reaching the stage where the dogs would salivate at the sound alone, without any food being present. The example of Pavlov's dogs evidences many key behaviourist notions, and it is from these that the main terminologies arise. Table 5.1 uses this example to outline these main ideas.

This can seem a long way away from the music lesson! However, behaviourist views on education have evolved somewhat from the early work by

Table 5.1 Behaviourist terminologies

Conditioning:	The stage where the animal is presented with food and the sound heard. This will take place on a number of occasions over time.
Stimulus:	That which is presented to the respondent, in this case the sounds which were played whilst the dogs were given food.
Response:	That which results from the stimulus, the dogs salivating.
Reinforcement:	Quite complex in classical behaviourism, but essentially something enjoyable which reinforces the desired response—often, for animals, food.
Punishment:	When an undesired response is obtained, something which is not pleasant is given. In some behaviourist experiments, the animals involved were subject to mild pain!

Pavlov, and later by Skinner, into a coherent view on learning. For behaviourists the key aspect of learning is the stimulus-response (s-r) cycle. They further refine this by saying that complicated activities are best broken down into a series of smaller stages, with mastery of each stage being required before moving onto the next. Reinforcement and punishment are also considered to be a part of the system, the latter often taking the form of withholding reward, rather than the infliction of pain! The main issue that contemporary cognitive psychology has with behaviourism is that aspects of 'mind' are discounted by behaviourists, who claim that observable behaviours are all that matter.

However, it is possible to see the influences of behaviourism in many aspects of music teaching and learning; indeed, Hargreaves argues that 'This learning theory approach is almost certainly that which has had the widest practical application in the field of music learning' (D. Hargreaves 1986: 20). From behaviourism, for example, we can take the notion of breaking down complex tasks into a series of achievable steps. Indeed, it could be considered that learning to play a musical instrument according to the typical western model of practise and refinement is exemplification on a large scale of behaviourist principles. According to Sink, behavioural approaches considered from a music education perspective, and, especially, research into them, have stressed a '. . . teacher-centered instructional model and purposeful change of behavior' where '. . . the teacher leads and directs students to acquire and generate specific, clearly defined knowledge' (Sink 2002: 315). This can clearly be discerned when looking into sequenced learning of a musical instrument. However, as with the caveat from the last paragraph, music educators will want to argue that at some stage it is likely that a mind will be required, not just a set of sensory-motor responses.

The implications for assessment of behaviourist principles as expounded by Mary James could have been written with the traditional view of instrumental music learning in mind. Note here that she is not using 'performance' in its musical sense, but for us, this meaning can be superimposed upon it:

Performance is usually interpreted as either correct or incorrect and poor performance is remedied by more practice in the incorrect items, sometimes by deconstructing them further and going back to even more basic skills. (James 2006: 55)

This behaviourist view can apply equally to classroom learning of instrumental skills, as well as to those of the individual music lesson. But mere sensory-motor coordination is not enough to produce a musical result. After one lesson where I had been teaching a class of pupils some basic keyboard skills, one pupil observed, 'playing the piano is easy, you've only got to press the notes in the right order!'. Well, yes, basically this is true, but there is a little more to it than that, I suspect! We know that 'Identifying the range of musically appropriate mental strategies beginners and intermediate players adopt when learning to play an instrument . . .' (McPherson & Davidson 2006: 337) involves a notion of mind, and so the fact that strict behaviourists ignore the function of the brain in learning and action has led to a number of criticisms of this stance. As Gruhn and Rauscher observe, '. . . the behaviorists failed to do justice to the organization of human behaviour and the complex inner processes that are responsible for generating it' (Gruhn & Rauscher 2002: 445). And so it is to a learning theory that foregrounds the brain that we now turn.

Constructivist views

'At the core of constructivism is the belief that human beings build up knowledge in a slow process, that begins with simple sensory-motor schema during early childhood and progresses to complex schema . . .' (Roth 1999: 6).

The constructivist view of learning places the learner as an active agent with responsibility for development. One of the important early figures in constructivism is Piaget, and especially his work on developing mental structures and the stage theory of development (Piaget 1952). This claims that development occurs, and that what develops are mental structures for dealing with the world. Constructivism is therefore in opposition to behaviourism in that it places a notion of mind at its centre. Piaget's work has been developed by a number of others, including von Glasersfeld, who asserted that 'Knowledge is never acquired passively . . .' (von Glasersfeld 1989).

In constructivism it is knowledge which is held to be constructed, and this knowledge is located within the individual. Von Glasersfeld's observation concerning the non-passivity of knowledge acquisition is key in this view. This contrasts strongly with the behaviourist view that notions of mind are not involved and that an individual simply responds to a stimulus. This means that 'Students in the constructivist view do not merely react to experience. They reflect on it and theorise it, developing mental structures or schemata for understanding it' (Desforges 2000: 69). One of the implications of this view is that learning is meaningful for the learner if they are able to make use of existing knowledge, and build their new understandings upon it. In other words, the learner is able to understand that what they are learning has some connection with prior knowledge (Ausubel 1961).

Building on this notion of prior learning Bruner posited the notion of the *spiral curriculum* (Bruner 1966, 1971). The idea of a spiral curriculum has been hugely important in music education, first of all in the Manhattanville Music Curriculum Programme (MMCP 1970), and then in Swanwick and Tillman's *Sequence of Music Development* (Swanwick & Tillman 1986). The notion of the spiral curriculum has found particular resonance with music educators as it provides a theoretical underpinning to the idea that musical topics can be undertaken with differing degrees of depth at different times in a learner's education career. For example, the area of study of the Blues involves learning about chordal structures, bass lines, and melody, and can be undertaken with pupils with differing degrees of depth, challenge, and complexity throughout their time in school. Figure 5.1 shows a visual representation of this, using topics associated with melody and harmony.

Another of Bruner's contributions to constructivism is the idea of *scaffolding* (Wood et al. 1976). This is where the teacher supports the learning of the pupil, and the metaphor takes its name from the way in which a scaffold supports a building. In music learning scaffolding can often clearly be seen in operation, both in generalist classroom music and in the individual instrumental lesson (Kennell 2002). The ongoing use of scaffolding needs to be gradually and sensitively withdrawn as the learner achieves mastery of their instrument, and it is a decision of the teacher as to the extent and rate of this withdrawal (Vygotsky 1978).

Another aspect of constructivist thought is the notion of a novice-expert continuum, and of the corresponding shift which occurs as learners move along an axis from beginners to becoming more proficient. The terminology 'expert' is not used in its everyday sense, but to imply a level of knowledge, understanding, and proficiency which allows for an essential level of mastery. There are arguments that the shift does not necessarily involve knowing more, but being able to apply knowledge in an appropriate fashion.

The implications for assessment of constructivist views on learning are manifold. The importance of prior learning means that formative assessment needs to play an ongoing role in looking forwards to future improvement. The

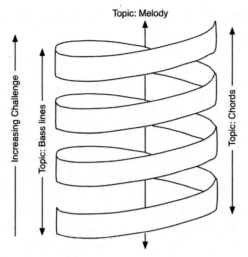

Fig. 5.1 Spiral curriculum

notion of scaffolding requires teachers to make a series of formative assessment judgments as to how much support needs to be offered to pupils, and to decide at what stage pupils will be able to work unsupported. The idea of a novice-expert shift can be seen to be operating in terms of musical skill development, particularly mastery of instrumental music skills, but also in the development of conceptual understanding.

Socio-cultural views

'Neither development nor learning occurs in a vacuum; both are located socially and, arguably, socially constructed . . .' (Welch 2001b: 202).

Socio-cultural views of learning stress the importance of the individual within society. One of the key proponents of this way of thinking about learning is Vygotsky, who observed that 'Every function in the child's cultural development appears twice: first, on the social level, and later, on the individual level; first, between people ("interpsychological") and then inside the child ("intrapsychological"). This applies equally to voluntary attention, to logical memory, and to the formation of concepts. All the higher functions originate as actual relationships between individuals.' (Vygotsky 1978: 57). What Vygotsky is saying here is that learning occurs as a result of the interactions of an individual with the people around them, the people being a part of society, and operating within a culture, hence socio-cultural.

One of Vygotsky's best known contributions to learning theory is that of the *zone of proximal development* (ZPD). The ZPD is the area between that which a learner is able to do with assistance, and that which they will be able to do by themselves in future; in other words, 'what the child is able to do in collaboration today he[1] will be able to do independently tomorrow' (Vygotsky 1987: 211). The implications of this for music learning are that learning takes place in a social sphere, and that 'group work is not an optional extra' (James 2006: 57). It is important to note that 'the zone of proximal development is not simply a way to refer to development through assistance by a more competent other' (Chaiklin 2003: 57), but that it can be used to account for very real differences in learning which lead to development.

Also important in the socio-cultural viewpoint are the linked areas of situated learning, distributed cognition, and activity theory. Situated learning (Lave & Wenger 1991) involves learners being involved in situations where learning by doing is shared between members of a group. The notion of *communities of practice* is important here, and '. . . learners inevitably participate in communities of practitioners and that the mastery of knowledge and skill requires newcomers to move toward full participation in the sociocultural practices of a community' (Lave & Wenger 1991: 29). From a music education stance we can clearly see examples of this: in learning to play an instrument, in group composing in the classroom, in junior bands through to advanced youth orchestras, in bands that rehearse in garages; all of these involve participation in communities of practice. Lave and Wenger describe how beginners start at the edge of a community of practice, and move towards the centre as they proceed towards mastery. Again, processes clearly visible in both formal and informal modes of music learning. The notion of authentic tasks, where pupils work on 'real' tasks, as opposed to non-real school-based ones, can be seen to have links to notions of communities of practice. Music education is quite well favoured here, as learning to play an instrument is an authentic task, as are many composing and performing activities.

Linking back to the ZPD, but thinking especially about conjoint work in, for example, a group context, then the idea that work which pupils do collectively, exceeding their possible individual capabilities, relates to the notion of distributed cognition, as propounded by Salomon (1993b), Cole & Engeström (1993), and Cole (1996). In this view the classroom music-making process of, say, composing can be thought of as being shared amongst members of a group, and being jointly 'owned' by the group. The terminology employed by Salomon is that of an artefact. This does not mean that the composing process

---

[1] Gendered specificity in original.

has been reified, but that 'artefact' is the labelling terminology for that which is shared among the group. The notion of a shared artefact makes it explicit that a group of students creating something together have joint ownership. Indeed the use of the everyday terminology that they are creating something 'between them' is most appropriate in this instance.

Closely allied with both situated learning and distributed cognition is activity theory. Activity theory takes as its unit of analysis '. . . the concept of object-oriented, collective, and culturally mediated human activity . . .' (Engeström et al. 1999: 9) It also '. . . insists upon, a pedagogic imagination that reflects on the processes of teaching and learning as much more than face-to-face interaction or the simple transmission of prescribed knowledge and skill' (Daniels 2004: 2). Activity theory is helpful in illuminating the way in which complex activity systems operate, and many classroom music-making processes could be considered in this way. This will be considered in more detail in Chapter 17.

The implications for assessment of socio-cultural approaches are to do with ways in which groups operate, group learning and assessment being features of some 16+ examination certificates, as well as ensemble performances. Authentic tasks also have a place here, with many teachers setting their pupils real-world problems, composing, or performing tasks to undertake. Indeed, it can be argued that the process of public performing at a school concert level is not different *in kind* from appearing at a gig, club, or other concert venue, and that the subsequent audience assessment will be made along not dissimilar lines.

Multiple intelligences

Howard Gardner's research work at Harvard on Multiple Intelligences (MI) is internationally known. In this, Gardner argues against the notion of IQ being simply measured by a single IQ score, and says instead that each individual has differing abilities in differing levels in a wide range of areas. He singles out music as one of these areas. This should be a powerful argument for the place of music in the curriculum alone, as it is one of the few school subject areas which has a one-to-one mapping with the notion of Multiple Intelligences! Gardner's theory does not detail *how* music should be learned, or about pedagogic approaches, which is helpful in that it retains a specificity which privileges the subject area.

One of the problems associated with the multiple intelligences approach has been its application in curricular terms by non-specialists. Even more concerning has been the proliferation of tests for MI, which are designed to measure the various competences of an individual in the differing areas of the intelligences. This can be problematic for music educators when the questions are as general as 'do you like music?'. However, these reservations aside, which doubtless were not approved by Gardner or his team, it is good to have music listed as a specific area of intelligence in its own right.

We have been thinking so far about theoretical approaches to learning. The terminology 'knowledge' has been used on a number of occasions during these discussion. Knowledge is often seen as the opposite side of the coin to learning, in common parlance what is learned is knowledge. But is it really that simple? Are there different types of knowledge? In this next section we look into these issues, again with a view to gaining a greater understanding of assessment, and how and why it can be used.

Knowledge

'Whole books on learning exist that have almost nothing to say about knowledge, except to treat it as the "content" of the learning process, i.e. something that is not affected by the process, and is itself not affected by the process.' (McCormick & Paechter 1999: xi)

If the content of music education courses was straightforward and unproblematic, then all units of work and programmes of study in all schools would look more or less the same. The fact that they do not means that there are different ways of organizing knowledge—assuming again that knowledge is the ' "content" of the learning process'. In the UK at least, class music teachers operating within a centrally imposed National Curriculum, still have control over the content of what is taught. Doing so involves making a set of decisions as to what should be included in a curriculum, and maybe more importantly, what should be omitted. Curriculum time is very closely prescribed by schools, and there is a problem with fitting everything in to a course of study. So what is it that should be included, and why? In order to answer this question we need to think first about the different types of knowledge that are likely to be included in a programme of study.

The branch of study concerned with knowledge is epistemology. Much has been written about the nature of knowledge, often starting from Plato's assertion that knowledge is a justified, true belief. For the purposes of this investigation, the main concern is with types of knowledge that will figure in music education, and the role assessment can play in developing them.

Let us start with two examples. A pupil in a KS3 music class is working on a group composing project where the pupils are making up a piece of music to go with a picture of a forest. What do they need to know to be able to do this? The list, in no particular order, will include at least these things, and probably a lot more besides, as shown in Table 5.2.

Table 5.2 Knowledge in a composing group

- What a forest is.
  - What the atmosphere/feeling of a forest is.
  - How to render the 'feeling' of a forest in sounds.
- How to play the instruments they have.
  - To be able to perform their piece.
- How to organize sounds in a musical fashion.
- How to work as a group.
  - How to communicate orally.
    - To be able to discuss their piece.
  - How to communicate musically.
    - To think creatively.
    - To know what a good composition will entail.
  - How to join their individual contributions together.
- To be able to generate new ideas.
- To work within the given time-frame.

In the second example we can consider a pupil having an instrumental lesson on the clarinet; the pupil is not a beginner, but has not been playing long, and soon they will doing their Grade 2 exam. What do they need to know to be able to play a piece? Again, in no particular order, and again doubtless there will be things that can be added to this list, as shown in Table 5.3.

It should be apparent from these tables that a number of different types of knowledge are involved. The knowledge of the fingering for a B♭ is a different type of knowledge from knowing how to work as a group. One straightforward classification of knowledge is to divide things into 'knowing how' and 'knowing that' (Ryle 1949). Another way of labelling these two types of knowledge is to use the terminologies 'declarative knowledge' and 'procedural knowledge'. Declarative knowledge, that which can be spoken, links closely with 'knowing that', as this tends to be factual knowledge which can be explained verbally. Procedural knowledge links closely with 'knowing how', as procedures are often of the 'how to' type.

Sometimes both types are needed for a single outcome. A non-clarinettist can learn the fingering for a B♭, knowing that a certain combination of keys need to be pressed—declarative knowledge—but be utterly unable to get a sound out of the instrument, as knowing how to get a sound out of the instrument is procedural knowledge. Mixing the two types of knowledge in this way

Table 5.3 Knowledge in an instrumental music lesson

- How to assemble the instrument
- How to make the instrument sound
- What being in tune involves
  - How to play in tune
  - The fingerings for the notes required
- To have a sense of timing and rhythm
  - To be able to play in time
  - How to read staff notation
  - How to breathe properly
  - How to phrase
- How to perform
  - Know what a good performance will look and sound like
  - What a musical performance is
- How to improve on what they are doing
  - To be able to practise
    - To know how to practise the difficult bits

is recognized in the philosophy of knowledge when defining the types of knowledge which are appropriate to a given pedagogic situation (Hirst 1981).

Specific to music education, Swanwick and Taylor took the two types of knowledge we have been discussing, and added two more:

- Know how: . . . to spell a word . . . to manipulate a musical instrument
- Knowing that: . . . $2 + 7 = 9$ . . . Beethoven wrote nine symphonies
- Knowing him/her/it: . . . a painting . . . specific knowledge of a musical work
- Knowing what's what: . . . what we like . . . what we value. (Swanwick & Taylor 1982: 7)

The third of these Swanwick expanded upon in a later work, 'the absolutely central core involved in knowing music can be appropriately called "knowledge by acquaintance". . . . We might call acquaintance knowledge knowing "this"; knowing *this* person, *this* place, *this* symphony, *this* song.'[2] (Swanwick 1994: 17).

---

[2] Italics in original.

Pedagogical content knowledge

The list of knowledge types under consideration so far applies primarily to the learner. Granted, these will have been duplicated in the teacher, both as the teacher enters the community of practice of music teachers, and as part of their learning experiences in the past. But teachers will also have an additional knowledge form of their own, this will be *pedagogical content knowledge*. Pedagogical content knowledge relates specifically to teaching, and as Shulman observes, consists of '. . . the most useful forms of representation of these ideas, the most powerful analogies, illustrations, examples, explanations, and demonstrations—in a word, the ways of representing and formulating the subject that make it comprehensible to others' (Shulman 1986: 6). Shulman goes on to note that, 'Pedagogical content knowledge also includes an understanding of what makes the learning of specific topics easy or difficult: the conceptions and preconceptions that students of different ages and backgrounds bring with them to the learning . . .' (Shulman 1993: 85). The acquisition and possession of pedagogical content knowledge are important aspects of the training and professional development of teachers, sometimes, admittedly, undertaken tacitly, but significant nonetheless.

Knowledge, competencies, and skills

'There is little agreement and much controversy on how pupils learn their musical knowledge.' (Philpott 2000: 24)

We have already discussed how there are different types of knowledge. In a music teaching curriculum there will be a series of 'bits' of knowledge which music teachers will want the pupils to acquire, and a series of activities in which they will want the pupils to participate. This dichotomy, between *acquisition* and *participation*, was expounded neatly by Anna Sfard (1998), who proposed that these two areas be considered as metaphors for learning, and that neither one by itself was inadequate. We can clearly see this operating in music education. There are aspects of knowledge which an individual needs to acquire, at a basic level perhaps a knowledge of where the notes are on an instrument, and of the concepts which underpin musical elements, such as pitch, rhythm, and dynamics. Then there are aspects of knowledge which require active participation by the learner; musical performance and group composing being two examples. Bearing this in mind, we can proceed to think about these metaphors for learning—the acquisition metaphor and the participation metaphor—in later chapters, as we think about different aspects of knowledge.

One of the aspects of knowledge that is frequently to be encountered in music education programmes is that of *skills*. A '. . . skill is a form of the representation of learning and it is the ability to do something that has been learnt' (Moon 2004: 15). The notion of skills encompasses a wide range of attributes, both physical skills of sensory-motor coordination, and ones which are essentially located in the mind: 'Music making entails perceptual skills (e.g., apprehending structural information as well as social information, including non-verbal cues exchanged between performer and audience), cognitive skills (e.g., memory, decision making, pattern recognition), and of course motor skills' (Lehmann & Davidson 2002: 542).

Many of the structural and cognitive skills associated with musicking are picked up implicitly due to enculturation. In other words '. . . almost every member of a culture is a musical expert' (Sloboda 2005: 248). For the music teacher, deciding on which skills are needed to be learned forms a major part of the curricular decision-making process. In the UK, this is governed to some extent by the developmental model espoused by the National Curriculum. Whatever model the teacher decides to adopt, skill acquisition needs to be thought of hierarchically, with more complex skills following on from the acquisition of simpler ones. Assessment of skill acquisition can be divided between those skills which are to some extent domain-specific, such as those appertaining to a particular musical instrument, and those which may have some form of general transferability between domains, such as the skills required to work well in a group situation.

This distinction between different types of knowledge leads to a fundamental question concerning the nature of knowledge itself, which means that, following Sfard, it is helpful to think of some forms of knowledge as existing separate from the learner, and some existing as jointly constructed by the learner. This means that rather than knowledge existing in one form only, where the teacher has it and tries to find the most efficacious way of 'giving' it to the pupils, it may be more helpful to think of knowledge as a continuum, to have: '. . . a conception of knowledge as external to the learner and fixed—at one extreme; and a conception of knowledge as constructed or co-constructed by the learner/s and as fluid—at the other extreme' (E. Hargreaves 2005: 224).

For the music teacher this may be less of a problem than with other subjects at school. After all, we have always known that instrumental mastery cannot be achieved simply by the teacher 'telling' the learner how to play; it has to be achieved by participation in playing the instrument. Although, as we have seen, specific information such as the fingering for B♭ on a clarinet is amenable to being imparted, we also know that simply being told how to play a B♭ does not guarantee that this will happen!

Competencies are related to skills, and some educational programmes use the terminologies in an interchangeable fashion. Competences can be considered to be skills which have been mastered, to a greater or lesser extent. The assessment elements of various skills and competences are considered separately in later chapters

Knowledge types in music education

What this discussion means for music education is that there is very little knowledge which we can consider to exist in isolation from other knowledge. This has implications for assessment purposes in that it can be very difficult to atomistically separate out one specific attribute upon which to focus. In other words 'clearly such rich activity cannot be reduced to just a single dimension . . .' (Swanwick 1994: 104). The differing notions of knowledge can be considered as operating in a number of dimensions simultaneously. Figure 5.2 attempts a visual representation of this complexity.

The left-hand column of this figure shows different types of knowledge which can be considered as being located within an individual pupil. The right-hand side shows the effect of how these aspects have been taught, and how the teacher chooses to deliver them to the pupil. The bottom of the figure shows the modes of encounter with the types of knowledge, whether aspects of these are acquired, participatory, or both. These modes of encounter might also have been in contexts in which the chosen pedagogy of the teacher has had a part to play.

On the right of the diagram is pedagogical content knowledge, which refers to the knowledge teachers have concerning how to teach topics and other aspects appertaining to pedagogy. This has an effect on the understanding of an individual pupil, as the manner in which a topic is presented and taught can influence the efficacy with which it is learned. Learning here can be viewed in some ways as being a product of interactions between teacher and pupil.

This is a complex diagram, endeavouring to represent a complex series of constructs, and which shows that assessment decisions are not going to be simple. However, we also need to balance the philosophical with the pragmatic, and realize that there are times when busy music teachers will need to assess atomistically, and so we have to think about what it is that is going on when this happens. Artificially separated atomistic assessment is not wrong *per se*, but a danger occurs when evidence from assessment undertaken in this way is mistaken for doing something it was not intended to. Thus the complexity of musical knowledge, achievement, and understanding represented by, for

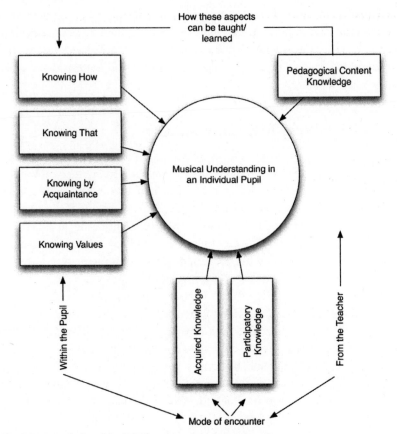

Fig. 5.2 Complexity of knowledge types in music education

example, National Curriculum level descriptors, grades, standards, or marks, cannot be achieved by evidencing attainment in a single task or from a single lesson. Single-focus assessments cannot possibly cover all the intricacies of music learning, skills, competencies, understandings, and knowledge which all pupils will have.

What is there in music education which can be assessed?

So, returning to Fig. 5.2, there are four principle domains of knowledge in music education: knowing how, knowing that, knowing by acquaintance, and knowing values. This means that these four domains form the primary areas of content which are amenable to assessment, and these are encountered by participation or by acquisition. At the most simplistic level, it is possible to think about assessment in music as being undertaken in these areas. This means that teachers will be asking questions of their learners in these four overlapping areas. This is the 'what' question of assessment, and so it is to the key philosophical 'why' question of assessment that we now turn.

Chapter 6

Why assess?

It is well known that historically many music teachers have had concerns and doubts regarding the use of assessment. In the early 1980s comments such as these were not uncommon:

- 'Is the subject [music] capable of assessment?
- Assessment—is it relevant? Or is it indulged in to conform with the rest of school procedure?' (Paynter 1982: 174–5)

The first of these statements relates to a position held by some music educators, that there are some aspects of music which are not amenable to assessment. What is often heard in relation to this argument is that the work that pupils do represents their best efforts at self-expression, that to assess this will be to inevitably diminish their self-esteem, and that for many pupils this is a price not worth paying. Others would argue that different types of music fulfil different functions and that to assess them involves giving voice to personal preferences, which begs the question as to why the preferences of one person should be any 'better' than those of another? The second statement is, in many ways, related to the first, in that it is saying that assessment for music education is divorced from the various realities of musical experience, and that its only purpose is to conform to legislation.

More recently similar questions have been posed:

- 'It is difficult to assess compositions
- Assessing music is a subjective thing and you cannot be objective about it
- Aesthetic education is to do with feelings. You cannot assess these.' (Bray 2002: 79)

So, against this backdrop, why should any assessments in music be made at all? Can teaching music take place without assessment? On a more pragmatic basis, given that there is in legislation nowadays an imperative to assess, what does this mean in practice, and why are music teachers conforming to it?

Teaching is assessing

It is hard to imagine teaching without assessing; indeed, Swanwick's observation, '. . . to teach is to assess' (Swanwick 1988: 149) has already been discussed.

In unpicking this statement, we need to begin by observing that there is no axiomatic linkage of teaching and learning. In other words that what is taught is not necessarily learned. This means that music teachers will always be undertaking processes of decision making, in terms of deciding both what to teach and how to teach it. This can be seen when a classroom teacher has to teach the same topic to three classes in a year group. By the second lesson the classes are more than likely to have attainments which differ somewhat from each other, which in turn means that the planning and delivery for the second and subsequent lessons will reflect this. Likewise, although an instrumental music teacher may have twelve different pupils all doing Grade 4, the lessons for each will not be identical. The decision as to what to do in each of these cases results from assessments which have been made, and acted upon.

Reasons to assess

In earlier chapters we have looked at purposes of assessment, and considered differences between formative and summative purposes of assessment. To some extent, these can be used as the basis for answering the question 'why assess'? But other areas also impinge upon this, with varying impact upon teachers and pupils, which means that reasons to assess include:

1. To help pupils improve in what they are doing
2. To measure what pupils have done
3. To measure what pupils have learned
4. To provide evidence for pupil progress
5. To indicate how much effort a pupil has put into their work
6. To ensure that standards rise
7. To provide indications as to how well pupils will do in the future
8. To provide information for parents concerning their children's progress
9. To check that specific topics have been learned
10. For a teacher to evaluate the efficacy of a Unit of Work
11. To measure how well pupils have been taught
12. To provide statistical data
13. To measure how effective a teacher is
14. To compare the results from different schools
15. To show that music is important in contributing to general education
16. To compare different geographical areas in terms of educational outcome

17. To evaluate the effectiveness of educational interventions

18. To evaluate the efficacy of governmental strategies in education.

This is a complex and disparate set of reasons for assessment! Many of these, and many more besides, will impinge at some point upon the work of the music teacher. What is also apparent from this list is that there are tensions between different uses of assessment. In essence, we can determine a number of such tensions from this list, which result in different four perspectives. These different perspectives are:

1. Those of teachers, who want to use assessment to develop the learning and improve the performance of their pupils

2. Those of school leadership teams, who want to audit the performance of different subject areas and individual or groups of teachers within their school. This information can also be used to provide data for . . .

3. School inspection regimes, such as Ofsted, who use assessment data to form judgements about how schools are performing, to identify failing schools, and to feed such information to . . .

4. Central and local government, who will want to demonstrate effective spending of public money, develop policy in this area, and prioritize spending.

The tensions in this list can be resolved still further, and be distilled down to two: the teacher in the classroom, and those outside the classroom. In other words: '. . . most teachers see assessment as a means of supporting their students' growth and development, many administrators, school boards, and test designers do not. The latter care more about using summative assessments to identify "failing" students and "failing" schools . . .' (Elliott 2006: 42). And maybe, some would add, 'failing' teachers. Tensions between the requirements of the teacher and the requirements of those beyond the classroom has led to a conflation of different purposes of assessment, which has led in turn to a blurring of different intentions, and the distinctions between them. This has been a bone of contention for music teachers, and those of many other curricula subjects too. Because the assessment regimes in many schools devour data, they have a non-stop hunger for more and more numbers to be produced, as this is the only sort of data that spreadsheets can handle. This has resulted, as we noted earlier, in teachers changing their own ways of assessing away from formative, and towards a series of mini summative assessments. This is particularly galling for music teachers, because of the traditional strength which music teachers had in the practices of informal and formative assessments. Moving away from the practice of regular formative assessment has happened for a number of reasons. These include:

1. '. . . the effective down-grading (in England, at least) of teachers' judgements in comparison with externally devised tests or tasks . . .' (Harlen &
   James 1997: 366)

2. 'Teachers feel obliged to "prove that they are doing assessment", this is usually expressed in terms of having to write something down, for example,
   ticking boxes.' (Neesom 2000: 5)

3. The feeling that talking with pupils is part of what a teacher does anyway,
   and is not assessment

4. The misunderstanding of formative assessment by school assessment
   managers, who are often from a background outside the Arts

5. 'Bullying' by heavyweight curriculum subjects, such as Maths and Science,
   who can easily produce reams of quantitative assessment data on demand

6. The desire for Music (and the Arts) not to be seen as peripheral

Add to this the pressures and tensions explored earlier in this section, and it
becomes clear that there has been a shift away from learning, towards auditing. This shift becomes problematic when auditing *replaces* teaching and
learning. As the old country saying goes, the pig doesn't get fatter by being
weighed frequently!

Confusions between assessment and testing

A number of the externally referenced modalities for assessment outlined in
the previous sections are achieved through testing, and, as has been observed,
this has resulted in a confusion concerning the interrelationship between
assessment and testing in the minds of many music teachers, with the result
that formative assessment has been downplayed in favour of summative testing. It may well be the case that the very notion of formative assessment has
become supplanted by requirements to produce summative assessment data,
and that this has resulted in a confusion wherein *all* assessment has become
viewed as summative, or, to put it another way, that all assessment involves
testing. This confusion has, in many cases, bypassed school assessment managers, who, as we have observed, often come from subject backgrounds outside the Arts, and so when these people tell music teachers what it is they
require, the busy music teacher—with concerts, rehearsals, peripatetic music
lessons, and a thousand and one other things to organize—simply comply, in
the mistaken assumption these people know what they are talking about! This
compliance is aided and abetted by the factors 2 and 3 in the list above. The
view that assessment has come to be synonymous with testing has resulted in
music teachers coming to believe that what they do when they are undertaking

formative assessment is not really assessment, as it does not involve testing; this results in them not feeling they can, as Neesom observes in point 2, 'prove they are doing assessment'. A corollary of this is that formative assessment data, which in music will often be musical, is downplayed in favour of statistical summative data. As one music teacher observed, 'When our school assessment coordinator asks to see my records, how am I going to be able to compete with the Maths and Science departments?' (Fautley 2004: 213), a situation which the heavyweight subjects have often tacitly perpetuated. Rather than admit their own possible weaknesses in formative assessment, they have adopted a 'quantitative is best' position, backed by the requirement for statistical data produced from evidence from test scores and the like. In music this can be a problem, and can result in numerical test-scores being produced which do not measure anything much that is worthwhile, as it is often easier to provide evidence for something simple, than to ask, and answer, something difficult. The mistake that this engenders is to measure whatever can be easily measured.

McNamara's fallacy

A classic version of this problem, that of measuring whatever can be easily measured, is known as McNamara's fallacy, named after an American politician who argued that in war, some statistics mattered more than others. The general principles he set out with relation to this have since been placed into a much wider arena. McNamara's fallacy runs like this:

The first step is to measure whatever can be easily measured. This is OK as far as it goes. The second step is to disregard that which can't easily be measured or to give it an arbitrary quantitative value. This is artificial and misleading. The third step is to presume that what can't be measured easily really isn't important. This is blindness. The fourth step is to say that what can't be easily measured really doesn't exist. This is suicide. (Handy 1994: 219)

This is a very real danger for music teachers. In a music lesson, assessing whether or not a group of pupils in a composing assignment had used a crescendo or not would be an easy thing to do, as either they did or they did not. Assessing whether in a performance unit a keyboard player used the correct fingers for playing a simple melody would be another easy assessment to make. However, both of these assessments ignore any form of musical judgement as to quality of response. Yet similar examples to these are to be found regularly in music classes, where that which is assessed is that which *can be easily* assessed, rather than that which is *worth* assessing. This mistaking is not done deliberately, but rather is an unintended side effect of the audit culture which exists in many schools and institutions today. As teachers we need to be aware that 'We start out with the aim of making the important measurable and end up making only the measurable important' (Wiliam 2001: 58).

Assessment as separate activity

Teaching and assessing, as we have seen, go hand-in-hand, and teachers will be constantly assessing as they teach. However, within the paradigm where teachers need to prove they are doing assessment, one way in which teachers have addressed this is to consider the notion of taking a series of 'snapshots' of attainment and using these as evidence of progression. It is quite possible that this idea comes from subjects such as Maths, where, with, say five lessons a week, teachers and pupils can afford ten minutes taken out of learning time each week for a quick-fire test. This is probably fine for Maths teachers, but in music, where typically, five lessons means five weeks, this cannot be done with anything like the same regularity, or in such an atomised fashion.

Assessment tests and tasks

The notion of 'doing assessment' in music often involves practical work of a specified type, and the commonest forms of these are assessment tasks and tests. Tests have a well-established place in educational practice, and form what could be called a standard element of pedagogic activity; they are what teachers do. In music, however, there are a number of different types, and tests can come in one (or a mixture) of four essential forms:

- Written tests—either in text or staff notation, where no sonic element is involved
- Listening tests—often involving written answers to audiation
- Practical tests—where some form of musical performance is involved
- Viva voce tests—where questions are asked and answers given in spoken form, sometimes with a musical instrument too.

Music teachers will be familiar with these, from their professional practice and from their own life stories. For musical learning purposes each of these are examples of summative assessments. They are looking back on learning, and providing a snapshot of achievement at a given instant and in a given situation.

One important aspect of practical tests in music is that concerning validity. Thus we will want to know that a guitarist has played their guitar in a practical test, we are unlikely to base our views on instrumental proficiency based on a written test (this is an obvious point, but, perhaps surprisingly, still needs pointing out!). Stobart's definition of a test is helpful here, '. . . it is a representation of a skill, so the closer it mirrors the skill, the more valid it is likely to be' (Stobart 2008: 108). This is what we want, so that tests mirror the skill being tested for. But playing an instrument is only one aspect of musicality. For example, for many musicians, ensemble performance is an important aspect of their music making. Sensitivity to the needs of an ensemble is harder to test for, and needs careful construction of appropriate testing conditions to be meaningful.

There are advantages and disadvantages associated with each type of test, and, where the music teacher is in control of the testing context, these need to be given some thought at the test design stage. Building on the types of knowledge discussed in Chapter 5, Table 6.1 shows typical examples of test types, and gives a brief outline of advantages and disadvantages of each.

What this table does not show, however, is possibly the most crucial question of all for the teacher, namely 'is a test the most appropriate format to gain the information I need?'. This, although again seemingly obvious, has a number of important sub-aspects to it which the teacher needs to think through. Again, this will be very much context dependant, but does require addressing on an individual basis. Sometimes it may be more appropriate for pupils to undertake an assessment task, but there are a number of significant differences between a test and a task.

Assessment tasks

A task differs from a test in a number of key areas. These are shown in Table 6.2.

Whether to use tests or tasks will be a matter of individual professional judgment for the teacher. We have already seen how assessment does not only take place during tests ('the assessment lesson'), and so it is important not to relegate thoughts on assessment solely to these infrequent moments. Tasks are an ideal forum in which assessment judgments can be made, and it is from the outcome of these that future learning can be planned for and executed.

Moments of assessment opportunity

Tasks are an obvious way for learning to take place in music. Musical learning will be evidenced throughout a wide range of what goes on in the classroom. Trying to record assessment judgements in manageable ways means that ongoing assessment for an individual is likely to be piecemeal, with 'on the fly' being a legitimate way of working. This gives rise to the notion of moments of assessment opportunity. Moments of assessment opportunity occur when the teacher notices attainment, understanding, or skill-acquisition evidenced by a particular pupil, and makes a recording of this in some form. Equally important will be evidence for *not* attaining, understanding, or acquiring skills, and

Table 6.1 Test types

Test type:	Typical uses	Advantages	Disadvantages
Written	'Knowing that' e.g.: Historical Knowledge Knowledge about instruments Music theory, e.g. note writing, scales, keys.	Easy to administer to large groups, can be marked away from the context. Some forms (e.g. multiple choice) very quick to mark.	Can only deal with some forms of knowledge. Not always directly appropriate (e.g. silent harmony tests). Some forms, e.g. essay, time consuming to mark.
Listening	Knowing by acquaintance: Knowledge arrived at by hearing music, based on prior learning; Specific aspects of music recognition e.g. cadences, key changes, time signatures.	Have face validity. Relate directly to music heard. Short answer questions can be quick and easy to mark.	Makes a noise, so cannot be done alongside other subjects! Requires preparation of audio material in advance, either recorded or to be played live. Mark schemes have to pre-determine a range of possible answers.
Practical	Knowing how: Playing an instrument: Ensemble performances Performances of compositions Conducting.	Validity of testing that which is relevant.	Time consuming if done on an individual basis. Can be hard to assess an individual in an ensemble activity. Mark schemes can have problems with inter-rater reliability.
Viva voce	Knowing that/knowing by acquaintance/ knowing values: Can follow practical, and deal with issues arising from performance. College/university/ conservatoire to examine e.g. dissertations.	Questions which require a conversation which are designed to be more in-depth than could be pre-planned, to reveal the extent of knowledge.	Time consuming if done on an individual basis. Require examiners to have an in-depth knowledge of topic to be able to develop follow-up questions.

again this can be recorded in some form. Doing this for every child with frequency is problematic in classroom music with limited contact, but building up evidence over time in this fashion is key to its success. Not only that, but utilizing moments of assessment opportunity means that more time can be spent on teaching and learning, and less time given to the artificial generation of assessment evidence. In England a version of this is supported by the Qualification and Curriculum Authority's work on assessing pupils'

Table 6.2 Assessment tasks

Formality:	A test is imbued with a degree of seriousness
Conditions:	Relating to formality, and often designed to test individuals
Opportunity:	Tests are often pre-planned, tasks are ongoing
Weighting:	Tests are often afforded more status by pupils and teachers than tasks
Validity:	In constructing tests teachers will try to form some intra- or inter-cohort validity. Tasks can be undertaken with differentiation for each class of pupils
Encapsulation:	Tests often focus on one aspect of learning or skill acquisition, tasks tend to be more general in nature
Readiness:	Often tests take place at predetermined times. Some flexibility can be built in ('take it when you're ready') but this can be problematic in classroom music learning
Formative potential:	The formative use of summative assessment is a common attribute of music teaching, and tasks can offer significantly more potential to improve learning

progress (APP): 'It reduces the need to use tests and specific assessment tasks to make assessment judgements by taking into account a far wider range of evidence. This gives a clearer and more accurate picture of learners' achievements and progress' (QCA 2008b: 6). Moments of assessment opportunity are very useful for the classroom music teacher and, importantly, allow assessment judgements to be used to improve learning.

Assessment as accountability

For many teachers, there are persistent feelings that their school leadership teams perceive music to be a fringe subject, and therefore vulnerable to cuts in both time and staffing. There are also issues of accountability in terms of assessment data, both locally within the school and more widely within communities and systems. Against this backdrop, many music teachers have the impression that public valorization of their role comes from what Salaman (1983) refers to as the *Kapellmeister* aspects of their work, organizing and directing concerts, and the associated tasks of extra-curricular music making, scheduling and taking rehearsals, arranging music for the forces available, and so on. Yet in league-tables and inspections this role can be downplayed in favour of the pedagogic function of the job, meaning that teachers can end up feeling torn. But, as David Bray observes (2000b: 6), Kapellmeister activities should not be the core function of the music teacher; this should be that of the *education* of all pupils through class music lessons. Important though these activities undoubtedly are, assessment of them normally comes in the form of evaluative comments from appreciative stakeholders, and it is the assessment of what goes on in the classroom, studio, and instrumental lesson that worries music teachers more.

The role of assessments made in educative situations are often wider than the immediate concerns of teacher and pupils, 'Policy makers, educators, and the public are looking to assessments to serve a variety of purposes, including gauging student learning, holding education systems accountable, signaling worthy goals for students and teachers to work toward, and providing useful feedback for instructional decision making' (Pellegrino & Goldman 2008: 7–8). Technically speaking this refers to uses, rather than purposes of assessment, but the issue remains pertinent, that of 'holding education systems accountable'. Historically, in the UK at least, one way in which music could be seen to be viable as an appropriate subject for teaching in schools was by emphasizing those aspects of it which most neatly fitted with what were perceived as academic. Doing this '. . . enabled music to be established more firmly as a "class" subject; if music could be shown to have its own grammar, literature, analysis and history then it could be taught like any other subject and deserved a place in the grammar school curriculum' (Shepherd et al. 1977: 203). This view has to some extent persisted to this day, with music teachers feeling that developing formal summative assessment is a way in which to show that music can coexist alongside other subjects. This has meant in some cases developing assessments which privilege the technical over the aesthetic, and finding ways to micro-measure skill acquisition. Public accountability for this aspect of their work is to be found in the publication of National Curriculum end-of-key-stage results, and in those of examination results at 16+ and beyond. For music this presents a slight problem. National Curriculum results are not subject to external moderation or verification; although seemingly great store is set by them, there is, apart from Ofsted inspections, no reliable way of knowing that what school A thinks of as being level 5 attainment is the same as the perception of school B. This means that music teachers, often working in small departments in terms of staffing, cannot be sure that their assessment results are reliable. Added to this is the temptation for schools to want their results to tend towards normal frequency distribution, and it is clear that there are all sorts of potential problems in store for music teachers! But what this does mean is that assessments which teachers give will have ramifications well beyond the immediacy of the educational setting. 'Why assess?' therefore includes notions of an evidentiary requirement beyond the immediate needs of the classroom.

Who is the assessment for?

Closely related to the question of 'why assess?' is that of for whom assessment is being undertaken. We have already encountered the notion of assessments having to do 'double duty' (Boud 2000). Asking for whom assessment is being undertaken adds another layer to this question, as in many cases there are multiple audiences and users of assessment data. The obvious answer to the question as to why assessment is taking place is to improve the learning of the pupils in the class or instrumental music lesson. This is the role of assessment as beneficial to learning improvement. On the other side of the equation, as it were, is the role of assessment to audit learning. These two roles can be conceived of as being complementary, but serving different masters. Auditing alone, as we saw earlier in this chapter, does not improve learning. Likewise, helping pupils get better in their learning needs to be undertaken against a reliable evidence base, hence some form of auditing is required. What tends to happen is that the teacher has to undertake a complex balancing act, juggling the various needs of pupils and systems in order to both promote and audit learning. Figure 6.1 gives a flow-chart representation of this stage of teacher thinking about assessment.

In this figure the shorthand 'systems' is employed for uses of assessment which are not directly concerned with classroom learning, such as data for assessment managers. This places a clear distinction between the different uses to which assessment data is put, and, if given to assessment managers who put pressure on music teachers for data, can be employed to demonstrate that there is a clear difference between assessment for classroom purposes which helps with music making, and assessment for auditing purposes, which serves a different set of functions. As has been observed elsewhere, many music teachers talk of having to 'do' assessment simply to provide data for others. This may have a purpose which the music teacher is unaware of (in which case some explanation by those responsible would be appropriate!), but given the time constraints in the music room, maximizing opportunities for musical learning, and for music making, will obviously be a priority. The balancing act needs careful handling!

Assessment as a political act

One of the factors of assessment which underpins its existence in education today stems from its historical place in society, and is one which we ought not to lose sight of. This is the place of assessment as a means for sorting out workers and managers, for determining the future place of an individual in society. As Patricia Broadfoot observes, 'Assessment procedures are the vehicle

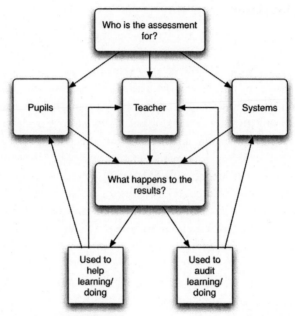

Fig. 6.1 Who is the assessment for?

whereby the dominant rationality of the corporate capitalist societies typical of the contemporary Western world is translated into the systems and process of schooling' (Broadfoot 1999: 64). This may seem like an extreme position when considering how to help pupils develop at classroom music, but it is important to remember that assessment procedures have not come from out of nowhere, but they have a history which has had social control as one of its outcomes. Indeed, as we saw in Chapter 1, to assess is to judge, and this in itself can be considered as a political act. Whilst this may sound uncomfortable, it is part of the problematic nature of assessment in general.

Chapter 7

Progression, development, and assessment

In educational circles it is common to hear talk of developmental education and of pupils showing progression in their learning. But what do these terminologies mean, and how can teachers use assessment to help with these areas? These are the key questions covered in this chapter.

Defining terms

In psychology, development usually refers to the maturation process, and developmental psychology investigates the ways in which cognitive and psycho-motor competencies change over time, and with education. The famous 'nature-nurture' debate can be seen to be relevant here. Progression, however, is less clearly defined. Piaget, for example, viewed progression in thinking as a result of cognitive accommodation. What most educational programmes refer to as progression often relates to moving forwards in some way, not doing more of the same thing, but of taking learning, to coin an apposite phrase, 'to the next level'. What we also find in educational parlance is that the terms are blurred, with 'developmental education' being used to mean education that takes things forwards, 'educational progress' to mean that something has been learned, and 'progressive education' to mean something trendy! In this chapter notions of progression and development are discussed with relation to music education, and following the normal usages of the domain, the two terminologies are not uniquely defined.

What develops in 'developmental learning'?

In cognitive terms, what is it that develops in 'developmental learning'? From biological and psychological perspectives, we know that as children mature over time changes happen, and we also know that these changes are more likely to occur as phases rather than stages (D. Hargreaves & Zimmerman 1992: 389), the difference being that phases are not hard-edged. Back in 1986 David Hargreaves observed that '. . . music education must have a firm foundation in developmental psychology' (D. Hargreaves 1986: 226). This is still an apposite observation, but the intervening years have not made the task any easier for music teachers! The issue of development raises questions as to what there is that can be developed in terms of musical learning. As in so many areas of music education, development is an issue which is not universally understood. As Pamela Burnard observes, '. . . conceptions of how development proceeds [are] not clear . . .' (Burnard 2006: 359). Building on the work of, amongst others, Hargreaves and Zimmerman (1992), Krumhansl (1990), Davidson and Scripp (1988, 1992), and the innovative Manhattanville Music Curriculum Project of the late 1960s (Thomas 1970), it is possible to propose four main areas for development in music education:

- Generative: original ideas, for example in composing and improvising
- Performance: skills for playing instruments or singing
- Perceptual: listening, appreciating, appraising,
- Representational: symbolic representation of music in (e.g.) notation

These are not discrete areas of potential musical development, but they operate in a complex joined-up fashion. The task for the teacher is to disentangle the various aspects of development that are suggested by each of these, and deal with them accordingly. In this book the first three of the four components of development are given separate chapters, whilst symbolic representation and the role of notation systems is dealt with in a number of places.

It is apparent that there will be some tension between the four proposed areas of musical development, and the knowledge types discussed in previous chapters. There is no obvious mapping between them. To exemplify this, let us consider the role of creativity. Creativity is patently involved in generative processes in music, and also in aspects of performance. Some would argue that listening to music can create new meanings for the listener, thus rendering it a creative act too. The problem with relying on knowledge transmission as a primary function of music education is that creative thinking can be missed, or missed out! Knowledge-based activities, particularly 'knowing about', in music do not always engage the learners personally with the very essence of the subject. 'Since creative thinking by definition goes beyond knowledge, there is explicitly or implicitly assumed to be a tension between knowledge and creativity' (Weisberg 1999: 226). In music education this tension can be readily seen in assessment. Summative assessment of knowledge is much easier to undertake than summative assessment of creative acts. This does not mean that creativity should be excluded because it is harder to assess, but that new ways of thinking need to have new ways of assessing associated with them. In creative music education, tensions between knowledge and creativity are not necessarily apparent, as Weisberg goes on to observe, 'A number of researchers have argued the opposite of the tension view, that is, knowledge is positively related to creativity. Rather than breaking out of the old to produce the new, creative thinking builds on knowledge' (Weisberg 1999: 226). This is clearly the case in the way in which in England the Secondary National Strategy for school improvement in music (DfES 2006b) views development, where skills and knowledge contribute towards musical understanding via the use of generative processes and creativity. In this sense, knowledge is a precursor to creative acts. After all, we would not want to set a class of pupils a creative composing task, and for them to come back with a model of a chair (Fautley & Savage 2007)! This might be a creative response, but it is not domain-specific creativity (Craft 2003; Csikszentmihalyi 1999). Creativity and knowledge acquisition, both participatory and acquisitive, are going to be involved in developmental music education.

Returning to the four areas of development—generative, performance, perceptual, and representational—the role of assessment in developing these needs to be considered. Specifically, how can they develop? There seems to be six main ways in which this can happen:

• Increasing depth
• Increasing breadth
• Enhancing skills (practical and cognitive)
• Allowing for personal engagement
• Formulation and articulation of value judgements
• Developing understandings

Managing all of these at the same time is yet another plate-spinning act for the music teacher to undertake! Realistically, however, development proceeds slowly, and so varying attention between these areas is the most likely way for teachers to deal with this. Indeed, so intertwined are they that atomistic separation sometimes becomes difficult. But for assessment purposes, this may be required, and subsequent chapters look at this in some detail.

These six areas are not the only model of musical development, however, and for a specific instance of where a developmental view of music education has been enshrined in statute, the case of the National Curriculum for music in England is worthy of consideration.

A regional diversion: assessment in the National Curriculum in England

In England there is an explicit model of musical development which is espoused in the National Curriculum levels of achievement (DfEE/QCA 1999;

QCA 2007). The National Curriculum (NC) is statutory in state schools. The situation is different between each member state of the UK, and the discussions here refer specifically to the NC for England. The statutory requirements are a slim document, and result in a situation where an interesting dichotomy arises between what Lave & Wenger (1991) refer to as the teaching curriculum, and the learning curriculum. What happens in this case is that the teaching curriculum is loosely prescribed, in that the content of what is taught is left very much up to teachers, whereas the learning curriculum is tightly defined in terms of assessable outcomes. This gives rise to a model of learning and progression to which it is expected that pupils will adhere, demonstrate achievement using the terminologies thereof, and for which teachers will be held accountable. The model of progression upon which the National Curriculum is based is not explicitly articulated. What arises is a layering of accumulated competences in a broadly neo-Piagetian framework of age-related delineations, with elements of behaviourism included, and an acknowledgement of Bruner's (or Swanwick & Tillman's (1986)) notion of a spiral curriculum, in that concepts can be revisited at higher levels of attainment. What this has meant for teachers is that they have had to engage in a fairly advanced process of hermeneutics in an endeavour to extrapolate retrospectively from the levels what it is that was wanted in terms of teaching. The acknowledgement of the differences between teaching and learning curricula was evidenced in a later incarnation of the National Curriculum (QCA 2007), where the language was changed from, 'pupils should be taught how to . . .' (DfEE/QCA 1999: 20) to, 'pupils should be able to . . .' (QCA 2007: 182).

To deconstruct the notion of progression as exemplified in National Curriculum levels, teachers are told that the first sentence of each level statement is the important one, and that other sentences in each level statement form a subsidiary role. Using this as a basis for a '. . . simple definition of progression . . .' (Ofsted 2009: 17), we have a model which looks like Table 7.1.

What this shows is that all of the six elements of developmental potential are used, but none of them are overtly identified as such. Indeed, by avoiding outcome driven statements ('pupils will be able to . . .') the wide range of starting and finishing points apparent in schools throughout the country can be encompassed. But although vagueness, when compared with closed-outcome statements, can be a strength, it can also be a weakness in terms of teachers and pupils understanding what progression and development 'look like', or, possibly more importantly, 'sound like'.

A potential problem that this view of learning can give rise to is a mistaken notion that what should develop in progression in musical learning is complexity (Swanwick 1999: 77). This would mean that on an outcome basis

Table 7.1 National Curriculum levels: first sentence

• *recognize and explore*	
o how sounds can be made and changed	Level 1
o how sounds can be organized	Level 2
o the ways sounds can be combined and used expressively	Level 3
• *identify and explore*	
o the relationship between sounds and how music reflects different intentions	Level 4
o musical devices and how music reflects time, place, and culture	Level 5
o the different processes and contexts of selected musical styles, genres, and traditions	Level 6
• *discriminate between and explore*	
o musical conventions in, and influences on, selected styles, genres and traditions	Level 7
• *discriminate between and exploit*	
o the characteristics and expressive potential of selected musical resources, styles, genres, and traditions	Level 8
• *discriminate between and develop*	
o different interpretations.	Exceptional Performance

Satie's *Gymnopédies* would compare unfavourably with Stravinsky's *Firebird*, and would be afforded a lower level; and North and Zaret's *Unchained Melody*, being less complex rhythmically than Jethro Tull's 5/4 composition *Living in the Past* would be similarly downgraded. This misinterpretation of progression can be viewed as a by-product of creating assessment criteria which leave the potential for ambiguous interpretations.

This problem of interpretation of National Curriculum assessment levels was further compounded in schools by teachers being exhorted to rewrite the official language of the wording of the statements into more user-friendly language for the pupils. What often happened then was that the 'pupil-speak' levels were prioritized in the minds of the teachers at the expense of the original ones, and much of the nuancing and inclusivity of the original language inevitably became 'lost in translation' (Fautley 2007) between the original levels and the re-written ones. These could then be used in a way far removed from the original intention. 'In one lesson seen, for example, students were told: "Level 3: clap a 3 beat ostinato; Level 4: maintain a 4 bar ostinato; Level 5: compose an ostinato." This demonstrated a significant misunderstanding of the expectations inherent in the level descriptions' (Ofsted 2009: 31). This rather trite and over-simplistic use of levels is not an isolated example though, and not dissimilar examples are to be found in many schools. Although this somewhat crass instance of level misinterpretation rightly drew Ofsted's ire, it is an inevitable corollary of asking teachers to do something, in this case paraphrase levels into pupil-speak, and then blaming them when they oversimplify it in ways the pupils can easily understand.

Further evidence of the dichotomy in which music teachers find themselves caught is to be found in the requirement many schools have of their music teachers to provide assessment information in National Curriculum levels which have been subdivided. As no such things exist in official documentation, teachers again have had to invent their own. The most common subdivision is into three, with variations on 'working towards', 'working at', and 'secure achievement'. Some schools, rather bizarrely, require subdivisions into tenths of a level, thus pupils can be at level 4.4, whatever that means! What Ofsted found with regard to the use of the subdivisions was that, '. . . such subdivisions did not take account of the National Curriculum guidance about progress within levels being seen in terms of increasing confidence, ownership and independence and so they ended up being based on arbitrary degrees of competence in separate and specific components of music' (Ofsted 2009: 32). 'Arbitrary degrees of competence' is a harsh condemnation, and might be construed as teachers making up things to assess, and then assessing them! McNamara's fallacy in action! This is obviously not going to be good assessment practice.

Linear musical development

One of the potential issues with the way in which National Curriculum levels have been interpreted by schools is that there is an assumption that they should be used to show a strictly linear model of progression. This means that there is an assumption that learners will make steady progress, and a graph plotting this progression would show a straight line. To add to this, many music teachers are told that their pupils *have* to progress by a predetermined amount, often expressed in terms of National Curriculum sublevels. As sublevels do not exist, progression using them is likely to be, at best, spurious, and, at worst, fictitious. Being told that pupils must progress by, say, two sublevels a term can result in the most pointless assessment data, where teachers simply add two sublevels to every pupil's last results. This might satisfy assessment managers, but it does nothing for pupil learning! This linear improvement also reveals another awkward facet of assessment data collection: that a tacit assumption has evolved that not only is progression linear, it is relentlessly upwards. A moment of reflection will reveal that this is problematic too. As Gary Spruce observes, 'The linear model presumes predictable and common stages of development and ignores children's social and cultural backgrounds which so affect their perception of what music is and *means* to them' (Spruce 2001b: 20). A pupil might be thoroughly inspired by a music project on, say, songwriting, and do some really good, original, and interesting work, showing a high level of attainment. The same pupil, for all sorts of reasons could be disengaged by a project on, say, the waltz, and not work at anything like the same level. In her work with Musical Futures, Lucy Green observed a very clear dip in attainment, from an initial level, before picking up again. She calls this a '. . . cycle of success, deterioration, then improvement . . .' (Green 2008: 52). Similar evidence can be found in many other areas of musical learning, as well as in other school subjects, yet the relentless upwards drive means that assessment snapshots which reveal that pupils should be awarded a lower grade cannot be translated into actually awarding a lower level for this piece of work as all sorts of problematic consequences will ensue. Can this be right?

Assessment and progression

As the role of assessment should be to improve learning, then the main role will be for formative assessment in developing progression. Increasing depth and breadth will obviously necessitate different foci at different stages in the learning process. However it is that music teachers determine progression, the role of summative assessment should be to audit attainment, and not to simply demonstrate skewed notions of 'best fit' linearity. The specific role of formative assessment is again key to this, and its role in developing learning in various aspects of musical endeavour is considered in subsequent chapters.

Chapter 8

Quality, values, and the affective domain

Music is an art form, and perceptions of art can be extremely personal. So, in music, one person's love of the Sex Pistols may not be shared by a Country and Western aficionado, and both may be reviled by a Wagnerite. What does this mean for assessment? How do notions of quality affect this, and what is the place for values in this? This chapter endeavours to address these issues.

Quality and values

Many of the discussions which teachers have with pupils will inevitably involve some talk concerning quality. One of the early writers on formative assessment noted that 'The essential conditions for improvement are that the student comes to hold a concept of quality roughly similar to that held by the teacher . . .' (Sadler 1989: 121). But quality is itself a problematic construct. What is quality?

Quality—you know what it is, yet you don't know what it is. But that's self-contradictory. But some things are better than others, that is, they have more quality. But when you try to say what the quality is, apart from the things that have it, it all goes poof! There's nothing to talk about. But if you can't say what Quality is, how do you know what it is, or how do you know that it even exists? If no one knows what it is, then for all practical purposes it doesn't exist at all. But for all practical purposes it really does exist. What else are the grades based on? (Pirsig 1974: 178)

Pirsig was not describing music, but classes in English, yet this quotation is apposite. If quality is so difficult to pin down, how can grades be based upon it? To address this difficult question, we need to ask what quality is in the case of music, and then specifically what this means in terms of music education.

Cantwell and Jeanneret discuss quality as operating in three areas in music education assessment. Firstly there are 'Quality of Instructional Objectives', which are informed by assessment; secondly there are 'Quality of Learning Processes', which are reflected by assessment; and thirdly there are 'Quality of Learning Outcomes', which are measured by assessment (Cantwell & Jeanneret 2004: 13). These are useful starting points, and move assessment from the 'folk view', centred on learning outcomes, towards a stance which includes teaching and learning. This inclusive viewpoint is very much in line with assessment for learning strategies, and takes us some way towards the sharing of views of quality between teacher and pupil which Sadler recommended in the quotation at the beginning of this section.

The issue of assessing quality in English National Curriculum music runs through the level statements like an *idée fixe*, without ever being articulated fully. Quality can exist at level 1 as much as at level 8; it is the shading of quality which is different. Whilst trying to find ways of assessing quality in music is problematic, as shall be explored below, nonetheless it is important for teachers to have expectations that all work done will display some qualitative facets.

In music education, it is possibly helpful to think of quality as being centred within three interlocking domains: those of technical quality, conceptual quality, and aesthetic quality. Technical quality is that which appertains to technique, and is reflected in control of the medium, be it instrument (including music technology) or voice. This takes us into the area of *skills*, which many assessment structures endeavour to measure. Conceptual quality refers to concepts involved, such as notions of musical structure, phraseology, dynamic contrasts, and so on. Aesthetic quality includes aspects of expressiveness, musicality, and what might be termed 'feelingful-ness'. (Of these it is technical quality which seems to offer the most accessible way of sharing criteria with pupils, and it is this aspect which is discussed in greater detail in Chapter 10.)

Each of these three domains come together to be valued, and then to evidence musical understanding, a process which is shown in Fig. 8.1.

So, with regard to the issue of quality, key questions for music educators to ask of their pupils are these:

- What are the key characteristics of this type/style/genre of music?
- Is this a good example of a piece of music of this type?

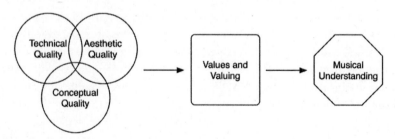

Fig. 8.1 Three domains of quality

- Is your composition/performance contextually appropriate within the requirements of this type/style/genre?

And a further question, to tease out understandings, would be:

- Why?

The purpose of these questions is to foster notions of quality concerning what is done in the music lesson, and this links in many ways to critical thinking and developing personal learning and thinking skills (PLTS). This in turn leads to the question of assessment of aesthetic quality. Writing criteria for assessing aesthetic matters is a notoriously difficult task, as the quotation from Pirsig above shows. But whilst we can recognize that aesthetic quality exists, rather than try and formulate assessment criteria for it, maybe the most sensible approach is to use the questions above, particularly 'is this a good example of this piece, and if so why?'. It may well be that the best standpoint is that of negotiation with the pupil as to what understandings of quality involve, 'If criteria are considered to be necessary . . . the community decides on criteria for assessment, but we need to determine the size of the community; I would advocate that the learner's own criteria be used, which means that the community is a minimum of two people . . .' (Hickman 2007: 84). This means that it is the teacher and the learner between them who make decisions concerning quality. The implication of this is that assessment judgements can be made, and discussed between pupil and teacher. It places ownership for qualitative aspects in the hands of the learner, and it enables formative feedback to be targeted effectively. What it does not do is grade. We have already seen that in the UK National Curriculum levels have a qualitative underpinning, but not a separate scale of values, so this way of working seems perfectly acceptable within published criteria.

Values and valuing

Rather like quality, developing pupil notions of values is going to be somewhat problematic. Notions of personal value are tied up with self-awareness, and are unlikely to be amenable to assessment in the summative sense. Valuing, however, is a different matter. It is probably not too hard to decide if a violin is being played in tune, but it is much harder to decide if a thrash metal song composed by pupils is worth fifteen or sixteen marks out of twenty, or, indeed, some might argue, why it should have to be awarded marks at all. How far would music teachers go in agreeing with the philosopher Roger Scruton that:

It is surely not difficult to establish the superiority of Cole Porter over R.E.M.; one has only to look at the incompetent voice-leading in Losing My Religion, the misunderstanding of chord relations, and the inability to develop a melodic line in which the phrases lead into one another with a genuine musical need.

But once you look at modern popular music in this way, you will come to see how gross, tasteless and sentimental it mostly is, and how far it is from our tradition of meditative polyphony (Scruton 1996), cited in (Green 2000: 92).

To consider this, we need to unpick what is being referred to when we talk about assessment and evaluation of, and in, music. This is an important area for assessment in music education and one which warrants some discussion.

In music education, it is helpful to distinguish between assessment of processes and products in terms of musical styles and genres, musical achievement within those styles and genres (in other words the development of skills), the notion of progression towards musical understanding which encompasses skill development, and separate this from evaluative statements concerning the relative worth or merit of different types, styles, genres, and contexts of music. Assessment, the main focus of this book, is concerned with improving learning and performance in the case of formative assessment, and certificating and auditing pupil attainment in the case of summative assessment. Evaluation, on the other hand, is concerned with placing worth on various activities, in terms of social status, social capital, cultural status and capital, and views of cultural worth. Here judgements are made which say that some sorts of music are *better* than other sorts. These evaluative judgements have often been mistaken for assessment judgements and the two conflated. Evaluation compares the worth of one piece of music against another, and this is a notoriously difficult thing to do:

... one key reason why evaluation seems to be such a cause for concern at the moment is because we are living through an era which seems to celebrate diversity, pluralism and relativism in the field of culture. Sometimes going under the name of postmodernism, it is suggested that the cultural domain has lost the boundaries and distinctions characterising the strict traditional hierarchies of cultural taste and instead values forms of popular culture ... (Sefton-Green 2000: 221).

So, how has evaluation become mixed in with assessment in music education? For answers to this, we need to go back in time a little. In a textbook for classroom music teachers written in 1965, the author, Charles Proctor, was able to affirm that,

... vocal music must, *per force*, receive its proper place in enlightened education as an essential part of culture and development not only of the individual, but of the community as a whole ... education only begins to function when a tradition of behaviour is engendered and stimulated for the better fulfilment of a personality and to the ultimate service to the community. On this civilisation depends. (Proctor 1965: 14).

The sort of songs which should be sung were obvious, 'National songs are the very musical fibre of a nation's music, and no self-respecting British-born subject should think himself an educated man who cannot sing and play his national songs' (Proctor 1965: 44). It may now seem a rather bizarre notion that the future of civilization should depend on 9Z singing 'The Ash Grove' on a Friday afternoon, but this evaluative statement was made without external reference or justification; it was a logical and obvious value judgement in the context of music education at the time!

It is probably unsurprising that a mere three years after Proctor was deliberating on the role of singing *Enquiry 1* was published by the Schools Council (Schools Council 1968), which noted that many of the students in schools at the time had become disaffected by music in education. Quite possibly, at the time of the Beatles and Rolling Stones, they were fed up with singing national songs! The figures that were produced were categorized under the heading of subjects that the students found to be 'boring' and 'useless'. Music came top of both, 48% of boys and 34% of girls said this was the case for them. Conversely 20% of boys and 35% of girls were noted as saying that pop music was an important issue for them. At around the same time a study in the United States noted the problem of the apparent lack of interest by school students in music in schools. This led to the publication of the Manhatanville Music Curriculum Programme. This noted that, 'By the junior high school level music classes are often problem classes. Where music is required there is often resentment . . . and schemes employing extrinsic motivational factors are often considered necessary' (MMCP 1970: ix). Having identified that a problem existed, and that many American students, like their English counterparts, were not happy with the role of music in education, MMCP proceeded to ascribe causes for their rejection. The authors decided there were two 'significant clues' which may have some bearing on the problem:

1. The period when rejection of the study [of music] appears to begin coincides with the time of intellectual development described by Piaget . . . where in the earlier stages of intellectual development concrete operations were easily followed by the student, in this later stage considerations of logic, variables, and relationships become important to him. Indeed, the students acceptance or rejection of any discipline will often be contingent upon the logic and reason he finds in the subject matter.

2. Signs of rejection are almost exclusively limited to those areas of the art which have often been involved with the education program. Interestingly there appears to be a converse relationship between disinterest in the school music program and participation in some activity outside the school. (MMCP 1970: x).

Following on from *Enquiry 1*, and drawing to some extent on the work of the MMCP, the Schools council project *Music in the Secondary School Curriculum* was initiated in 1973 and was an important area of research and dissemination of examples of what were regarded as being good practice. A major change compared with the music education programmes of the nineteenth and early twentieth century was that the pupils were treated as active participants and creators of music, rather than as recipients of a curriculum in which they were not empowered.

Prior to this time it would seem that the enthusiasms of the pupils were to be totally disregarded. The pupils themselves were often viewed in a similar manner to that in which the nineteenth-century church viewed wayward sinners, that they should be brought to the '. . . final reward of virtue and punishment of vice' (Paley 1820: 415). Vice being seen as the students 'falling' into the sinful mode of pop music, and virtue being an acknowledgement of their errors. To help with this, music lessons often had an element of 'musical appreciation':

The primary purpose of musical appreciation is to inculcate a love and understanding of good music. It is surely the duty of teachers to do all they can to prevent young people falling ready prey to the purveyors of commercialised 'popular' music, for these slick, high-pressure salesmen have developed the exploitation of teenagers into a fine art. (Brocklehurst 1962: 205).

This is an unashamed evaluation of musical typologies, where the assumption is that the music to which the students should be aspiring is 'high' art western European music. 'In terms of Young's (1971) sociological analysis of the school curriculum, "serious" music is defined as high status knowledge, and "pop" music as low status knowledge' (Shepherd et al. 1977: 207). What this is doing is to evaluate high status music, in this case western art music, as being superior to popular music. Evaluating music in this way means that statements can be made such as this, '. . . there is no excuse for allowing school music lessons to be infected with the prevailing values of the pop industry, which require nothing more musical from children than the ability to dip into their parents' purses to buy gormless videos of posturing idols' (Morrison 1991).

The use of the music curriculum as a place for social engineering is another area where evaluative judgements were to be found:

Britain's unelected cultural commissar Dr Nicholas Tate, chief executive of the School Curriculum and Assessment Authority, called for 'educators' to impress on children that 'high' culture is good, profound and moral, whereas 'low' culture is base and worthless. Dr Tate is convinced that the threat posed by Blur to Schubert is so serious that unless we return to basics (in culture as well as morals) the core values on which Western civilisation was based will crumble away for good. (Wilkinson 1996)

However, this seems to be a view that even then was past its sell-by date. As the author of the piece in *The Independent* went on to observe, 'It is particularly odd that this argument is being made now. After all, during the past three decades the boundaries between high and low culture have virtually disappeared' (Wilkinson 1996). Janet Mills is also scathing about this attitude:

Today this is just not good enough. First in a multi-cultural society our culture is not just European. Second, a notion that high art is great and other forms of European music are not great is open to question. Third, the transmission of our cultural heritage, whatever we mean by this, is only one part of music education. (Mills 1991b: 108)

The quasi-nineteenth-century views cited above can still pervade aspects of music education at times, and of these we need to be wary. Returning to the present, in many ways the music curriculum, in the UK at least, has now taken the opposite stance to this position, and many music departments are rightly proud of their rock bands and techno musicians. Indeed, classroom learning of popular music is now a normal part of the KS3 and KS4 curriculum (Green 2006). In the UK, the work of the 'Musical Futures' project where pupils learn directly how to play in styles of their own choice, has widened musical horizons considerably (Price 2006). What all this means is that valuing music is felt to be important and pupils are encouraged to '. . . communicate ideas and feelings about music, using expressive language and musical vocabulary to justify their opinions [and adapt] to different musical roles and respecting the values and benefits others bring to musical learning' (QCA 2007). This means that pupils valuing a variety of types of musics is felt to be worthwhile, and the process of valuing, and of valuing quality, is now seen to be an appropriate part of music education and, moreover, contributes to the wider development of the pupil in the social sphere, 'When good music teachers guide students as they "enter into" unfamiliar musics through active music making, students engage in self-reflections and personal reconstructions of their relationships, assumptions, and preferences about other people, other cultures, and other ways of thinking and valuing' (Elliott 2006: 51).

John Finney notes that there '. . . have been contentious issues related to whose music it is that is fit to study . . .' (Finney 2007a: 14). This is an important evaluative question, and one which teachers will need to consider as they think about which of Elliott's 'unfamiliar musics' will be most appropriate to use. This is a point which will be picked up at later stages in this book.

Possible sources of confusion regarding evaluation

Having identified that there is a danger of confusing evaluation with assessment, it is appropriate to consider possible sources as to how this confusion may have come about.

One possible reason is that of the differing ways in which music has been taught and learned in schools over time. Up until the changes in the 1970s outlined above, the focus of the music lesson was to treat music as if were an ossified object in a museum of works (Goehr 1992). This required the focus of the subject to be one where knowledge was one step removed from music. In Chapter 5 different types of knowledge were discussed, and so we can clearly see that 'knowing that' is but one kind of knowledge. Nowadays music lessons are also concerned with other types of knowledge too, 'whereas the traditional . . . syllabus demanded that children should be knowledgeable *about* music, more recent assessment schemes have encouraged children to be actively engaged *with* music, with knowledge seen as a by-product of performing, composing and listening' (Pitts 2000b: 147) (author's italics).

This shift from 'knowing about' to 'engaging with' has had a concomitant effect on the way musical evaluation is viewed. In the earlier paradigm the stratification of musical types was an integral component of the music lesson, and the unchallenged hegemonic views we examined earlier are proof of this. Once the emphasis of the music lesson changed towards one of direct engagement with practical music making, then the role of the pupil in the music lesson shifted too, from disinterested (or uninterested) passivity, to one of active participation in the production of music. With this approach the pupil became an active agent in the lesson, and had ownership of their production. With ownership comes engagement, and with engagement comes valuing. For the teacher to decide that the musical tastes of the pupils was 'inferior' to their own, which had been the case in the former paradigm, became a counter-productive and untenable position. A teacher assuming a position that is diametrically opposed to the enthusiasms of the pupils will not result in a fruitful relationship. Far better to take the advice of Mrs Curwen's Piano method. 'Proceed from the known to the related unknown' (Curwen 1886). Undertaking an evaluative process of this sort is not a case of applying hegemonic stratification of musical types, but of moving pupils towards proficiency.

Implications for the teacher

What may well be the case is that teachers do not need to shy away from evaluating within types, styles, genres, and contexts of music, as, after all, their pupils will be doing this:

. . . it's the easiest thing in the world to get kids to make aesthetic judgements. They do it all the time. The hardest thing in the world is to stop them. Oasis are better than Blur. Eastenders is better than Brookside. The question is how well they articulate it . . . and distinguish between the things which are personal and the things which are not necessarily universal or transcendental but are shared (Raney and Hollands 2000: 21).

What it does mean is that ownership of musical taste is not the sole province of the teacher, with pupils 'looking up' to them. So, with regard to evaluative statements, whilst we need to be aware that 'Teachers cannot avoid making judgements about musical value' (Green 2000: 93), we also know that pupils are able to do this too, and a fruitless argument as to whose judgment is 'best' will not help progression. What this means is that progression in musical understanding and proficiency is not linked to the status of the music in question relative to other musics, but that developing skills and knowledge in a particular style, type, or genre is done in a way which is appropriate. After all, all instrumentalists want to get better! This is the realm of assessment. A Fado singer will want to develop style-specific proficiency, as much as the rock guitarist, folk fiddler, or classical trumpeter. The role of assessment is to establish criteria against which judgements concerning progression can be made. Management terminology refers to interested parties as 'stakeholders', and in music there are a number of these: pupils, teachers, parents, school leadership teams, examination boards, local authorities, government departments, and many, many more. But the primary stakeholders must be the pupils and their teachers. Assessment needs to tell them as much, if not more, than it tells other stakeholders. We shall look in later chapters at managing learning, and it is in this area that assessment is particularly appropriate in that it provides the key stakeholders—teacher and pupils—with useful information.

Music education requires a number of choices to be made: choices of curriculum content, choices of approach, choices of material, choices of musical style, and, importantly (and relating to the evaluative discussions above), choices of what music to include and what to leave out. It is possible to construct curricula which tacitly downplay certain types, styles, and genres of music by omitting them from the taught programme. This is as much a statement of values as what is included! We have seen how it is important not to confuse the two. The focus of this book is on assessment, but we still need to be on our guard with regard to evaluative issues that might impinge upon the main purpose of assessment from the perspective of the teacher—to help pupils improve!

Bloom's taxonomy of the affective domain

Having investigated evaluation and from a historical perspective, it is also useful to consider aspects of valuing from a theoretical standpoint. To investigate this from an assessment perspective in music education, the work of Bloom and his co-researchers in America in the 1950s and 1960s seems a logical place to begin. Bloom's taxonomy (Bloom 1956), discussed in Chapter 4, is well-known in educational circles and figures in many current publications and directives. What is being referred to here is, strictly speaking, Bloom's taxonomy of educational objectives in the cognitive domain. There is also a much less well-known taxonomy of objectives in the *affective* domain (Bloom et al. 1964). Bloom and his colleagues found this much harder to research and write, and say so in the introduction, along with the observation that they were less happy with the results. However, we have had little else since which sets out to look into notions of affective matters. Bloom and his colleagues developed a taxonomy of affective objectives in a similar fashion to their previous work in the cognitive sphere, producing a hierarchy of affective responses, as shown in Fig. 8.2.

This is complex set of constructs and space precludes detailed analysis of its implications for music education. But for thinking about notions of *valuing*, then it has a direct relevance. The construct *valuing* appears halfway up the taxonomy, as the third item. Bloom subdivides this further into three categories:

3.1 Acceptance of a value (e.g. continuing desire to develop the ability to write effectively and hold it more strongly[1])

3.2 Preference for a value (e.g. seeks out examples of good art for enjoyment of them to the level where he behaves so as to further this impression actively)

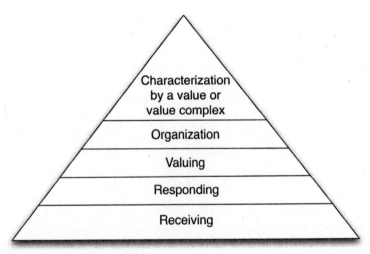

Fig. 8.2 Bloom's taxonomy: affective domain

---

[1] Examples are those employed by Bloom.

3.3 Commitment (conviction) (e.g. faith in the power of reason and the method of experimentation). (after Bloom et al. 1964: 35)

In assessment terminologies this presents a hierarchy of valuing, but what can be done about it in practical terms in the classroom or studio? Does holding a preference (in Bloom's terms a conviction) that certain rock bands are worthwhile, and where the pupil actively seeks them out, warrant a higher (or lower) grade than someone who likes renaissance music? This takes us back to evaluation, which, as we saw above, can be a minefield for assessment judgements. Bloom and his colleagues recognized this, and, interestingly, used music education as a specific instantiation for this:

For instance, if we wish to determine whether a humanities course has resulted in 'an interest in seeking and enjoying a wide variety of musical experiences,' we may attempt to appraise the variety of musical experiences the student has voluntarily participated in prior to, during, and subsequent to the humanities course. We hesitate to trust the professed evidence that a student has developed such an interest, because we have difficulty in determining the difference between a natural or honest response and one that is made solely to please the teacher, and we may even have some question about the accuracy of the student's recall of such experiences. On the other hand, if our objective is 'the development of the ability to become sensitive to and perceptive of different aspects of a musical work,' we may present him with a series of musical selections which are likely to be unfamiliar to him. Then, by careful questioning, determine which elements he has perceived and which he has not. We would not hesitate to assign him a grade on the second objective, but we would have considerable hesitation about failing the student or giving him a high grade on the basis of our evidence on the first objective. (Bloom et al. 1964: 17)

This is at the heart of assessment of values in music education, can it be done? Indeed, what is the role of the affective? '. . . assessment of composing, performing or tasks related to listening activities is not just about "correct notes" or accurate reproduction of factual information, but is also about musical attainment having an affective as well as a cognitive facet' (Durrant & Welch 1995: 122). This surely is the point of good music making. It is not just about playing the right notes in the right order. Computer programmes can do this. It is about being musical, and assessing musical values from a standpoint which is reliable and valid is going to be problematic.

Assessing aesthetic responses

There is considerable debate concerning the role of the aesthetic in music education.[2] David Elliott (Elliott 1995) argues cogently against taking an aesthetic

---

[2] For an overview of the debate, particularly between Elliott, Reimer, and Swanwick, see Regelski (2005), Panaiotidi (2003), and Plummeridge (1999).

view of music education in favour of one based in praxis, whilst others, including Reimer (1986) and Swanwick (1996) take a different position. Aesthetic development in terms of music education is concerned with '. . . the education of human feeling, through the development of responsiveness to the aesthetic qualities of sound' (Reimer 1970: 39).

In England, back in 1986, the Music Advisers National Association observed that aesthetic judgments were key to musical understanding:

Aesthetic judgements are, then, in one sense personal but in another, communicable, open to inspection and capable of negotiation. . . . It is now suggested that musicians can best demonstrate the rationality of their aesthetic judgements by ensuring that, to some degree, they comprehend *consciously* what happens in the music they are judging and refer to aspects of it as occasion arises. (MANA—Music Advisers National Association 1986: 10)

According to this view, it is clear that assessment is going to be highly problematic. How can teachers do this? Csikszentmihalyi writes of attending a conference on aesthetic education where assessment was discussed:

How do we measure the impact, the outcome, the effects of an aesthetic experience? What is the proper way to assess aesthetic learning? . . . The entire enterprise depends on what measures are selected because the method of assessment will dictate the answer to the most fundamental question, namely: Is this program worth doing? Because of its centrality, assessment lurked underfoot . . . like an unexploded bomb. Several times, I heard people refer to 'the "A" word' when they were talking about it. Some presenters said that a thorough evaluation was the most important task of the entire enterprise, while others made the point that it should be avoided as long as possible. (Csikszentmihalyi 1997)

This issue goes to the heart of the music education as aesthetic education (usually abbreviated to MAEA) debate.

In the aesthetic view, a truly musical experience serves no practical purpose. An aesthetic experience is (and must be) intrinsic, immediate, disinterested, self-sufficient, and distanced. Any meanings, functions, or experiences not directly related to a work's structural patterns are deemed incidental, irrelevant, referential, or non-musical. (Elliott 1995: 124)

Again, this makes classroom assessment distinctly difficult! However, whilst these issues cause considerable debate amongst philosophers of music education, they are likely to have passed by many music teachers. In the UK a pragmatic perspective would be that:

For many music teachers, differences of opinion over the theoretical foundations of music education are far less important than what they see as a threat to the status of their subject. With an increased emphasis on the utilitarian purposes of education there is a fear that music and the arts might be further marginalised. (Plummeridge 1999: 121)

But for assessment purposes, the problematic nature of the influence of aesthetics continues to be felt. This issue is returned to in later sections, particularly with regard to the assessment of listening in Chapter 12.

Final thought

Ludlow's challenge: 'If it exists, it can be measured; If it can't be measured, it doesn't exist.' (Ludlow 1996)

If values exist, then they can be measured. Or can they? This particular assessment issue has a long history in the positivist tradition. Back in the 1920s, Thorndike observed that 'Whatever exists, exists in some amount. To measure it is simply to know its varying amounts' (Thorndike 1921). Is this true in music? One phenomenon of music listening is the 'tingle factor' (Juslin & Sloboda 2001), created within the individual by certain phrases within a piece of music. Measuring this in pupils would be quite difficult; let us hope we are not required to! This is but one aspect of music which is unlikely to be amendable to measurement, certainly in the classroom, yet to say it does not exist is nonsense. Many other aspects of music fall into this category too. Einstein, who knew a thing or two about measurement, had a sign hanging in his office at Princeton which read, 'Not everything that can be counted counts, and not everything that counts can be counted', and this seems an important point to bear in mind when thinking about what matters in assessment in music education!

Chapter 9

Developing appropriate criteria for assessment

The notion of assessment criteria has already been mentioned a number of times. In this chapter the issues surrounding them, what they are, how they can be constructed, and how they can be utilized in the classroom are introduced, discussed, and developed.

Specifying learning outcomes

In many schools it is now commonplace for teachers to plan learning outcomes for each lesson that they teach, and it is a matter of policy in many schools to share these with the pupils at the outset of each lesson. What this means for teachers and pupils is that this is an opportunity for assessment to take place. Many teacher education and training programmes ask student teachers to plan differentiated learning outcomes, along the lines of 'all—most—some'. For example:

All pupils will learn to compose an ostinato on the keyboard

Most pupils will learn to compose an ostinato on the keyboard which is at least 4 bars long

Some pupils will learn to compose an ostinato which is at least 4 bars long, and begin to add a melodic accompaniment to it

Learning outcomes of this sort have one major advantage and one major disadvantage built into them. The advantage is that carefully written learning outcomes can become their own assessment criteria. The disadvantage is that they can exclude other learning taking place.

Using learning outcomes as assessment criteria

Using learning outcomes as assessment criteria means that the teacher can form a rapid assessment judgement concerning the achievement of a class. Thus in the example learning outcomes given above, it is possible to decide relatively easily whether or not the class, or individual pupils within the class, have achieved, and at which of the three outcome statements. However, this does not mean that all learning outcomes are suitable as assessment criteria for all forms of classroom activity in the music lesson. One of the key areas which needs to be explored here is that of the interrelated, but distinct, notions of 'doing' and 'learning'.

Learning and/or doing?

It is worth taking a step back from the example of a differentiated learning outcome given above, and thinking more generally about them. We know that many designated learning outcomes which are pre-specified by teachers are not *learning* outcomes at all, but rather *task* descriptions, 'It is important to distinguish between the regulation of the activity in which the students engages and the regulation of the learning that results. Most teachers appear to be quite skilled at the former, but have only a hazy idea of the learning that results' (Wiliam & Thompson 2008: 65). This concentration on tasks has historically been seen as a strength of music teachers. Indeed, published programmes for music education can be found which are not much more than collections of activities for pupils to undertake, with little by way of drawing out any learning which might be involved. This is also understandable in terms of the requirement many teachers have to keep their pupils busy. This leads to the assumption that busy pupils are learning something. However, although we want music to be an active subject, and we want the pupils to be engaged with the materials of sound, we also want them to be learning something. So, what are these elements of doing and learning, and how are they affected by assessment?

Understanding

For assessment purposes the nature of what is going on in a music lesson needs to be considered. If learning is evidenced in *doing* then assessing the activity might be one way of assessing the learning; but, if doing involves little by way of learning then it is the doing alone that will be assessed. This may, of course, be what is required! Occupying a third layer is understanding, and 'teaching for understanding' is a key phrase in current educational parlance. This gives a model of understanding in music which involves iterative processes of doing and understanding, as is shown in Fig. 9.1.

But understanding is a slippery construct! What is musical understanding, how can it be fostered, and what is the role of assessment in this?

The Secondary National Strategy for music defines pupils' musical understanding in terms of combining two areas of learning:

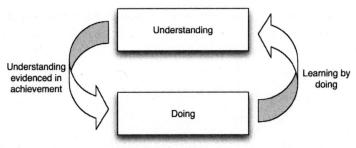

Fig. 9.1 Understanding in music education

a) knowing about musical conventions, processes and procedures
b) exploring a range of diverse musical styles, genres and traditions through practical music making (DfES 2006b: 4).

The document goes on to comment on the practical nature of music making as being a key part of understanding:

The ability to work practically with music—to be a "music maker"—is an essential part of understanding. However, it is seen as the means to an end rather than the purpose of the work itself: performing, composing and listening or appraising skills enable pupils to explore understanding effectively, and to demonstrate what they have learned (DfES 2006b: 4).

The twin peaks of understanding in terms of the National Strategy for music are acquisition and application:

It is important to recognise the twin aspects of 'acquire' and 'apply' . . . acquiring information about music aids understanding, but musical understanding can only be firmly embedded in pupils' learning when it is explored, applied and demonstrated through practical musical making (DfES 2006b: 4).

In terms of learning potential it is the twin areas of *acquisition* and *application* which need further unpicking. Looking into other ways of thinking about understanding proves helpful here, 'Understanding shows in the ability to organize knowledge, to relate it actively to new and past experience, forming "big" ideas . . .' (Harlen 2007: 30). And, '. . . "understanding" [is] the capacity to use current knowledge, concepts, and skills to illuminate new problems or unanticipated issues' (H. Gardner & Boix-Mansilla 1999: 79). So, taking these two examples, and returning to the model shown in Fig. 9.1, understanding arises as a result of organizing existing knowledge, and is a way of reframing information so as to be able to use it in new and as yet unforeseen situations. In other words '. . . understanding is an indicator of the quality of learning' (Newton 2000: 2).

What this means for assessment purposes in music is that we have the three elements of the model to think about—doing, learning, and understanding.

Taking this further, three questions arise concerning assessment, and the roles it has to play with regard to learning, doing, and understanding, namely:

- How can assessment be used to
  - o *identify* doing, learning, and understanding
  - o *quantify* doing, learning, and understanding
  - o *help* to improve doing, learning, and understanding?

Figure 9.1 can now be redrawn to include these key questions, as shown in Fig. 9.2.

This gives a far more complex picture. Let us consider each of the aspects shown in the triangles at the bottom of Fig. 9.2 in turn to try to unpick this further.

Identify

Identifying and planning for doing is, as we have seen, more straightforward than identifying learning. When pupils are working at a performance, or at a

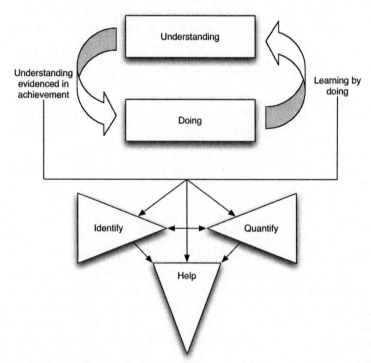

Fig. 9.2 Key assessment questions

composing task, it is not difficult to make rapid observations, starting from whether or not the pupils are on-task, through to more complex judgements about what it is they are actually doing. These judgements, it is important to remember, are formative assessment judgements; they may not be written down, or recorded in any way, but they are assessments. More complex identification will, inevitably, move towards the area covered by the second triangle, that of quantification.

Quantify

Ludlow's challenge, and the related assertion by Thorndike, discussed in Chapter 8, states that anything which exists does so in some quantity. For music teachers this notion of ascribing a quantitative value to musical performance has often caused headaches. However, 'It is important that we know what differentiates a good performance from a merely adequate one' (Johnson 1997: 275). Music teachers tend not to have a problem with this, in that they can tell a good performance from a poor one, where the problem lies is in detecting shades of variation between good and not-quite-but-very-nearly-as-good performances, and then placing a numerical value onto this difference. It is with grading, putting numbers onto the performances, where difficulties lie. For class music making we need to ask whether doing this is important. Quantifying a performance can be done numerically, but it can also be done holistically. Sometimes there is a feeling that something has only been assessed when a specific number, grade, mark, or level has been placed upon it. This need not be the case. In the quotation from Peter Johnson above, he wisely observes that we need to know 'what differentiates a good performance', he does not say we need to know by how much. This means that as teachers we can help someone improve by concentrating on qualitative aspects of their musicality, rather than by saying, say, they need to improve by 43% in order to be a level 4c; we can say instead that the pupils need to develop their breathing, posture, stick technique, rhythmic accuracy, or whatever. This is of far more benefit to the learner than a series of spurious statistics. To put it another way, if child A has two apples, and child B has an apple, two oranges, and a banana, we can say child B has more fruit than child A. Trying to statistically quantify *how much* more fruit child B has is hard, as we can wonder if an apple is equal to a banana! Often teachers try and do this, whereas the simpler observation will, in many cases, not only be sufficient, but more helpful and meaningful. To quantify in assessment terms need not always mean to measure accurately, but to be able to say whether something is present or absent.

We have seen that teachers are able to detect an average performance; the challenge is then to tell the pupils what they need to do to improve, this is the 'help' triangle, which we consider now.

Help

If assessment is to be of use to the teacher and the pupil, then identifying and quantifying performance needs to be translated into something that has meaning for the learner, and which they can use to improve their performance. This is where the professional judgement of the music teacher will come into play. As we saw above, the teacher may have to record a quantitative grade for external statistical purposes, but this will be of little use to the students if it is not mediated through some form of textual or verbal discussion. Oral feedback is key to this, in that it is immediate, tailored to the individuals concerned, and should involve a dialogue concerning what they need to do to improve.

What is to be assessed?

To begin to address key assessment questions we need to think about assessment criteria, and the uses and purposes of the assessments which will be made. The first thing for the teacher to do is to decide what it is that they wish to assess. Out of the doing/learning/understanding trio, it is 'doing' which is by far the easiest to make assessment judgements about. Most music teachers will be familiar with ABRSM-type graded examinations, which focus on 'doing'. Applying these principles, even if somewhat obliquely, provides the teacher with something specific to focus upon. This means that criteria for 'doing' can be written relatively straightforwardly. For example:

- Can play keyboard melody with more than one finger
- Can play xylophone with two beaters
- Is able to play chords correctly
- Can play bass line accurately
- Is able to keep in time when playing drum rhythm
- Holds bow correctly

All of these work perfectly well as 'doing' criteria. (At this stage there is no concern with any notion of musicality—in the western art tradition that often comes later!) Having established these as criteria the next stage is to decide how to assess them. In quantifying assessment judgements, then, and thinking of the issues discussed in the 'quantify' section above, the first stage is for the teacher to ask themselves the question 'does this need a numerical grade, or will another form of measurement be more appropriate?'.

Here are six examples, all of which have the same assessment criterion:

Assessment criterion: Can play keyboard melody with more than one finger

1. Tick the box[1]

   ☐ Always   ☐ Nearly Always   ☐ Usually   ☐ Sometimes   ☐ Never

2. Tick the box

   ☐ Working towards   ☐ Can do   ☐ Can do well

3. Tick the box

   ☐ Yes   ☐ No

4.

   Mark out of 10: ☐

5.

   Mark out of 100: ☐ %

6. (National Curriculum linked):

   N.C. Level (3–5)   Sublevel (a–c)

Each of these ways of assessing are looking at the same thing, if a child can play a keyboard melody using more than one finger. With the possible exception of number 6, whether or not these are worthwhile may well depend upon the use to which they are being put. Number 6 is dubious for many reasons, including the stated NC aim that assessment levels should not be used to assess individual pieces of work, and the fact that sub-levels do not officially exist. Most teachers would happily accept the rough-and-ready nature of number 1 above, and would not object either to the very bluntness of number 3. However, what is six out of ten fingering? What is 63% fingering.[2] How does knowing this help the learner to improve? Asking these questions links identifying with quantifying, and gets to the very heart of thinking about the uses of assessment.

By far the most common form of assessment grading used in schools is the tripartite form shown in number 2. Here the 5-point scale of number 1, usually referred to as a *Likert Scale*, is simplified, making the three categories representing attainment which is not meeting the expected level, then that which is,

---

[1] Some of these 'tick the box' methods can also be done using 'smiley faces' instead of descriptors to make them more pupil-friendly.

[2] I have observed lessons where the melodic content has been counted for notes, divided into a percentage where each note equals, say 2.6%, and then the teacher counts the number of right notes and multiplies by 2.6 to give a total. I am not sure this helps much!

and finally attainment which exceeds expectations. The wording of the three grading categories can be rewritten to suit the task, and can be conveniently represented by the shorthand –/=/+ to help with recording information. This methodology has a number of factors in its favour, which are described in more detail later in this chapter.

Here are some questions that it would be useful for the teacher to ask at this point:

- If the aim is to help the learner, what is the most helpful way of doing this?
- If the aim is to compare the learners, one with another, and let them know how they are doing relative to each other, what is the most helpful way of doing this?
- If the aim is to produce statistics, because I, the teacher have been asked to, what is going to happen to this information?
- If the aim is to report to parents, what do they need to know?
- Why am I assessing fingering in this way?
- Does a musical performance matter (or not)?
- Is a musical performance with wrong fingering better than a non-musical performance with the correct fingering?

What this means is that having devised an assessment criterion, what also needs to be done is to devise a suitable mark scheme for it.

Grading criteria and mark schemes

What the previous section tells us is that *grading* is an important component of assessment. To explore this further, let us pursue the notion of an assessment criterion based on keyboard fingering. What happens next? What is the *use* of this assessment? Here is a list of possible next steps in the use of this assessment, which can occur singly, or in combination:

- The mark is entered into a markbook
- The mark is given to the school's assessment coordinator
- The teacher devises the subsequent programme of study to help with keyboard playing
- Harder keyboard pieces are found for those with high marks
- Those with low marks are made to play the melody again
- The teacher explains to those with low marks why they got them
- The teacher explains to those with low marks what they could do to improve

- The class moves on to the next unit of work
- Those with high marks are given a merit
- Those with low marks have to come back at break

It is here that distinction between *uses* and *purposes* of assessment can be starkly seen. Some of the uses of the assessment data outlined above seem relatively restricted. There might be a school situation which requires assessment data to be entered into a markbook, but this seems a topsy-turvy way of teaching if there is no other purpose to the assessment activity. As John Finney puts it, 'A culture of "performance" negates a culture of authenticity and meaning making. New orthodoxies emerge. Music comes to be taught upside-down' (Finney 2006: 4). In other words, music education needs to be about musical matters, not devising things which might be musical in some way, but which are easily assessable. What is likely to be better is for the teacher to decide what the use of the assessment data is likely to be, and then devise appropriate ways of eliciting it from the pupils.

However, in the real world of the busy music teacher, with too much to do, and too little time in which to do it, it is likely to be the case that not only will teachers want their learners to improve in their music making, they will also need to be able to prove to those in authority that they are doing something about this! This means that assessment judgements which are made in the classroom will, in many cases, have to be multifunctional, and both help learners improve and fulfil some requirements of data collection. In order to achieve this, we saw earlier that Boud (2000) talks about assessment doing 'double duty', and in Chapter 6 the question of for whom assessment was undertaken was discussed. It was shown that what this meant was that teachers are using the assessments they undertake in the classroom both to help their pupils improve, and to produce assessment information which will help show they are doing this. What is likely to be needed is a careful balancing act by the music teacher, and this is the topic to which we now turn, that of trying to maximize assessment opportunities by designing criteria which will be meaningful in the classroom.

Three dimensions of assessment

'In the hurly-burly of contemporary teaching we need clear criteria that help us to say "yes, that is effective music-making", or "this is astute appraisal" ' (Swanwick 1997: 209).

Owing in part to the elevated status of externally validated summative assessments, we do not have the clear criteria that Swanwick referred to, as the confusion between summative and formative purposes has meant that assessment criteria which are produced by the teacher to help with musical progress are undervalued in favour of grades showing statistical progression. But assessment judgements made by the classroom music teacher which are based upon clear criteria do have a helpful role to play in the development of learning. The problem for the teacher is in deciding exactly what it is that should be assessed in a learning episode. If this is done too strictly, then the teacher will end up 'teaching to the test', if it is not clear enough then neither teacher nor pupils will know what is going on:

> One of the key elements of AfL is the emphasis on making explicit both what is being learned and what successful learning would look like . . . However, achieving clarity in this process is like walking a tightrope, if [it] is not clear what is being learned (and why) and what success would look like, then learners will remain bemused, if it becomes too tightly specified then it becomes an exercise in compliance (Stobart 2008: 155).

For music teachers, the effect of tightrope walking is magnified by the learning/doing dichotomy. Teachers want their pupils to be composing, performing, and listening in ways which are musically appropriate, but they also want them to be learning how to do this. This means that in thinking about devising assessment criteria a series of stages need to be gone through in order to arrive at something which is meaningful.

Assuming that the purpose of assessment is to develop pupil learning and attainment, then what will be needed is for the teacher to ask themselves a series of questions about what it is that is important to them and their pupils in the specific piece of work in question. Bernstein (1971a) described the differences between *framing* and *classification*, where classification '. . . refers to the nature of differentiation between contents', and framing '. . . refers to the form of the context in which knowledge is transmitted and received' (Bernstein 1971/2003: 248). Bernstein went on to describe differences between strong and weak framing and classification. This is helpful for our purposes, as the notion of strong and weak classification, where some aspects are deemed more important than others, can be developed with relation to assessment.

What will be taking place in a music lesson will normally involve the conjunction of music making and music learning. These can be thought of as being, in Bernstein's terms, classified on a continuum from strong to weak.[3] Strong classification will involve the emphasis placed on each of the areas. Thus, for instance, in a composing project which has as its origins in work on

---

[3] Swanwick (1988: 122) also discusses these matters in musical terms relating to a lesson on the 12-bar blues, and Savage (2006: 89) with regard to Gifted and Talented learners.

African drumming, pupils may produce a piece of music which is only vaguely related to its African stimulus, but which evidences a good deal of musical learning, for example about instrumental control, rhythmic accuracy, dynamic contrast, and so on. The assessment that the teacher will make for developing the work of the pupils will be informed by the ways in which they think about the classification of the task. Thus, to continue the African music example, the importance of being authentically 'African' could well be outweighed by other aspects of learning which is taking place. This means that the teacher will be juggling classifications across three dimensions: those of music making, learning, and assessment, as Fig. 9.3 shows.

The limitations of two-dimensional representation are problematic here, in the classroom all three will be operationalized simultaneously. This means that the teacher will be making assessments based on their judgements along these three axes. This will involve classifications like this:

Weak ◄─────────── Music Making ───────────► Strong

In this axis, it is the music made by the pupils which is deemed to be important. A strong classification will mean that this takes precedence over learning, in other words at this stage there is an expectation that learning will have been accomplished in earlier stages of the unit of work, and what is being looked for here is musical proficiency. Weak classification can occur at the outset of a unit, where, for example, being stylistically exact might take second place to getting notes in the right order.

Weak ◄─────────── Learning ───────────► Strong

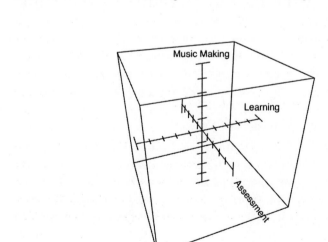

Fig. 9.3 Three dimensions of music making, learning, and assessment

When thinking about learning, the teacher will be concerned with a number of aspects of learning, including the acquisition of skills, concepts, and competencies, and of developing understandings within the style and genre of the music being worked on. It is also likely to be the case that non-musical factors will be important here, including groupwork, cooperation, creativity, and personal learning and thinking skills.[4] Strong classification here will mean that the teacher places emphasis on the development of these aspects of learning, a weaker classification will mean that less of an emphasis is placed here. It is important to note that the two axes of music making and learning should not be thought of as operating in inverse relationships with each other; simply because strong classification of learning could be achieved at the expense of music making does not mean that this has to be the case, equal emphasis could be placed on each, the two axes operate independently of each other. The assessment axis will be based in part on such judgements as these. It has already been described how all music making involves an assessment of some sort. In the classroom, the teacher will be deciding whether the assessment axis involves a weak or a strong classification:

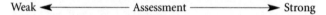

Weak ◄─────────── Assessment ──────────► Strong

In a weak classification, assessment judgements are kept to a minimum, possibly limited to impression comments. In a strong classification, assessment will form the main focus of what is taking place. By linking the three axes we can see that this could be based on a mixture of music making and learning, the decisions for this being in the hands of the teacher. What this also means is that the teacher is operating assessment judgements all the time in the classroom, a situation we know to be the case, but has control over the uses and purposes of assessment. What is also important is that these three dimensions do not need to be applied equally within a classroom. Thus a teacher in the situation where a number of groups are working simultaneously could decide to prioritize learning for one group, and music making for another.

Developing assessment criteria

Thinking about assessment operating in three dimensions means that the teacher can decide the aspects upon which to concentrate. This will involve producing separate criteria for learning and music making. These criteria can be formal, and written down, or can be based on spur-of-the-moment reactions and responses, building on the professional experience and knowledge of

---

4 For further discussion of non-musical aspects, see, *inter alia*, Hewitt (2003, 2006) and Maugars (2007).

the teacher. What many teachers have found helpful is to have a series of criteria which are predetermined, can be shared with pupils, and used for formal assessment purposes. Here the classification of assessment is strong, whereas other criteria which arise from the instantaneousness of classroom interaction with regard to music making may not have been worked out in advance.

In designing formal assessment criteria the problem of how to begin can seem to be an overwhelming one for some teachers. There seem to be too many variables to be considered at one time, 'Authentic musical assessment tasks, by nature of their similarity to real-life situations, contain numerous variables and potential confounding factors that are uncontrollable because of the authenticity of the task' (Brophy 2000: 50). So, how to deal with this? One way is to prioritize that which is important in terms of learning and/or music making. This seemingly obvious point is often neglected at the expense of McNamara's fallacy where things which are easily assessed are prioritized instead. So, what is important? This requires decisions by the teacher about learning and music making (or doing) separately.

Prioritizing aspects of music making means deciding what is important about the particular context being worked upon. At Year 7 in the secondary school it could be getting a feel for a piece of music which has three beats in a bar. At the conservatoire level it could be conveying meaning through musicianship. It may be the case that as competence increases a progressively weaker classification of assessment becomes in order. Thus attending a performance in Symphony Hall will entail evaluative assessment judgements, but that is unlikely to be the primary motivation of the audience attending. Music critics can disagree with each other, but the essence of their reviews serve a different function from the comments of a panel of examiners for a conservatoire student's final performance. In the school classroom, instrumental lesson, or school ensemble rehearsal, what is important needs to be decided upon, and enacted accordingly.

Here are some common KS3 topics:

The Blues	Film music
Minimalism	Songwriting
The Waltz	African drumming
Theme and variations	Binary and ternary form
Scary music	Reggae

Each of these will have a different set of importances, and these can reflect the value placed upon them. A useful exercise is for teachers to think about what matters *for them* in each of the topics in their syllabus, and then to design a short series of, say, three assessment foci which really look into these. Table 9.1 shows some aspects of each of the KS3 topics listed above which could be considered important, and which might form the focus for assessment.

Table 9.1 Assessment focuses for KS3 topics

The Blues	Knowledge of chords I, IV, and V
	The Blues scale
	Repetitive lyric structure (AAB)
Minimalism	Repetitive melodic framework
	Small changes over time
	Regular beat pattern
The Waltz	Triple time
	To be danced to
	Nineteenth-century importance
Theme and variations	Origins in Classical era
	Develops from melody
	Allows for rhythmic shifts
Scary music	Idea of atmosphere in music
	Suspense and fear
	Tension and release
Film music	Idea of atmosphere in music
	Mood to fit with images
	Sounds to fit with action ('Mickey Mousing')
Songwriting	Importance of lyrics
	Structure of verse-chorus
	Relevance to pupils
African drumming	Importance of rhythm
	Call and response
	Turn-taking
Binary and ternary form	Knowledge of Classical era
	Structure
Reggae	Repetition of material
	Knowledge of cultural origins
	Rhythmic emphasis
	Instrumentation used

These evidence a range of importances, and are likely to vary between different teachers, but what can be taken from this list is the notion of assessment focuses changing with the topic.

However, what one teacher values in the blues, could be discounted by another teacher. Here is a teacher talking about his views on this:

I went to a conference once where someone was doing a thing about Blues, and he'd bought with him a CD of some stuff that kids had been doing in his classroom, and he played you this backing track thing, and he said 'Now I don't think that's a very successful blues composition, why not?' Then we had to sit round and discuss it. And it was like a chord sequence with a bit of blues scale improvisation over the top, right-hand chords, left-hand automatic chords keyboard. And, well, I thought it's just not the blues, that's what wrong with it. He wanted you to say, 'Well you know, they haven't really used the scale properly, or sometimes the improvisation over this chord doesn't, like go, and they stray away from the arpeggio here.' It wasn't blues. Blues is gutsy real-life music first and foremost. Now there are blues singers who do 12 bar blues, there are blues singers who do 9 bar blues. Blues singers, if you read about them properly and find out about them, then when they were standing on Beale Street with an acoustic guitar trying to play for their pennies, sometimes it was 13 bars long, sometimes it was a bar of 7/4 because it didn't fit the words properly. But what it was really was real-life music, in a real situation telling you a story about something real, and about real-life. And a kid sitting behind a keyboard poking away at random notes out of the blues scale is not blues. I don't care what you do with it, that's not blues.

What this teacher values in the blues is obviously very different from a teacher who wants accurate performances using the standard 12-bar I-IV-V based chord sequence. These are matters for individual teachers to decide, and central prescription will not help! Priorities here include authenticity and feeling, matters which will derive from, not be replaced by, technical issues.

But this leads into the second of the three dimensions, that of learning. Although music making and learning operate independently, there are obviously relationships between them, and in order to improve and develop music making at any level then some form of learning will be involved. Indeed, it has been observed that concentrating on performance (in the non-musical sense) can actually be detrimental to improving it, '. . . a focus on learning can enhance performance, whereas a focus on performance can depress performance' (Watkins 2001: 7). So thinking about learning can pay real dividends elsewhere! There will also be developmental issues which may be subsumed within a unit of work, and which will have subsequent effects on learning later in the programme of study. These can be considered as being examples of subsidiarity in terms of learning outcomes. For example, a unit on the blues, using keyboards as its focus, may have the subsidiary intention of developing pupil understanding concerning chords and harmony, which will be needed for a later unit, on, say, songwriting. Thus whilst there will be a learning focus on understanding the conventions of the blues, there will be subsidiary learning foci on developing chordal knowledge. This was the purpose of the spiral curriculum diagram shown in Chapter 5 (Fig. 5.1). Thinking about learning like this helps with issues of development discussed in Chapter 7. This leads to a multi-layered approach to assessment, which helps explain why thinking about assessment across three dimensions is useful for the teacher, because where subsidiarity is important, it ought not to be lost in a focus on what might seem more overt topic-centred learning outcomes.

Developing manageable assessment criteria

The notion of assessing across three dimensions, as exemplified by Fig. 9.3, is also going to present challenges in terms of the ways in which teachers can undertake their day-to-day assessment activities. One way in which this can be achieved in a straightforward fashion in the classroom was looked at earlier in this chapter, in the form of tripartite grading criteria. To add extra dimensions to this inevitably involves diluting the more complex 3D aspects, but for the busy music teacher a system of assessment recording which is not manageable will simply not be used. The way this can be worked in practice is to produce a simple assessment grid, with the criteria set against the grades. Figure 9.4 is an example from a teacher's markbook of such a grid.

In this example the pupils were working at a task which involved composing a melody and an ostinato. This assessment example is noteworthy on a number of counts. It allows the teacher to exercise a degree of professional judgement in a number of areas, including what it is which is 'felt' to be an ostinato; the assessment can be applied to a group of pupils (which might make for manageability in the first instance) as well as to individual pupils, and there is scope for thinking about the musicality of responses. This last point is an important one, as it gets to the heart of assessing musically. All too often assessment schemes for music attainment can be found which miss out the very essence of that which is desirable—musical responses. Music teachers can at times be afraid of writing assessment criteria of this order, and yet it is important; an ostinato could be produced by a machine (a repeating pattern of notes is not a complex construct) and yet some pupils will produce results from this task which are inherently more musical than others. Music teachers need not be afraid of having assessment criteria of this nature. Indeed, it could be argued that by having an assessment criterion which allows teachers to use their judgement in this area, the validity of the assessment increases.

	Not yet	Satisfactorily	Well	
Makes appropriate use of Ostinato				
Appropriate use of melody				
Works cooperatively as a group				
Produces musical results				

Fig. 9.4 Markbook assessment grid

Criteria for criteria

The issue of teachers being concerned about writing criteria which allow for affective responses, and judgements which appertain thereto was the point at which Chapter 8 concluded. Here that point is resumed, and we need to think about what makes a good assessment criterion. Issues of reliability and validity obviously impinge upon this, but there are other points that we need to consider too. A number of points seem to be relevant here:

- A criterion should have a degree of exclusivity
  - It should be specific enough to measure a single item/skill/construct without too many extraneous variables coming into play
  - A criterion should, if possible, relate to a singularity
- A criterion should be assessable in some way
  - It should be possible to ascribe a rough valuing to the criterion, along the lines of the example above −/=/+
- A criterion should have some relationship to the whole
  - It should not be evaluating an irrelevant aspect of musical accomplishment, such as one observed which was 'has tie done up'!
- A series of criteria which deconstruct a whole should, when taken together, go some way towards formation of an overall impression of the whole
  - The isolated deconstructed aspects of criteria should not simply be an amorphous mass of unrelated trivia, but should have an overall meaning.
- Just because something is hard to assess does not mean it should be ignored!
  - The example of a criterion looking at musical results mentioned above is an example of this. It is probably the most important aspect, and so should be assessed in some way. It does rely on professional judgements, but so does neurosurgery!

These are important aspects of assessment criteria construction. Spending time getting criteria right is a worthwhile task for the music teacher, as this will make the key learning more straightforward to focus upon. It is also worth pointing out that music teachers should not be afraid of making *and defending* these judgements. Too often music teachers seem to be under the impression that they can only assess easy to access micro-behaviours (such as fingering), and it is these criteria which will help them carry weight with their colleagues in Maths and Science, but this need not be the case. A maths teacher can recognize an elegant solution to a problem, even if the answer is wrong, in the same way the music teacher knows a musical performance when she hears one.

Assessment criteria for tests and tasks

In Chapter 6 differences between tests and tasks were discussed. At this point it may be helpful to differentiate between assessment criteria which are devised for tests, and those which are devised for tasks. Fig. 6.1 ('who is the assessment for?') presented the notion of different uses for assessments, particularly the differences between auditing and improving learning. A test is that which occurs at the end of a learning episode, a task is something which is employed along the route. Teachers are used to constructing assessment criteria for tests, but tasks too need some attention in terms of what it is that is to be assessed.

In many primary, and some secondary schools, teachers use the acronyms WALT (we are learning to . . .) and WILF (what I'm looking for) to introduce learners to the outcomes and success criteria for what they are learning. For tasks the useful acronym here would appear to be WILF (however, this can obscure a range of outcomes which appear unintentionally!). In a similar fashion some teachers have adopted the formulation 'to do this well, you will . . .', which has the advantage of homing in on those aspects which will form the focus of assessment attention.

So, are assessment criteria for tasks and tests different? The answer to this question lies partially in the areas of validity and reliability. Assessment for a task will often be designed to use the results to take the learning of the pupils forward in some way. The results do not have to be reliable across contexts, they are relevant for that pupil in that lesson on that day. This contrasts with testing, however, when the teacher wants to be able to say with some accuracy that all year 7's results have some degree of reliability (even if only within that school). Tests and tasks will inevitably form a component of music education, and the appropriateness of their utility with regard to performing, composing, and listening are dealt with in later chapters. For the moment, it is important to note that a test contains an element of formal procedure about it, and can be considered as being 'done to' pupils, whereas tasks will involve ongoing learning and attainment, and can be considered as being 'done with' the learners.

Holistic or atomistic

So far this chapter has considered atomistic approaches to assessment criteria. This is where separate aspects of the musical whole are treated as the important distinguishable components of the whole, and marked and graded accordingly. There can be good reasons for doing this, including the issues of reliability and validity discussed so far, but we need to be on our guard against assuming that atomistic assessment is the only methodology available. Janet Mills wryly notes:

As I leave a concert, I have a clear notion of the quality of the performance which I have just heard. If someone asks me to justify my view, I may start to talk about rhythmic drive, or interpretation, or sense of ensemble, for instance. But I move from the whole performance to its components. I do not move from the components to the whole. In particular, I do not think: the notes were right, the rhythm was right, the phrasing was coherent, and so on—therefore I must have enjoyed this performance. And I certainly do not think something such as SKILLS + INTERPRETATION = PERFORMANCE (Mills 2005: 176).

This does seem to have an inner logic to it. Assuming that quality can be derived from a summation of the components in the simplistic fashion Mills talks about is going to be problematic. Indeed, as Swanwick observes, 'The conflation into a single figure of two or more observations hardly seems to be very meaningful in assessment and loses important information on the way' (Swanwick 1994: 106). And yet this is increasingly what accountability and the standards agenda seems to have required teachers to do.

Holistic assessment, on the other hand, eschews atomistic criteria, and simply grants an overall grade to, say, a performance, based on the professional judgement of the teacher. Arguments against this method say that it is subjective, and yet, as Janet Mills argues, '. . . all assessment is subjective, in the sense that human beings determine how it is done' (Mills 2005: 177). Indeed, even when endeavouring to be objective in assessment, shades of subjectivity often creep in, '. . . music teachers described many different assessment criteria and their equivalent marks which relied on subjective judgments. Accuracy, musicality, performance, pleasure, emotion, beauty, and students' musical ability were not "objective" assessment criteria . . .' (Maugars 2007: 17).

Maybe the issue for music teachers has been that they are concerned that holistic judgments will be derided by their colleagues, yet surely the issue is for assessment in music to be musical, rather than aspire to some pseudo-scientific quasi-objectivity. This should not be seen as a weakness of the subject, but a strength. It is the different nature of music and music education that should afford it a place on the curriculum. Diluting those differences and only assessing knowing about music is unlikely to help it maintain its place.

Endnote

Having discussed the importance of developing criteria for various aspects of musical achievement, specific instances of assessment criteria and their employment are considered in next three chapters, focusing on performing, composing, and listening. In these chapters many of the threads from this, and earlier chapters, are picked up and considered from the very particular perspective of educational music making and learning.

Chapter 10

Developing classroom performing by the use of assessment

This chapter, and the two which follow it, look at the role of assessment in developing the key music curricular activities of performing, composing, and listening. Separating them out in this fashion does not imply that these are distinct and discrete activities, which can be thought of as functioning in their own separate bubble with no connection to other core activities. The National Curriculum talks of 'Developing knowledge, skills and understanding through the integration of performing, composing and listening' (QCA 2007: 180), and it is this integration which remains at the heart of our discussion of these interlinked areas. However, pragmatically and philosophically, an integrated notion of 'musicking' (*cf.* Small 1998) is, in many of the world's cultures, also associated with the separate and specific notion of developing skills in using instruments and voices. For the teacher in the classroom there can be logical reasons for dividing the emphasis in Programme of Study between the differing aspects of performing, listening, and composing, and therefore assessment will have a different role in the development of each.

Limitations of this chapter

In many ways, this chapter is attempting the impossible. Assessing performing in the classroom using criteria is always going to be problematic, because the very nature of assessment criteria themselves will be suspect, 'The assessment criteria for performance are ultimately infinite, as they can be endlessly broken down into sub-criteria' (Dixon 2000). Writing criteria for assessing performing will therefore inevitably involve only a small subset of what is involved, in other words '. . . criteria-based assessments emphasise a narrow view of music performance characteristics' (Stanley et al. 2002: 53). Alongside this, and building on the previous chapter, we need to be aware that atomistic assessment of performing components does not tend to take place in real-world settings, where the whole experience is more of concern. Janet Mills writes of '. . . performances that have overwhelmed me, despite there being a handful of wrong notes. I remember others in which the notes have been accurate, and the interpretation has been legitimate, and yet the overall effect has been sterile. A performance is much more than a sum of skills and interpretation' (Mills 1991a: 175).

The alternative to having assessment criteria is to adopt a holistic stance, and assess the totality of a performing experience without resorting to micro-specification of subcomponents. Whichever way we choose, it is helpful to think of performing as a continuum from novice to expert, and the role of the teacher being to facilitate the journey along this trajectory. This novice-expert continuum probably has no fixed end points, especially at the expert end! This means that there will constantly be more steps along the journey, which implies that there is no definite point of arrival at the position of expert. What is helpful, though, is to recognize the milestones along the route. Lehmann & Davidson (2002: 549) describe three stages in skill development: the pre-instruction phase, where play is the main form of encounter with music; guided instruction, which is the phase of most concern to primary and secondary school music teachers; and the final phase where an individual makes a full-time commitment, this is an important phase, but nonetheless one which the majority of school students will never make. The concern for the majority of school teachers will be with ways in which, returning to the quotation from Janet Mills above, moving pupils towards a more expert performance, account can be taken of, and allowances made for, handfuls of wrong notes in order to help our pupils along their own personal journeys.

Assessment of performing

It has already been observed that of all the various aspects of musical achievement, performing has the most developed assessment schedule associated with it. For classroom purposes this can be both a blessing and a hindrance. The ubiquitous nature of ABRSM type of performing examinations can act as an unwitting model for the promotion of performing in ways which, ultimately, might not be overly helpful. This is because ABRSM examinations are rightly concerned with a hierarchy of instrumental performance aimed at performing to the highest standard. The sequence is designed to build up to this, and quality in performing is the end result. In the classroom, performing is more likely to be a part of a general musical education, and, in keeping with models of musical learning previously looked at, performing in the classroom can be seen as a means to the end of musical understanding. These distinctions are represented visually in Fig. 10.1.

Figure 10.1 shows the different modalities of musical learning, with learning to play an instrument at the top, and classroom learning at the bottom. There is

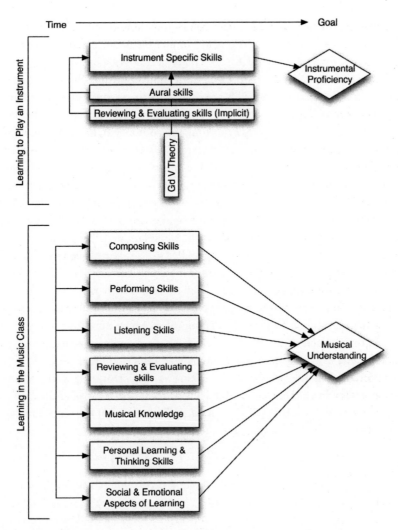

Fig. 10.1 Differing modes of musical learning

a clear difference in emphasis between the two, with learning to play an instrument having a specific outcome in terms of its end goal. Notice too that other aspects of instrumental achievement are subsidiary to this main end product. I have known of peripatetic instrumental teachers who would enter pupils for Grade examinations, and then expect someone else to 'do' the aural skills component, so detached was it from their day-to-day teaching. For ABRSM there is the 'one hit' of Grade 5 theory, a separate examination, which needs to be taken before progress to higher performing grades is allowed. Again, this tends to have very limited transfer to learning to play an instrument, and often occurs as separate and isolated from the instrumental learning situation.

This contrasts with the classroom learning model shown in the lower part of Fig. 10.1, where performing skills are there to serve an entirely different end goal, that of musical understanding. Here learning is deliberately designed in a more 'joined-up' fashion, and performing is a component, not a goal in itself. In the classroom, performing is often used as a servant to other skills, and, as we shall see, this is particularly true in the case of composing.

What Fig. 10.1 also shows are a range of skills and knowledge which may seem tangential to the original learning intention, but which are nonetheless important components of musical thinking. For commonality of nomenclature, these have been labelled with current National Curricular terminologies. Thus personal learning and thinking skills (PLTS) are not seen as optional 'bolt-on' extras, but as an integral part of the music curriculum. This is where higher order thinking, creative acts, and attributes of learning are situated. Metacognition, another key aspect of music learning, is located here too. Social and emotional aspects of learning (SEAL) have an important part to play in the affective components of music learning, and have a key role in the development of rounded musical thinking and understanding.

Understanding the two ways of thinking about performing is important, because what is unlikely to be effective is where a teacher has grafted on to classroom work a 'watered down' version of instrumental learning. The two types have very different end goals, which will affect pedagogy, and so this needs to be recognized, and appropriate ways of learning and teaching devised accordingly.

So, how can assessment be used to develop classroom performing? Here we need to think about some of the aspects of learning which have been discussed above, as well as in earlier chapters. Although performing has been seen to be a component of a wider learning outcome, there are still specific skills for different instruments that teachers will want to develop in service of those wider goals. We also need to bear in mind that, '... a curriculum that consists of performance could shrink in on itself until it ceased to be creative or imaginative, and failed to involve students in musical activity away from the instrument or voice ...' (Mills 2005: 52). And so the consideration regarding performing in this chapter will always need to be read with a view to its wider application, and to the purpose of developing musical thinking and understanding.

In order to think about performing in a little more detail, we need to consider a number of aspects simultaneously. These include:

- Reasons for performing
- Type/range of instrument(s) used
- Specific skills in question
- Links with composing
- Links with listening
- Conceptions of quality
- Self-regulating development aspects

Many teachers also use classroom performing to develop skills in staff notation reading, or in graphic scores. Whilst this will obviously depend very much on the context it is important to note that reading staff notation is not itself an instrumental skill, although in the western classical tradition it is very much bound up with it, as has been discussed earlier. Whilst it may well be deemed appropriate to be using staff notation alongside the development of instrumental proficiency, we have established that the two are cognitively unrelated. Assessing performing is not intrinsically linked to assessing note-reading. For this reason this section, and those which follow, deals with notation as a separate component of learning, not necessarily as being integral to performing, composing, or listening.

For classroom performances, many schools have a limited range of instruments available to them. Typically these include percussion, tuned and untuned, guitars, electronic keyboards, and a range of ICT equipment, often centred around computers. It is patently obvious that developing skills in playing the guitar are different to those for playing percussion. However, what they have in common are elements of control, and of a relationship between control and sound output. This means that assessment of performing needs to recognize these differences, and so we need to deconstruct the notion of performing in its classroom variant.

In Fig. 10.1 above, the second box in the list of classroom attributes for musical learning is labelled 'performing skills'. But is this a unitary attribute? Is there a single skill-set which is particular to performing? Sadly the answer to this is 'no', as otherwise we would all know what it was, and would be employing it on a daily basis! So, what is involved in performing? To return to our earlier discussion of theoretical approaches we can consider two aspects to performing: those which are primarily behavioural, and those which are primarily cognitive. The notion of 'behavioural' here is *not* being used in the sense of not involving any notion of mind at all, here behavioural aspects of performing are deemed to arise from a mental aspect, and then be transmitted in a sensory-motor fashion via motor skills to the fingers, hands, and feet of the musician. Cognitive aspects here are separated into those which do not translate directly into an embodied response. There is a causal link between the two, but for the purposes of classroom assessment, we need to separate out those which are amenable to intervention and assessment, and those which may not be.

Although some types of musical knowledge clearly exist outside of performance (Davidson & Scripp 1992), for assessment of performing it is in and through performance that instrumental and vocal skill acquisition in the classroom is primarily going to be evidenced. Mastery of skills required therefore needs breaking down into those which are assessable in performance of a whole piece, and those micro-skills which can be assessed separately in sub-species of musical performing. Assessment of classroom performing is therefore going to focus on a number of factors. According to McPherson and Schubert there are at least four main types of competences used to define assessment criteria, these being technique, interpretation, expression, and communication (McPherson & Schubert 2004: 64). Swanwick also posits four areas for this, alongside other classroom music making: 'sound materials, expressive characterisation, structural sequencing, valuing' (Swanwick 1994: 108). For many classroom teachers, working with the shadow of school assessment managers behind them demanding simple regular assessment data, some of the more complex aspects of performance assessment can be subsumed within a mindset which includes, at or near the top of the list, skill acquisition and technique. So, let us begin with a consideration of technique in relation to classroom performing.

Technique

On its own, technique is too big an aspect to be assessed as a unitary construct; as we saw in Chapter 9, it is helpful if assessment criteria can be uniquely defined, and notions of technique do not possess this attribute. What teachers will normally be looking for in technical terms is some view towards accuracy. This can be thought of in terms of sensory-motor control which results in accurate performance. How accuracy is defined will depend on the context, but usually involves a notion of playing right notes, with attention to rhythmic details.

Accuracy is not the only domain which affects technique, but is obviously a key one. Also important in thinking about performing are notions of *intention*. Here it is possible for the classroom teacher to not rely on a final performance, as listening to ongoing classroom performing work will provide information as to whether intentionality of an individual's performance is undertaken consistently. This does not mean simply that the pupil intends to be correct, rather that they have a degree of control over their performance.

Once a degree of mastery has been achieved, then the sensory-motor movements of an individual tend to become more fluid in nature. This results in acquisition of a sense of gesture. To conceptualize this, an accomplished performer playing an arpeggio will be able to do so in a smoother fashion than a beginner. Gesture also involves facility with bodily movement in an appropriate manner—appropriate to the instrument that is. Some forms of gesture are domain-specific to the instrument, such as smooth movements of a violin bow, others are learned by imitation, such as the circular arm movement of an electric guitarist playing power chords. Whichever method of acquisition/ participation has been used, there will be a degree of instrumental specificity about them.

In the western classical tradition, it is not uncommon to think of learning 'the notes' first, and putting in the expression later. In some world musics the two are intrinsically bound up one with the other. This is potentially the hardest to assess of this already hard area! Absolute rules concerning expression cannot be formulated, as notions of expression will always have to be mediated through the listener. This involves a process of communication from the performer to the listener. The performer needs to know that their performance is being listened to, and make it 'a performance', the listener has to be made aware of what is going on during the course of the performance: 'The communication of expression is more effective when listeners can detect variations in performance and interpret them.' (Hallam 2006: 102)

To assess this area, therefore, the affective dimension does not only have to be recognized, it is part of its very *raison d'etre*.

What this discussion concerning technique has tried to do, is to bring a number of elements into play which will have some effect on the way in which classroom performing takes place. These are represented diagrammatically in Fig. 10.2.

Figure 10.2 shows technique being subdivided into the componential aspects discussed above, and then being evidenced in performance. An alternative to breaking down assessment of performing into the atomistic components of the middle column is to treat it as an indivisible whole, and then for the teacher to use professional judgement to comment on the quality of what they have heard. This avoids the necessity of trying to decide what aspects of performance technique are in need of attention, and treating it instead as a complex whole. To do this the music teacher needs to be quite clear that what is being done is that professional judgements are being made, and that whilst

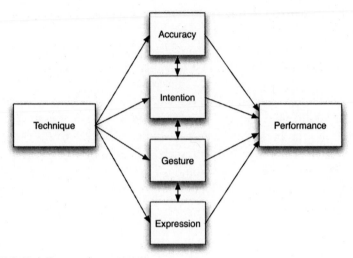

Fig. 10.2 Technique and assessment

possibly personal and subjective, these are in keeping with the ethos of the subject, after all '. . . the acquisition of informed subjectivity is one of the aims of arts education . . .' (Spruce 2002: 127). The effect of holistic assessment is to say, in essence, that we are able to make informed judgements as to the quality of a performance. Interestingly, for some reason we as music teachers are often less willing than our Art and Design colleagues to say that something is good 'because we say so':

> Common criteria have value in helping to focus the assessors' attention on particular concerns but they do not provide absolute measurement standards—assessment of the arts in schools still requires aesthetic judgement and connoisseurship based on experience of what pupils at a particular age can achieve. (Mason & Steers 2007: 15).

And what music teachers seldom do is to overtly use the notion of connoisseurship as the basis of a judgement. Does this matter? The problem with connoisseurship is that it presupposes that the person making the judgements can do so with some degree of accuracy and reliability, but this is not necessarily the case:

> The process of assessing musical performances is often based on several implicit and often flawed assumptions. One is that the musical value of a performance can be assessed accurately and reliably. a second is that experienced listeners are able to make consistently accurate judgments. This leads to a third assumption, that expert judges possess the ability to make finer discriminations than average listeners due to their

more refined abilities to determine which of the components of a performance were effective and which were not. (McPherson & Schubert 2004: 65)

As we have seen elsewhere, it may be the case that the concerns music teachers have with objectivity places them in the position of believing that this will 'cut no ice' with science and maths colleagues, and that music education does need to at least nod towards objectivity. But are we really being objective when we say we are, or are we using a spurious pseudo-objectivity as a cover-up for being subjective? After all, '. . . teachers aim at being objective by using many criteria for assessment and markings, but rely more often than not on subjective judgments (accuracy, musicality, and interpretation)' (Maugars 2007: 1). Music teachers probably already trust their judgements; maybe they need to be given confidence that these judgements are considered trustworthy.

Different modalities for classroom performing

Because performing skills can only be evidenced in performing itself, then teachers are likely to set up opportunities for performing at a number of points during the course of a music programme of study. These will normally occur in one of the following organisational routines:

- Performing as individuals
- Performing in small groups
- Performing as a whole class

The type of things that will be performed are likely to be one of the following:

- Pieces of music complete in themselves
- Pieces of music to help with specific aspects of technique
- Technical exercises to help with specific aspects of technique

So it follows that reasons for performing might include:

- Performing for its own sake
- Performing in service of another of aspect of musical achievement e.g. composing or improvising

This means that a complex series of linked dimensions are operating in the music class, and it is up to the music teacher to sequence these activities carefully. The complex interlinking between these various elements of performing is shown in Fig. 10.3.

There are separate aspects of musical endeavour involved in each, and performing as a whole class involves a different set of skills being employed than performing solo; likewise the repertoire performed will affect what is assessed,

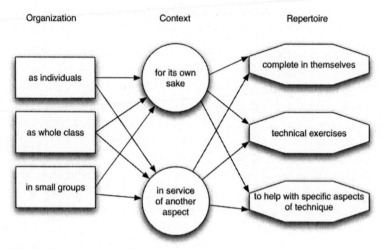

Fig. 10.3 Performing modalities

in the sense that specific stylistic matters and details will assume differing levels of context-specific prominence.

The sequencing of musical learning matters here, as it is important to ascertain that pupils are involved in music which is appropriate for them to perform, not only within their capabilities, or aspirant capabilities, but for which there is a logical reason for doing. In a similar fashion, using performing to evidence understanding of composing needs to be structured in such a way that the performing skills are of a suitable level at which composing skills can be evidenced. Whether this means treating them as separate, or as linked activities will be a matter for the teacher. What it does mean is that the multi-faceted nature of performing in the classroom requires subtly different assessment approaches.

Beyond technique

In the discussions concerning assessment of performing so far we have concentrated our attention upon technique, and placed expression as a component thereof. But what of other aspects of performing? What else might there be to assess?

Brophy identifies six areas for assessment of musical skills for performing in the general music class. These are: pitch, rhythm, sight-reading, vocal range, vocal acquisition, and dexterity (Brophy 2000: 116). In the UK context, assessing vocal range and acquisition smacks of the 'sheep and goats' divisions of music classes of the mid-twentieth century, when in many schools, the music teacher placed his ear by the pupil's mouth, and then divided the class into those who would spend the lesson singing, and those who would be involved with music via worksheets! Sight-reading we have already discounted as being performance-related, rather than an intrinsically performance-based skill. This leaves pitch, rhythm, and dexterity. There is some debate in the neuro-science community as to whether cognitive systems for perception of pitch and rhythm exists as separate, or unified dimensions (Boltz 1999). Whatever the outcome of this neuroscientific research, for practical classroom purposes many music teachers treat pitch and rhythm as part of the same musical knowledge-set, as it is difficult to separate them out in a meaningful fashion, and are probably best considered in terms of accuracy.

Assessment of doing or assessment of learning?

'Any valid and reliable assessment model has to take account of two dimensions: what pupils are doing and what they are learning . . .' (Swanwick 1999: 84).

It is in the assessment of doing, or of the assessment of learning, that music teachers really start to tie themselves up into knots! If it is *learning* which is valued, then why assess it by *doing*? If *doing* is important, then what part has *learning* had to play in arriving at this level of doing-ness? Teachers talk of having learning outcomes, but then assess whether these have been reached via the use of task outcomes. The assessment of performing falls right into this, and so we need to be clear as to whether what is being assessed is the per-forming, or the learning which has taken place in order to arrive at the per-forming stage. This is a complex concept to grasp, and an even harder one to enact! If we consider classroom performing as an example, using classroom percussion, guitars, and electronic keyboards it is possible to see a series of layers operating in terms of a developmental assessment.

Skills specific to the instrument in question are likely to form a first layer to this. Then onto this, as base-level skills become acquired, we can overlay fur-ther requirements of musicianly thinking in terms of the ways in which devel-opment takes place within the individual. This point was recognized by Swanwick and Tillman in their spiral sequence of musical development (Swanwick & Tillman 1986), which although appertaining to composing, places sensory and manipulative aspects of musical learning at the base level of the spiral. In terms of assessment of performing we need to ask questions about how skills are learned, and then how learning of those skills might be assessed separately from demonstration of those skills being put into practice.

Task analysis

Theoretical accounts of learning, explored in Chapter 5, allow for different explanations of the ways in which people learn. Both behaviourist and cognitive approaches allow for breaking a complex task down into a series of smaller steps or stages. This procedure, known as task analysis, varies in its employment in the music classroom from a rough-and-ready deconstruction by the teacher, to step-by-step instruction books purchased specifically for the purpose. However this is accomplished, task analysis with regard to performing is an important aspect of the teacher's role, '. . . different learning outcomes require different forms of assessment and different kinds of instructional or learning strategies to foster them. An essential skill of instructional designers, then, is the articulation of the kinds of learning outcomes for which they are assisting learning (i.e. task analysis)'[1] (Jonassen et al. 1999: 1).

For classroom performing this is going to be harder than it sounds! What the teacher is likely to want is going to be an accelerated transition through the initial early stages of skill acquisition. For example, in learning to play the side drum, some tutors begin with a protracted period of stick holding, before beginning to play the instrument. In the classroom situation this may not be an appropriate methodology. The teacher will want to get the pupils performing as soon as possible. This means that the task analysis which the teacher will have done, even if unarticulated, will involve developing a technique which is good enough for the next stages to be reached. This 'good enough' technical facility can be seen to characterize much classroom performing, in that the ultimate aim is musical understanding. Certainly, pupils who show some form of aptitude may well be pointed towards further and deeper study, but the learning outcome for all pupils will contain this notion of being good enough. What 'good enough' involves is likely to vary from teacher to teacher, and maybe from instrument to instrument. The 'good enough' potential of the descant recorder, for instance, may involve reducing the over-blowing headache-inducing potential, whereas for Spanish guitar it may involve holding the instrument in a way that reduces danger to the instrument and other pupils!

Formative and summative assessment of performing

It is at this point that the differing purposes of formative and summative assessment assume primary importance. Put at its most simplistic, formative assessment will be used for making assessments of learning, and summative

---

[1] Parentheses in original.

assessment will be used for auditing developing mastery and skill acquisition. Of course, this overly simplistic description belies a complex series of other judgements which the teacher will be making, but this is, in essence, what will be taking place. This means that the assessments which will make a difference to pupil learning will be formative ones. The entire learning process will be scaffolded by formative assessment judgements made by the teacher during the course of the learning programme. In order to explore this in more detail, the distinctions between formative and summative assessment of performing need unpicking somewhat.

Formative assessment of classroom performing

The ongoing nature of developing skill acquisition in classroom instrumental playing is best served by formative assessment, in that learning is supported and scaffolded by appropriate formative assessment. The class teacher will establish learning-to-perform activities which are sequential, and which offer the potential for development. The important point to be remembered here is that there are the differences explored earlier in this chapter between different modes of learning to perform. The instrumental music teacher will be concerned with developing mastery of the instrument, whereas the classroom teacher will be focusing on developing understanding, which requires a skill-set in order to underpin cognitive development.

Day-to-day formative assessment of performing will be very much concerned with structured interventions, with giving feedback and feedforward, and with personalizing learning to suit the needs of the individual concerned. As we have seen, the function of performing in the classroom is very much one where the activity can be both an end in itself and a means towards musical understanding. Due to this duality of purpose, different modes of assessment will be appropriate when assessing classroom performing. This links to the three dimensions of learning, doing, and assessing, as the teacher will be thinking separately about them. There is a steady pendulum-like swing between a focus on learning and a focus on evidencing learning in doing. To take a concrete example, at KS3 the use of electronic keyboards is a regular part of the music programme. In the early stages of such work, teachers will establish differentiated learning tasks for pupils with different levels of attainment in keyboard playing. Thus for complete beginners a structured programme of note-naming and simple melodic playing will be in order, which would be thoroughly inappropriate for pupils with some degree of pre-existing proficiency. Formative assessment of the novices would take the form of the teacher being assistive with the learning tasks that were being engaged with. This represents a focusing on the learning. Once a degree of competence has been established, then it is quite likely that the teacher will set a group performance of some sort, where the focus is likely to be on music making which has resulted from learning. Similar and more complex instances will be found throughout generalist music classes.

The use of moments of assessment opportunity will be important here, as ongoing development of performing skills can be formatively assessed as pupils work at a variety of learning tasks in the music lesson. These will not necessarily arise as a product of formal testing, but will be the result of teachers' ongoing classroom observations. Being formative assessments, and therefore focusing on improving learning, the teacher will make comments and give feedforward as to how the performing skills can be developed, and what each individual concerned needs to do themselves in order to raise their attainment.

Summative assessment of classroom performing

Summative assessment of pupil performing will normally take place at the end of a learning episode or unit of work. Its purpose will primarily be that of measuring, auditing, and certifying pupils' performances. There are four questions which it is worthwhile to ask here:

1. Why is summative assessment of classroom performing taking place at this particular juncture?
2. How is it to be assessed?
3. How is it to be graded?
4. What will happen to the results?

In many ways the first of these questions is the most telling, and is the one which teachers should address at the outset. If the main answer is 'to improve it', then that end might be better served by formative assessment. If, as we have seen previously, summative assessment is being undertaken in the belief that a series of mini-summative assessments constitute formative assessment, then maybe a truer type of formative assessment might be more appropriate. Which leaves a number of other reasons, including:

1. To provide material for a test
2. To compare students with each other
3. To provide data
4. To put students 'on the spot'
5. To give the students a chance to achieve
6. To judge the effectiveness of teaching
7. So I (and they) can see improvements over time

A number of these are interrelated, and also link to questions 2 and 3 from the first list. There are valid reasons for using summative assessment of performing, but if not thought through properly, there can be a potentially destructive effect for some pupils. Summative assessments do not have to be public events, and the individual pupil may feel that to publicly perform may be a step too far, and this can have a detrimental effect upon their self-esteem. This does not mean that the pupils should never be asked to perform in public, but the teacher, who will know their class, might want to address this issue for some pupils. Indeed some individual education plans (IEPs) might have something of this nature in them. However, each of these can be valid reasons for undertaking summative assessment of performing, and so are explored in some detail.

To provide material for a test

It has already been explored as to how the notion of a test is different from that of a task, and performance-as-task is different from performance-as-test. Some music teachers value the gravitas that tests have, and welcome the comparability they give with the other subjects. It can also be an opportunity to undertake an assessment 'snapshot', and as such, is likely to be worthwhile. For many teachers and pupils, having a test focuses attention onto a specific point when, for example, a unit of work comes to an end. This can act as a motivator for many pupils in its own right.

Pragmatically, this reason for testing might be in response to impositions from school management teams. It can also become part of what pupils expect, and be built into the calendar of the school. But we do need to beware of tests for tests' sake: 'Grades really cover up failure to teach. A bad instructor can go through an entire quarter leaving absolutely nothing memorable in the minds of his class, curve out the scores on an irrelevant test, and leave the impression that some have learned and some have not' (Pirsig 1974: 204). 'Failure to teach' being a sad by-product of the over-utilization of testing.

To compare students with each other

Norm-referenced assessment is concerned with statistical information about the placement of individuals in terms of attainment within a given population. Some schools require this information in terms of pupil data, where a class is placed into rank order. This can have a motivating and affirmational effect for pupils in the upper quartile of such a ranking, and a demotivating effect upon those in the lower quartile. For the classroom teacher the issue would be why this is being done—what information is being gained from this?

To provide data

A common cry from music teachers is, 'I need to provide my data manager with grades'. Often, the easiest way is to have a test. This seems to be an example of what John Finney calls '. . . the creation of data efficient systems capable of telling an official truth . . .' (Finney 2006: 2), and he goes on to refer to this way of working as '. . . music comes to be taught upside-down' (Finney 2006: 4). Certainly assessment data can and should be used for tracking and monitoring purposes, but fabricating potentially pointless and spurious data simply to feed into a spreadsheet is unlikely to be the most efficient way of doing this!

To put students 'on the spot'

Being able to be confident in public is obviously a useful skill. Being able to perform musically is an important part of music learning. Putting students 'on the spot' in terms of a solo performance can be seen to be a useful precursor of subsequent solo examinations. However, for many people, performing in front of their peers is a tough act, and this aspect need to be handled sensitively by the teacher.

To give the students a chance to achieve

For many students in schools, performing can be something they enjoy. Rock bands, for example, relish the opportunity to perform in front of their peers. For some pupils musical performance can be an unusual example of an area in which they excel, and so having an assessed performance is something with which they are entirely happy. This category also includes those pupils who rise to a challenge, and where the notion of an assessed performance is a motivating factor

To judge the effectiveness of teaching

It can be the case that a teacher wishes to evaluate the effectiveness of their pedagogy, and so to do this they assess the pupils concerned. This can reveal gaps in knowledge, or of common mistakes, and the teacher can use this information to develop their teaching in the future.

So I (and they) can see improvements over time

Sometimes it can be hard in the day-to-day work of the classroom for learners to realize that they have made progress. The use of audio recordings of performances facilitates listening back to performances from an earlier time by the pupils.

Many of these reasons hark back to issues of who assessment is for, and what the uses of the assessment data will be. Many of the comments concerning performing so far have been specifically concerned with using an instrument. Whilst these can in many cases also be applicable to singing, there are some specific ways in which assessing singing is unlike assessing performing on an instrument, and it is to that which we now turn.

Singing

Singing features as a performing activity throughout music learning, and we know that there are specific aspects of the teaching and learning of singing that assessment feeds into. Singing can be a much more personal activity than instrumental performing, and many teachers are very aware that young people can feel particularly conscious of themselves whilst singing. Assessment of singing therefore needs to take account of this, and teachers need to be sensitive to this. We know that singing is an important feature of musical development (Welch 2006), and, as part of the National Curriculum, figures in many units of work in schools, and as a part of instrumental music learning too. However, balanced against this, John Finney observed that singing, '. . . despite its statutory place in the English secondary school music curriculum, it has in practice a twilight existence and marginal role' (Finney 2000: 203). This 'twilight existence' might go some way towards explaining its problematic assessment. If the activity itself does not figure widely, then assessment practices must reflect this. To address this 'twilight existence', we can consider a range of assessment uses and purposes for singing. For the classroom, assessment can be considered as happening across a continuum from individuals, via pairs and small groups, to whole class or larger ensembles.

Summative assessment of singing does not seem to take place anywhere near as frequently in classroom music lessons as summative assessment of performing does. Reasons for this probably relate to the issues of self-awareness of young people, and of the problematic nature of undertaking such as assessment. Indeed, it may well be the case that summative assessment of singing might have a detrimental effect upon the individual, and a consequent reduction in their capabilities. As Graham Welch observes, 'The artificiality (in terms of customary classroom musical activity) can have negative effects on a child's ability to make sense of the singing task and to demonstrate *proficiency* as opposed to inadequacy'[2] (Welch 1994: 7).

Where summative assessment is to be found, however, is in the realm of competitive musical festivals and the like, where external assessment of (typically) group singing is a normal event. The emphasis on group singing is important, as this takes the onus away from the individual pupil.

---

[2] Parentheses and italics in original.

Formative assessment of singing is far more commonplace in the classroom, and here carefully targeted supportive comments are appropriate when aimed at individuals and at groups. Patrick Allen recommends the use of targets, such as '. . . posture, self-discipline, well sustained phrases, [and] clarity of diction . . .' (Allen 2003: 31). Many of Allen's targets can themselves become formative assessment criteria for class singing in their own right too.

Whole class instrumental and vocal tuition

In England, whole class instrumental and vocal tuition (WCIVT) has been promoted via the Governmentally funded 'wider opportunities' programme, whereby classes of Key Stage 2 pupils receive music tuition focused on instruments or the voice. It is pertinent to note that the wider opportunities programme is not solely concerned with teaching youngsters to play instruments, but that:

> . . . central to programme is the belief that learning a musical instrument is not an end in itself but the means by which children can develop their musical learning and understanding through direct engagement with making music. The instrument is the means not the end and the focus is on the learning child not the instrument. (Spruce 2008: 3–4)

One of the implications for assessment of having whole classes learning through instrumental work are that enormous demands are placed on the teacher, who has to make rapid formative assessment judgements which will not only help the learners to improve, but will also involve attention to future teaching, as individual and small group pedagogies are unlike that which is required for whole class teaching in this fashion. In that sense formative assessment has an important role to play in this way of working.

Assessment of instrumental learning using notation

In Chapter 4 the role of staff notation as a symbolic reference system, rather than a thinking system was discussed. This is an important point to revisit here, as there is a common assumption that learning to play an instrument has to involve reading notation.

> A curious contradiction in music pedagogy is that teaching practice is often in conflict with theories of instrumental teaching about how to introduce notation to a child. Whereas most children learning an instrument in Western styles of education are introduced to musical notation from their very early lessons, prominent instrumental teachers throughout history have advocated that ear playing should he emphasized before the introduction of notation. (McPherson & Gabrielsson 2002: 99)

There are a number of reasons that this confusion exists. Janet Mills (2007: 140) tells how, when she began teaching the violin, she unconsciously did so in a similar fashion to her own violin teacher some years previously. This is a common reason, and carried to its inevitable conclusion could mean that violin teaching has not altered much since the time of Mozart's father! Whilst playing from notation is an appropriate skill for many instruments, it is not the only way, or, for some pupils, the best way to learn.

For many expert musicians, staff notation has become a system which they can use to think about sounds with. It is not altogether an accurate analogy, as few expert musicians could transcribe, say, extracts from Stravinsky's *Rite of Spring* as they listened to it, but as a basis for organizing instrumental performances, it works for individuals. Having grasped it, it then becomes difficult to conceive how musicians could possibly manage without it, and yet they do, from pop, rock, and jazz musicians, to world music, and karaoke singers. A mistake is to confuse assessment of thinking, or assessment of performing, with being able to play from notation. This need not be the case, and the notion of 'sound before symbol' is an important one. Thus teachers can be heard to observe that pupils don't understand syncopation, when what they mean is they are having trouble decoding it from staff notation. Again the symbol is not the concept. After all, the pupils will have been doing playground games involving rhythmic fragments such as the well-known 'na-na-na-na-na', or, in staff notation:

from a very early age.[3] The problem lies in working out what notation means. It is not conceptualization which is the problem. Pieces such at Scott Joplin's *The Entertainer* use syncopation, which pupils have no problems at all in recognizing, or of clapping along to, or of spotting the beat. Decoding the score however, is a different issue!

So assessment of concepts need to take place separately from assessment of notation of those concepts, 'The symbols are therefore not introduced at the same time as the musical concepts, but serve as mnemonics for the performance of musical concepts with which the children are already familiar' (Tan et al. 2009: 20). To help with developing musical proficiency, many music teachers introduce basic music notation reading classes. Indeed, some music educators have devised systems which are predicated on simplifying notation by the use of coloured notes, or rearranging staff systems, although these may

---

[3] Thanks to Helen Coll for this observation.

not necessarily be any more effective than standard musical notation (Tan et al. 2009). As staff notation is a construct, it has to be taught and learned. Having an application for the employment of notation is logical, and there are different reasons for its employment in instrumental lessons than there are for it to be taught in isolation.

For no particular reason, some staff notation learning seems to involve the notes C-A-B-B-A-G-E and B-A-G-G-A-G-E, and pupils are set tasks to write the longest word they can using musical notes without having a clear understanding (for which, in many cases, read 'any idea') what they or doing, or why!

The students do not hear what they sound like, they just decode the staff notation to produce words . . . CABBAGE and BAGGAGE typically appear in these lessons because they are examples of relatively long words that only use the letters A-G, and not because of any aesthetic qualities of the melodic motifs they generate. (Mills 2005: 24–5)

This is likely to be an example of what Ofsted refer to as 'inappropriate use of notation' (Ofsted 2009: 15). Although assessment of notation knowledge can be undertaken separately, there seems little point in teaching, learning, and assessing, until the conceptual basis upon which the notation structure is superimposed is secure. Although some would have it that the notation structure develops at the same time as the conceptual one, there seems little purpose in multi-layering a range of different and, to the child, potentially unconnected aspects of learning, and an associated fragmentary assessment system. There would seem little point teaching the Cyrillic alphabet to someone who did not yet have at least a rudimentary knowledge of spoken Russian. Gary McPherson writes of his

. . . unease with conceptions of musical achievement that focus on children's ability to perform repertoire from notation which they have practised at home. The problem with this conception is that it is possible to learn a piece of music through mindless drill and practice with little or no understanding of the task . . . (McPherson 2005: 9).

Understanding is surely more of a multifaceted construct than simple regurgitation.

Endnote

Ray Cramer asks a key question: 'What materials are you going to use to teach "about music" "through music" while "performing music"?' (Cramer 1997). As this chapter has shown, performing music can be both an end in itself and a means towards musical understanding, where a number of other factors are involved. Performing is a highly visible part of music education, and, for many teachers, is the component which makes music different from other areas of the curriculum. But music is a complex set of human activities, and although expert performing is privileged in western views, it is only a part of the totality of musical experience, albeit one where valorization in the public sphere is most forthcoming. Teaching and learning about music through performing is important, and it is through performance that many attributes of musical understanding will be evidenced. It is to these other attributes that the next chapters address themselves.

Chapter 11

Developing classroom composing through assessment

Composing is the means by which pupils' original thoughts and ideas in musical terms come to be realized. In the classroom context composing occurs as both an individual and a group activity. Collaborative composing is common in the novice stages, and then there is a trend increasingly towards solo composing as pupils get older. In the UK there is a cut-off point for this, with much of the composing that is undertaken up until the end of Key Stage 3 taking the form of group work, and then from Key Stage 4 onwards, roughly aged fourteen and over, composing tends towards becoming a more individual activity, in line with external examination syllabi. This chapter considers the ways in which composing happens in educational settings, and discusses how assessment can be used to develop composing, both in group situations and in solo working.

Summative assessment of creative products is normally more straightforward that that of creative processes, '. . . the identification of a thought process or subprocess as creative must finally depend upon the fruit of that process—a product or response' (Amabile 1996: 33). For the music teacher dealing with composing, the key assessment questions will be those which were discussed in Chapter 6, in other words, 'who is the assessment for?', and 'what happens to the results?'. A simplistic approach to this would be to say that, with regard to the process of composing, the primary function of assessment will be to make pupils better over time, for which formative assessment will be the tool for the job; whereas the product, the composition, can be subject to criteria-based summative assessment. But contained within this simplistic approach are a number of intriguing complexities, and this chapter will endeavour to disentangle these.

Process or product?

Composing is a process, and is one which is undertaken intentionally and deliberately with the aim of producing a piece of music. For educational purposes we need to distinguish between the *process* of composing, and the compositional *product* that results from it (T. Bunting 2002). During these discussions the verb 'composing' will be used to denote the process, with the noun 'composition' being used to denote the product which arises from the process; this linguistic nicety is not always observed in the literature! In assessment terms, a consideration of the process of composing needs to be considered separately from the product which results from it. In externally assessed work it is normally the compositional product which is the focus of attention; the composing process which has been undertaken in order to arrive at the endpoint is, by and large, ignored, or considered irrelevant. The opposite situation is often the case up until KS4, however; here it is the process of composing which is often the main area of attention, and teachers want to work with their pupils to develop this. In this case, although the resultant composition is important, it is developing the process that normally matters most.

Assessment of process is clearly going to be a different matter from assessment of product, as process involves action and activity, and is undertaken by a pupil, or group of pupils. A problem for the teacher can be that, as Keith Swanwick observes, 'Musical processes are inaudible without musical products' (Swanwick 1998: 2). The resultant composition is an object in its own right, and assessment of it can take place according to criteria, either designed by the teacher, or, in the case of external and examinable composing, by an outside agency. Each of these involves different things, and so will be considered accordingly.

Composing and creativity

The notion of creativity is often invoked when discussing composing, and this is an important area in current educational thinking and practice. In educational terms we need to think what is really meant by the term 'creative', what does it mean, and particularly what does it mean in terms of composing?

Margaret Boden draws a distinction between two forms of creativity which are helpful when thinking about composing. Music teachers will be familiar with pupils producing compositions which have a certain similarity of sound about them. What the pupils have done is to produce responses which are creative for them, in the sense that they have not heard them before. Boden calls this sort of creativity being 'P-creative', where P stands for psychological. This she distinguished from H-creativity, H standing for historical, which would be an idea that is thoroughly original.

P-creativity involves coming up with a surprising new idea that's new *to the person who comes up with it*.[1] It doesn't matter how many people have had that idea before. But if a new idea is H-creative, that means that (so far as we know) no one else has had it before: it has arisen for the first time in human history. (Boden 1990: 2)

---

[1] Italics in original.

This distinction is useful in music education, as it enables us to think of musical utterances that we have heard many times before as being creative, as they are new for the pupil concerned. Boden goes on to observe:

... a P-creative idea need not be unusual. It is a novelty for the person generating it, but not necessarily for anyone else. We may even be able to predict that the person concerned will have that P-creative idea in the near future, yet its being predictable does not make it any less creative ... children's minds develop not just by learning new facts, and not just by playfully combining them in novel ways, but also by coming to have ideas which they simply could not have had before. (Boden 1990: 48)

Pupils composing with a xylophone and sweeping the beater up and down are doing something that thousands of other pupils will have done before them. But for a certain pupil this is a P-creative act; it is original to that pupil. What this means for music education is that P-creative acts are going to be met on a daily basis, and that they can be dealt with as original utterances, and developed accordingly. Items of H-creativity, budding Mozarts as child prodigies, can be dealt with if and when the need arises!

Much of the research on composing and creativity contains echoes of Wallas' (1926) pioneering work on the creative process. Wallas identified four stages in the creative process:

- Preparation: where initial work is undertaken, which will ultimately result in creative work being undertaken
- Incubation: when issues are mulled over and considered
- Illumination: the 'Eureka' moment, or the point at which ideas come into being
- Verification: where ideas are trialled and evaluated in context

This model has influences in the field of composing in music education, as it can be seen that the stages offer a glimpse into the process, and mean that music teachers do not have to treat composing as a singular endeavour, but can access aspects of what is going on.

Developmental composing

Accessing aspects of what is going on is useful when it comes to assessing the process of composing in ways which will be useful to the people who are actually doing it. As such, it forms a way in which composing can be considered as a developmental activity. Composing is a complex part of music education, and we know that there have been issues with music teachers' own background and training with regard to teaching it (Berkley 2001; Byrne & Sheridan 1998; MacDonald et al. 2002). The notion of composing as a developmental activity received particular attention from Swanwick and Tillman (1986) who produced their spiral diagram showing the sequence of development. More recently Pamela Burnard and Betty Anne Younker have investigated a number of aspects of pupils' composing (Burnard 2000, 2002; Burnard & Younker 2002, 2004; Younker 2000), and found that there are complex pathways taken by pupils when they undertake composing activities.

To be able to treat composing as a developmental activity it helps to have a view of the *process* of composing which pupils go through when they are composing. To this end it is helpful to think of the composing process as happening in a series of stages (Fautley 2005a). In essence, for assessment purposes, eight stages in classroom composing can be identified and labelled. These are:

1. The composing stimulus
2. Initial confirmatory phase
3. Generation and exploitation of ideas
4. Organizational matters
5. Work-in-progress performances
6. Revision
7. Transformation and development
8. The final performance

Each of these contains within it specific sub-aspects of the process of creating a piece of music. For assessment purposes this means that teachers can gain access to the process, which is helpful in taking learning forwards. (Fautley 2004). Figure 11.1 shows a diagrammatic representation of these stages in the composing process, with the multiple potential routes through it too.

The composing stimulus

For much composing which happens in schools, the starting point is often a stimulus of some sort, which is normally provided by the teacher, 'We need to provide varied opportunities for children in music-composition tasks if we want to encourage and nurture the most creative musical-thinking processes.' (Hickey 2003: 35). So, in order to try to provide a varied range of opportunities, music teachers tend to offer a variety of differing composing starting points. There are other good reasons for this too, as Janet Mills notes: 'An effective stimulus helps composers, particularly those working in groups, to spend less time deciding what to do, and more time deciding how to do it' (Mills 1991b: 38). A wide range of stimuli are employed in school composing, and teachers tend to select those that they believe will be the most effective

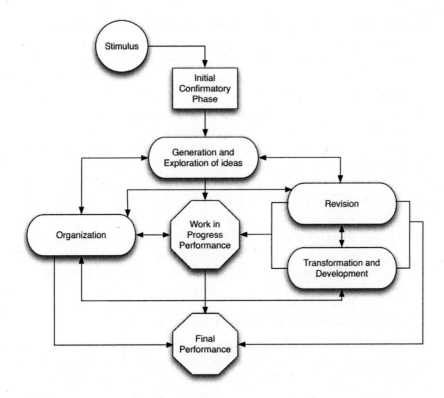

Fig. 11.1 The composing process deconstructed

with their pupils (Savage 2006). Stimuli for composing tend to fall into a number of categories, including

- Visual: a picture; an object; a video with the soundtrack removed; textures (e.g. rough/smooth)
- Aural: a pneumatic drill; an aeroplane; a short verbal phrase (as used by Philip Glass in *Different Trains*)
- Literary: a poem; a story
- Expressive: a journey (e.g. my walk to school; crossing the Ganges); a mood (e.g. happy/sad); the haunted house; the sea; fog
- Musico-technical: ternary form; accelerando; dynamic change
- Musico-referential (start with the chords of Pachelbel's *Canon*, compose your own version)
- Abstract: 2+3; a line; a single word (e.g. 'bookcase').

These composing starting points can also be thought of as being closed or open-ended. An open-ended task will involve little, if any, sense of the finished product in the starting point. A closed task will lead directly to an outcome limited deliberately by design. There will be times when teachers will want to use one sort rather than another.

In assessment terms the stimulus will, as we have noted, normally be provided by the teacher. This means that evaluation will take place as to the efficacy of the stimulus in providing the sorts of results that were hoped for, or whether the stimulus was considered to be generally effective.

Initial confirmatory phase

Following the presentation of the stimulus, there will then be a relatively short phase in the composing process where the pupils work out the implications of the starting point, and how they can go about achieving the task. Formative assessment dialogues will be useful at this point, as the teacher can help the pupils clarify what it is they will be doing in subsequent stages.

Generation and exploitation of ideas

This can be an iterative stage in the composing process, where pupils generate ideas, and try them out. Some of these early utterances in the composing come in the form of gestures, which relate in many ways to Gibson's (1979) notion of *affordances*.

Pupils play classroom instruments in ways whereby the instrument itself 'affords' opportunities to the player. A triangle produces a different affordance to a Glockenspiel. Composing gestures are therefore affordances. Chained gestures are chains of affordances. From these affordance-based gestures, emergent sonic utterances are afforded the status of music, or maybe more correctly what we might call proto-music, sounds which with 'refining' could become musical. (Fautley 2006: 29)

The notion of 'refining' is where the teacher has an important role, and where assessment comes into play. Formative assessment here will play an important part in refining these gestures. In discussing P-creativity above, the example of the xylophone beater being swept up and down the notes was posited. This can be considered to be a musical gesture, and, according to Peter Webster, 'Initial music gestures, or what I have called primitive gesturals (PGs) are very easy for children to create . . . Children can easily string together a series of PGs, creating a wide variety of timbral effects, spatial distance, and textural diversity' (Webster 2003: 56). Having noted that pupils have created their initial composing gestures, Webster then asks, '. . . once these primitive gesturals are formed, how can we guide children to a more complete and extensive compositional experience?' (Webster 2003: 56). This is where formative assessment comes in.

We know that a key role of assessment is to help improve learning; by appropriately intervening in the composing process at this stage, the teacher is able to affect the future direction of the learning in terms of the composing process. There may well be cases too where the appropriate formative assessment judgement is to *not* intervene in the process! As Ofsted observe, 'Good teachers judge carefully when to interrupt or intervene, so as not to disturb the flow of activities; it is often appropriate to listen or to participate, rather than use verbal discussion to gain evidence of progress' (Ofsted 2003: 4).

There is a difference between generation and exploitation of ideas which the teacher will want to draw out of their pupils. Often an idea which has been generated can be a single phrase, gesture, or rhythmic figure. Exploiting this single idea can again be achieved by appropriate formative assessment strategies, including feedback and feed-forward. Selection, acceptance, and rejection can be helped by the teacher modelling this, possibly by demonstrating, using groups of pupils, how ideas can be generated and then exploited.

Organizational matters

Having generated ideas, the next stage is for the pupils to put their ideas together in some structured fashion. Sometimes this can involve drawing on knowledge of conventional musical structures, and sometimes it can involve the pupils in devising their own ways of organizing the musical materials in less formal ways which arise from their own needs.[2]

It is with organizational matters that many music teachers feel to be on solid ground with regard to intervening in the composing process, and able to provide useful formative assessment commentaries. It is at this stage that the pupils move from 'proto-music' to something which has the potential to be more inherently musical. Careful structuring of musical ideas is important in moving from ideas which could become music to musical ideas. The knowledge and expertise of the teacher is important in this, and so making appropriate formative assessment judgements is a logical way for teachers to intervene in the composing process at this stage. We also see in Chapter 12 how novices perceive music unfolding over time as a single continuous and contiguous event. In composing terms what this can mean for beginning composers is the impression that a piece of music that is three minutes long

---

[2] An interesting example of this can be seen in an exemplar materials video for the English National Curriculum, to be found at www.newsecondarycurriculum.org/content/library/music_other.aspx#, where pupils at Coundon Court School are organizing a group piece with the phrases: 'It goes "I want a drink and I want it now", and us three go: "Beans on toast, beans on toast . . ." '.

involves three minutes' worth of original non-repeated material. Organizing the ideas generated by the pupils, with the help of carefully chosen listening examples, can help address this misconception. Composing being, as the old saying goes, one percent inspiration and ninety-nine per cent perspiration, the one per cent of ideas need to be put together carefully in order to maximize their effectiveness.

Work-in-progress performances

The role of the work-in-progress performance is integral to the ways in which many pupils compose. This can occur at almost any stage in the process, and can be considered as being central to its success. What happens is that pupils use the work-in-progress performance to assemble their music into a coherent structure. Novice pupil composers tend to need to play the whole piece through in its entirety, whereas more experienced pupils are able to identify which particular aspects of their work they wish to address, and then concentrate on playing through the particular point in question.

Work-in-progress performances can occur in two ways: opportunistic or systemic. Opportunistic work-in-progress performances occur informally as the pupils work through their composing. Systemic performances are occasioned by the teacher, for example by listening to them at key moments during the course of the lesson or lessons.

The work-in-progress performance offers a number of possibilities with regard to assessment. Formative assessment is clearly something which the teacher can put into practice here, by intervention in opportunistic performances, or by deliberately setting up systemic ones. Systemic work-in-progress performances also offer the possibility of peer assessment. Peer assessment of the work-in-progress performances gives the opportunity for targeted constructive criticism of the work the pupils are doing. Teachers who have used this effectively set up supportive environments in which suggestions are given by the pupils in the class. This establishes the members of the class as a community of practice (Lave & Wenger 1991) who are jointly concerned with developing their own composing. Peer assessment in this fashion can be undertaken in a variety of ways, from the immediacy of spoken contributions, via written observations and notes, through to blogs and e-comments on school intranet sites.

An important factor of the work-in-progress performance is that it is *in progress*, and so there is an expectation that the piece of music is still in a state of flux, and will alter. A key element for formative assessment opportunity is to be found in audio or video recording of the work-in-progress performances.

This can be undertaken during systemic performances, for example at the end of a lesson when the composing work will be continued on future occasions. Ending a lesson with class performance which is recorded means that a starter activity for the follow-on lesson can be listening to the recording. This serves two purposes: it reminds the pupils of what they did, and it allows for self-assessment of listening to be undertaken, removed from the immediacy of the performing situation. Self-analysis of a performance from a recording is of an entirely different order to self-analysis directly after a live performance. This use of recordings allows for ongoing formative assessment, and helps the pupils with improving what they do. Apparently schools do not do this regularly: 'Across all the schools visited, audio recording was not used enough as a means of ongoing assessment but tended to be used only at the end of a unit of work. As one pupil said, "It is good we record our work, but it would be better if we could listen to it more and find out how we could improve it" ' (Ofsted 2009: 18). Recording work-in-progress performances in the way described would help with learning, and, as described in Chapter 14, is a straightforward task using modern technology.

Wherever and however the work-in-progress performance occurs, and whether opportunistic or systemic, the assessment potential of this stage alone is enormous, and, because of the notion of the music still being in flux, pupils being able to act on formative assessment comments means that significant progress can be made during the course of a series of lessons.

Revision, transformation and development

There are two separate aspects to the ways in which pupils are able to develop their pieces of music in the later stages of the composing process. These are revision, and transformation and development. The difference between the two is that revision involves essentially reorganizing or reconfiguring extant material, whereas transformation and development involve manipulation of the musical material in a more substantial fashion. This stage in the composing process may need modelling for novice composers, as the notion of stream of consciousness composing, where ideas unfold in real time, and require a large supply of material, needs, as discussed above, to be dispelled. We know that encouraging revision is a useful skill in composing (Webster 2003). What is helpful here is for the teacher to model the process of developing ideas in composing. This itself is an assessment activity, as the teacher will be judging what level of revision will be appropriate for the pupils at their current stage of musical development. The process of revision may not be one that pupils arrive at of their own account, so this is where teacher intervention is appropriate.

The final performance

Classroom composing often tends to happen as an interface between cognitive processes which take place in the mind (Sloboda 1985), and the practical affordances of realizing ideas using musical instruments. This process, as we have seen, results in a compositional product, expressed through the work in progress performance, and, for educational situations, culminates in a final performance. The final performance has traditionally been the point at which assessment takes place. Hopefully the discussions above have shown that there are moments of assessment opportunity which happen throughout the process of composing, and relate specifically to the task in hand, in other words to *composing*. The reason for this seemingly obvious statement is that there is a danger that assessment of composing can become summative assessment of the final *performance* of that composition. In many cases this is what is meant by assessment of composing, the process is ignored, and assessment tends to be based on performance aspects, such as being on the beat, playing together, dynamic contrast, and so on. This is an important distinction to draw, and needs some further discussion.

Composing is a process, and so throughout the discussions of the deconstructed activity which have taken place so far, the focus of attention has been on formative assessment which is used to develop learning. It is at the final stage of the composing process where a finished, or at least completed, piece of music has emerged. For classroom composers this will have been a process which has been undertaken entirely using sounds. Jo Glover writes of how educational composing is '. . . wholly dependent on the skills of producing sounds from the instrument' (Glover 2000: 67). This is another reason why summative assessment of composing needs to distinguish between process and performance. This is compounded when the ideas that pupil have are not translatable into reality because of their lack of technical accomplishment in terms of musical instrument performance skills, 'For the class music teacher the mismatch between what the learner wishes to attain based on his or her well-developed musical schemata and his or her generative skills, particularly those relating to technical skills, can create problems' (Hallam 2001: 71).

The implications of this are that three separate aspects of musical endeavour present themselves, those of composing (process), composition (product), and performing, all of which are candidates for assessment.

The issue for the music teacher is in deciding which of these three is going to be the focus of assessment, or, if they are all to be assessed, how this is to be achieved? Jonathan Savage writes of inauthentic treatment of composing, and of how '. . . pupils' latent interest is often suffocated by an over-prescription of content and formalisation of ideas' (Savage 2003: 82). Presenting pupils with

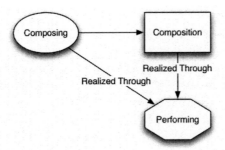

Fig. 11.2 What is assessed in composing?

authentic tasks for composing is a challenge for teachers, and the same is true for the notion of authentic assessment too. We want assessment of composing to be that—assessment of composing, not assessment of performance, or assessment of ability to explain, and so teachers need to think about the validity of composing assessments, which is the point to which we now turn.

Summative assessment of final performance

Having a valid assessment of composing is clearly important. Knowing why assessment is taking place will inform the teacher as to which purpose of assessment is going to be adopted. At examination level there will be no choice; summative decisions need to made, criteria have to be interpreted, and grades applied. Given the three interrelated areas of composing, composition, and performing, summative assessment criteria need to be clear as to where the main focus lies. Most assessment criteria for external examination purposes are centred on the final composition. Typical criteria are those of the Edexcel examination board, where the assessment criteria for GCSE music (Edexcel 2006: 83) are:

- Use and development of ideas
- Exploitation of the medium
- Structural interest
- Understanding the brief

This makes any performance largely irrelevant, as the criteria are aimed squarely at the compositional product. (It is to be noted, though, that process is to some extent inferred through retrospective extrapolation, as 'use and development of ideas' contains elements of the processual about it.) Composition at this level involves submission of '. . . a notated score (either hand-written or printed) or written commentary . . . and a recording' (Edexcel 2006: 24). In other words although the performance is notionally not assessed, it has to exist. This can be problematic when the performance is the reification of composing, in other words when what comes into being through being played is the composition in question. This raises the question, '. . . what exactly is the line that separates composing and performing? Is there a clear line of demarcation, or are what we call "composing" and "performing" better understood as two facets of one activity?' (Benson 2003: 2). In the GCSE criteria, the submission of a 'written commentary' alongside the audio does clearly co-mingle the two facets.

The existence of a staff notation score, however, is a different thing entirely. This sort of a score is, '. . . a medium through which the act of composition takes place, not in sounds, not in company, and not in real time as it passes but in silence, solitude and imagined time . . .' (Small 1998: 114). Here, the score *is* the composition, and performances of it can only approximate to it. Assessment of ideas from the score, then are not subject to the vicissitudes of performance, and so assessment can take place directly from it. Of course, having a performance on which to base judgements helps, but such a score separates composition from performance.

Making summative assessment judgements of the finished product at this stage of a pupil's development, then, co-mingles elements of compositional technique with aspects apparent from the performance. The preferred modality of the individual submissions will to some extent determine the decision-making process which is undertaken. This is fine and appropriate for pupils at the age of sixteen and over, but for younger composers the distinction between composition and performance is likely to be more blurred. So what criteria can be applied for younger pupils? Brophy (2000: 166) suggests that the teacher chooses the 'assessable components' in advance. This can be done, but there is a danger that assessment criteria will focus too much on 'the elements', which can result in artificial distortion, and pupils over-emphasizing, say dynamic contrast, at the expense of general musicianship. Jonathan Stephens suggests that assessment categories could include communication, musicianship, and technical skills. As he observes, 'The purpose of these categories is to assist examiners in the analysis of specific aspects of a composition, not to encourage a separation of music into disconnected areas' (Stephens 2003: 133). This non-divisibility of assessment criteria has been met before, and is analogous to the notion of holistic assessment as previously discussed.

As an alternative to this list, what teachers might wish to assess in pupil composing can be reduced in essence to two areas:

+ Intentionality: what is it that the pupil-composer(s) intended to achieve?
+ Effectiveness: were they effective in achieving this?

For novice composers, assessment in this fashion reduces the need for artificial isolation of elements, and can subsume notions of technical skill and communication. In order to achieve summative assessment of this sort codings of grades such as those discussed in earlier sections can be employed, with fine gradation determined by the stage of development of the pupils. Thus, taking a three-point grading scale of $-/=/+$, an intentionality score which is above average ('+') for pupils of age eight years will be different to the same grade for pupils who are some years older.

Portfolio assessment

With the continuing rise in affordability of technology, it is becoming increasingly straightforward to develop sophisticated portfolios and e-portfolios of pupil composing, as we shall discuss in later chapters. At this stage it is pertinent to observe that although audio or video recording of final performances should be commonplace in schools, these need to be thought of in terms of assessment evidence. This contrasts sharply with many other subjects on the school curriculum, in that the evidence of something can often take the form of textual responses from the pupils. Thus the notion of submitting pupil writing books to internal or external agencies for verification of progress is not appropriate here. It may well be the case that in a history lesson knowledge of, say the Norman conquest, can be evidenced in an essay, but music educators would be very unhappy with the idea that compositional knowledge should be codified in textual form. Recordings of pupil composing and compositions are evidence, and need to be recognized and treated as such.

Formative assessment of final performance

For occasions other than final examinable components, formative assessment will normally be appropriate for assessment of the finished composition, with teacher comments and peer assessment being appropriate. However, teachers may want to use formative assessment alongside summative assessment in order to provide evidence of progression over time, and that is where the formative use of summative assessment would be appropriate.

The formative use of summative assessment in composing

The formative use of summative assessment is apposite in the case of composing, as teachers will want to keep records of progression, but also be able to use these in a developmental fashion. This is where formative assessment can feed into summative assessment. The classroom teacher has been involved in the process of composing with the pupils, and has proffered formative assessment suggestions in the form of feedback and feed-forward during the composing process. The teacher has moved between multiple simultaneous pupil composers in the class, and helped them progress along the continuum from novice towards expert. These formative assessments can now be used to help inform the summative assessment judgement which is made. Having done this, the teacher can then use this information to help the pupils achieve at a higher level in the future. Summative grades, as we have seen, can be viewed as shorthand reductions of more complicated observations of performance (both in the musical and non-musical senses!). To this end, not sharing grades for composing is considered as good practice by many teachers, with comment-only marking being employed for this purpose. Where grades are shared, teachers can use these to help pupils improve, both in terms of realistic target setting, and in the way that achievements develop with practice, experience, and over time.

Group composing

So far in this chapter composing has been discussed in general terms, without distinguishing between solo composing, and that which is undertaken in group situations. Group composing is a common activity in educational settings, and this can be for a variety of reasons: it makes optimal use of scarce resources; it allows for whole class engagement with the process; it makes use of social construction of knowledge, it enables pupils to work in their zones of proximal development; it allows conjoint activity; and it distributes the cognitive process across multiple individuals. As Kutnick and Rogers observe, '. . . shared perspective taking with groups increases the likelihood of cognitive understanding; the effective use of small groups promotes greater achievement through co-operation than do comparative whole-class and individualized grouping approaches' (Kutnick & Rogers 1984: 4). The process of composing as a cooperative activity finds its most common expert situation in the music of pop and rock bands, where corporate endeavour, composing pieces of music directly into sound using the instruments that band members play, is considered entirely normal (Green 2002). This contrasts sharply with the western classical model, where the normal model is that of the lone composer.

For pupils in the classroom, the process of composing as a group activity means that aspects of the generation of the piece are shared among and between the members of the group. In cognitive terms this offers the possibility of distributed cognition, where the cognitive process of composing is shared between members of the group. This is not only useful as a way of addressing the issues noted above with regard to reasons for composing in groups, but also enables a complex cognitive load to be shared amongst a number of pupils. 'Two heads are better than one', and more than two heads allows for more of the process to be distributed. This allows straightforward accessing of what might otherwise be a difficult task for pupils in schools. This is not only a worthwhile thing to do in its own right, but takes the pupils a stage further forward in their individual journeys, '. . . one should regard situations of distributed cognitions not only as ends in themselves but, more important, as means for improving mastery of solo competencies' (Salomon 1993a: 135). What this means is that there are sound educational reasons for undertaking group composing, as well as the practical and pragmatic ones of which teachers are well aware. Given that this is the case, what can be problematic for teachers is the assessment of group composing. External examination syllabi often disallow conjoint submissions, and so it will be nearer the novice stage of composing that this issue needs addressing.

Once again it is summative assessment that is likely to cause problems here; formative assessment of group work will follow the paths established through-out this chapter, and will include elements of developing group work as a way of working. Summative assessment is a different matter, however, and will centre around the key issue of whether each member of the group should get the same mark or not. There are three potential solutions to this issue. One is to ignore it, and to give everyone the same mark anyway; the second is to find a way of differentiating in some way between the pupils; the third is to give two separate marks, one for the group, and the other for the individual's contribution to the group. In the latter model the views of the group can be important, and this methodology offers a potential for the involvement of peer assessment. The teacher can be responsible for grading the overall achievement of the group, according to whatever criteria they deem appropriate, but the individual members of the group take responsibility for negotiation of marks available for individual contribution, based upon criteria such as cooperation, participation, and willingness to contribute ideas. This hands some responsibility for assessment to the pupils, whilst retaining authenticity in terms of teacher assessment. Whichever route for summative assessment is taken might well depend on one of the usual questions—what (or whom) is the assessment for?

Chapter 12

Developing listening through assessment

In order to develop pupil listening through assessment, we need to begin by considering what it is that is being assessed! Listening to music is, on the face of it, a seemingly simple activity, that most people in Western cultures do almost unthinkingly on a daily basis. Research into music listening is extensive, and encompasses a wide range, from perceptual and psychological investigations, through to aesthetic responses. Indeed, the terminology 'listening' itself is open to a variety of interpretations, including active and passive listening, audiation (Gordon 2003), aural skills, dictation, and many more besides. To try to unpick a way through this maze is itself a complex task! The aspects which seem to be important for current purposes are those which appertain to the use of assessment in order to take pupil understanding forward via the employment of some aspect of listening. To some extent this rules out many of the more complex psychological studies, as they often tend to be concerned with atomistic aspects of music perception which are not amenable to teacher intervention. This still leaves a range of other ways in which listening can be addressed, and so this chapter will survey a range of these which may be of use to the classroom or instrumental music teachers and their pupils.

The purpose of listening

Listening to music in educational settings has a long, and, some would say, chequered history. Stephanie Pitts explains how, at the beginning of the twentieth century, divisions emerged between the proponents of 'musical appreciation' and those advocating singing, especially sol-fa, and dictation exercises (Pitts 2000b: 12). This legacy can still be felt to some extent today, and the educational use of listening to music, and the way it can be developed in educational terms, lags a long way behind the perceptual aspects discussed in the opening paragraph. This gives rise to a number of key questions in terms of listening and assessment which teachers need to think about when planning for listening:

1. What is there to listen to in music?
2. Why do we want pupils to listen?
3. What do we want them to listen to?
4. What does music listening involve?
5. What happens when music listening occurs?
6. What develops in music listening?
7. How can educational assessment help with this?

There seem to be two main reasons for listening to music in schools: for its own sake as a worthwhile activity, and as a means to access performing and/or composing. There are also inter-linkages between these two, as aspects of music which have been listened to, and learned about, can then be expected to figure in composing and performing work with which the pupils engage.

The function of music listening

'There is no such thing as music.
Music is not a thing at all, but an activity, something that people do.' (Small 1998: 2)

Small's view encapsulates a key dilemma which lies at the centre of music listening. On the one hand we have a view of the great milestones of the Western Classical repertoire, which many consider as being the cornerstones of our civilization, and on the other hand we have everything else! And every-thing else includes pop, rock, jazz, world music, folk music, and a myriad of other musics which are not Western Classical. This is an important distinc-tion, between which lie a range of subtle and not-so-subtle differences in the ways in which people listen to these differing musics.

The history of classroom music listening has its roots in the musical appreci-ation movement of the early twentieth century. This movement was predicated on the use of great masterworks, and of endeavour required on the part of the listener in order to gain some understanding and knowledge concerning the music itself. This is the notion that music exists as a separate canon of musical works, which require study to understand. The essence of musical appreciation was '. . . a knowledge of music literature through hearing standard works performed well' (Cox 2001: 10). This view, explored initially in Chapter 8, was neatly summarized by Stepharie Pitts: 'This concept of music as a "barrier" against untold degeneration draws strongly on the ideas of cultural (and, implicitly, social and moral) superiority that assured the place of music in the pre-war curriculum' (Pitts 2000a: 35). The purpose of listening to music was to do with bettering oneself, social advancement, and, possibly, social control.

One of the corollaries of this view is that classical music is difficult, and needs to be mediated by an expert—the teacher—before the novices—the pupils—can come to understand it. What this also means is that listeners need a great deal of background information, of the 'programme notes' variety, in order to be able to have a chance of understanding the music.

It does seem unfortunate that, in the name of education, people have been brought misguidedly to believe that they need such detail. Originally intended as background support, this information is transformed into essential knowledge which, although it may be interesting in itself, has nothing directly to do with what is experienced. (Paynter 2008: 180)

This is knowledge by acquaintance, or knowledge about, and it is not, of itself, musical knowledge.

We also saw in Chapter 8 how one reason to listen to music was that being inducted into the cultural aspects of western civilization was thought to be good for the pupils in some sort of elevating fashion. This viewpoint still hovers in the background where cultural education is concerned; it eschews popular music, and concentrates instead on classical masterworks. This can have cultural and political overtones of a hegemony which could well be at odds with the prevailing culture of the school. We know, for example, that in schools with a large Muslim population the choice of music, or even music itself, can be a contentious issue (R. Bunting 2006; Harris 2006).

Another common feature of the listening class was the notion that music needed to be listened to in silence, with the full powers of concentration being given over to it. This in itself was, and remains, problematic, as this is not how many people experience music. 'The nineteenth century ideologues of absolute music may have worked hard to make musical appreciation a purely mental experience, but this was hard work precisely because most listeners didn't listen to music this way . . .' (Frith 1996: 115). This leaves music listening in a somewhat difficult position, and for the music teacher, aware of the immediate ramifications of playing certain types of music to the class, there can be difficult decisions to make.

Evaluating

The National Curriculum for music in England contains the additional layers of 'reviewing and evaluating' when discussing listening (the terminology 'appraising', used up until 2008, having since been dropped). This means that pupils are required to '. . . communicate ideas and feelings about music, using expressive language and musical vocabulary to justify their opinions' (QCA 2008a: 182). Pupils having opinions about music is fine, but, some might say, potentially problematic. But being able to justify opinions means that music education has come a long way from the music appreciation approach, where it was the opinions of others that mattered.

We have already seen that the issue of aesthetics causes problems in music education. At its most primitive level, it can become reduced to a slanging match between teachers and pupils of the 'mine is better than yours' variety! Following Young's (1971) notion of knowledge status, and, to some extent, Bernstein's (1971b) work on social class, the notion of 'cultural deprivation' was used to explain this, 'In order to preserve the rigid stratification of knowledge in schools and the consequent rigid hierarchy between teacher and taught, the culture of the pupils has to be seen as a deprived one, so that cultural deprivation becomes a plausible explanation for educational failure' (Shepherd et al. 1977: 207). This has clear links to Bourdieu's notion of cultural capital, and, again, some would see a role for music education to address what might be seen as a deficit model on the part of the pupils.

What is there to listen to?

Against this rather complex background, it is perhaps unsurprising that listening remains, to some extent, the poor relation in music education. So, what is there to listen to? At least six sources of listening materials can be readily found in many schools. These are:

- Commercial recordings of music
- Live performances by others
- Live performances by the class/peers
- Recordings made by the class/peers
- Multimedia content
- Music specifically for aural tests

Music consumption plays a powerful role in the lives of young people, and so the choice of music to which to listen can be drawn from a wide selection of readily available materials. Many music teachers make use of internet sites to show videos to accompany music listening, and have access to music libraries which contain a wealth of recordings which cover the entire gamut of musical traditions. In addition live performances are becoming frequently more common in schools, and are encouraged in England by the National Curriculum.

Music for aural tests has been included as a sub-category as its sole purpose is to test for competence, and so although extant music can be employed, what is frequently found is that examples of atonal melodies, or rhythms in isolation from pitch are manufactured, which have no bearing on 'real' music. The assessment of this type of listening is explored in more detail below.

But knowing what there is to listen to is only a partial picture, as what music there is to listen to needs to be mediated by the ways in which listening takes place. Listening to a live performance by a visiting ensemble which captures the attention of the pupils is of an entirely different order to listening to background music whilst painting a picture in an Art lesson.

What develops in music listening?

One of the common features of the pedagogy of music listening is that of an understanding of musical structures and forms. Indeed, in many units of work, structural aspects of the construction of a piece of music form the backbone of reasons for listening to the music in question. This simple statement, however, opens up an underlying minefield. This is to do with the ways in which expert and novice music-listeners perceive and conceptualize musical structures. For expert listeners, the notion of blocks of musical structure which have relationships with each other, and unfold as a piece progresses, are part and parcel of their daily understandings of music. For novice listeners, however, music simply moves in a linear fashion from beginning to end in a constant stream. This gives rise to the observation that, '. . . any music teacher is likely to have encountered the surprise expressed by untrained listeners when they discover how much repetition, and therefore how little distinct material, there is in a great deal of familiar music' (Cook 1990: 45). But to get to this stage requires developmental education, and recognition of this issue on the part of the teacher. This means that the teacher has to understand the developmental notion of perception of music in this fashion, and structure their lessons accordingly. This approach to stages of development in music listening is an important one, '. . . once having learned to respond to the sign :|| as if by a conditioned reflex, we easily wipe out the fact that while this is an instruction for the performer to "turn back" in the score, within the culture of the novice listener, music like time, can never "turn back" ' (Bamberger 2006: 88). Although Bamberger uses behaviourist terminology, this can also be considered as a Piagetian standpoint, in that stages of development are deemed to occur, and the pupils need to be able to conceptually grasp the notion of temporal flow, and of perceptual structures within this, in order to be able to understand what is going on in the music. But this in itself is problematic. What form does knowledge of structures take?

There is, then a widespread consensus of opinion among twentieth-century aestheticians and critics that listening to music is, or at any rate should be, a higher-order mental activity which combines sensory perception with a rational understanding based upon some kind of knowledge of musical structure. Quite what form this knowledge might take, however, is not so clear . . . (Cook 1990: 21–2)

If it is not clear what form the knowledge takes, then this obviously makes assessing its development difficult! But if it is not clear what form listening knowledge takes in isolation, then this explains why it is subservient to making music. Or, to put it more directly: 'The kinds of musical knowing required to listen competently, proficiently, or expertly for the works of a given musical practice are the same kinds of knowing required to *make* the music of that practice . . .' (Elliott 1995: 96). Which then, in turn, renders assessment of knowledge about music more directly into assessment of musical knowledge. So this then allows the linkages between composing, performing, and listening to be thought of more directly, where listening becomes the glue that binds these activities together. As the National Curriculum states,

'. . . pupils should acquire and apply knowledge and understanding of:

♦ how music is constructed

♦ how music is produced

♦ how music is influenced by time and place' (DfES 2006b: 4)

By linking the acquisition *and* application of knowledge in this way, *pace* Sfard (1998), the DfES point the way for listening to become a developmental activity whose achievements are manifested in action, rather than in language. This means that assessment can have a role to play in listening, and that developmental understandings can be legitimized in units of work. This does not mean to say that listening should *only* be assessed by its applicability, but that this would be one way of allowing for its musical application to come to the fore.

Assessing developmental listening

The notion of transition from novice to more expert listener was posited above, and this gave rise to a Piagetian notion of cognitive structural development. This gives an important context for music educators to help foster increasingly complex understandings in their pupils. Whilst it is not entirely clear what form these mental structures take (Fodor 1983; Karmiloff-Smith 1992), for the music teacher this is probably less important than thinking about how they can be developed. What the teacher is likely to want is for increasing knowledge about music to become manifest in the music that the pupils produce, and that this knowledge needs to be developed alongside practical skill acquisition, in order to more further along the path towards music understanding.

Bloom's taxonomy of the cognitive domain, explored previously, is one of the few tools available to investigate and categorize thinking. In terms of listening to music it is not overly helpful in the stages of lower-order thinking, however (Colwell 2002), and, sadly, this is more-or-less true too for Bloom's affective taxonomy. The higher-order skill of analysis, at least in its strict western classical sense, needs to be preceded by lower-order music listening skills of identification—which links to knowledge and comprehension—and recognition, which might link to application. In music listening terms we can differentiate between varying levels of recognition. For example, at a fairly basic level we can identify which instrument of a family of instruments makes what sounds, and then refine it from there. This relies on knowledge and comprehension, but mixed, sometimes with deduction. For example, in identifying the sound of a Shamisen, if one has not been heard *and named* before, the listener can deduce from the timbre that it is a plucked string instrument whereas naming it requires specific knowledge. The same could be applied to listening to the sound of a lute; again, knowledge is being applied in a layered fashion. Developmental listening in this manner can be fostered, depending on the level of articulated response required; thus for a KS3 pupil the response 'saxophone' might suffice, for GCSE a desired response might be 'tenor saxophone'. These layered responses can be developed by choosing and listening to a range of music, beginning with straightforward examples.

Instrumental identification is, however, a relatively low-level skill up to a certain point. Beyond the initial labelling phase, however, it becomes difficult; thus distinguishing between the sound of a Stradivarius and another violin is not always simple (Fritz et al. 2006), and, moving to voices, Welch and Howard (2002) were able to demonstrate that identification of boy from girl choristers by sound alone was not always reliable. But for most teachers and their pupils this is not what is needed, and so a labelling of instruments and voices can be undertaken using deductive logic. Assessment for instrumental identification can be undertaken on two levels: the simple right/wrong for knowing the instrument, and that of making marks available for the demonstration of deductive reasoning. Thus in the case of the Shamisen, marks would be available for the response 'plucked string instrument', or 'plucked chordophone', with maybe further marks available for the identification of a plectrum. This type of assessment can be graded and scored at the appropriate level with relative ease by the teacher.

Moving to the next level of listening identification, we have already discussed how the English National Curriculum delineates a series of musical elements, namely, pitch, duration, dynamics, tempo, timbre, texture, and silence (QCA 2007). Assessment for detection of these can take place at various levels. In the twentieth century, fine distinctions in aural detection of a range of these elements (also referred to in the literature as 'primitives') formed the basis for tests of musical aptitude. For example, the 'Bentley Test' (Bentley 1966) required candidates to distinguish between pitch differences of less than a semitone. Whether or not tests of this nature are a reliable pre-indicator of musical ability is a contested area (Shuter-Dyson & Gabriel 1981). Certainly there are issues with the quality of the original recordings nowadays, and we now tend to think of ability and aptitude as being different constructs, both of which impact upon musical development. As is discussed in Chapter 15, although music teachers often long for a modern, reliable, and simple listening test which would produce National Curriculum levels after a single application, in reality such a thing is unlikely to be produced!

Assessment of detection of the elements of music via listening form a common part of units of work in Key Stages 1–3. We have already seen that it is a pedagogic error to confuse the signifier with the thing for which it stands; thus formative assessment of knowledge of the elements of music needs to be concerned first of all with whether or not the concept is fully embedded, before moving to assess whether or not correct terminology is being employed. We know that very young children are able to discriminate between quite complex auditory stimuli (Deliege & Sloboda 1996; Lamont 2001), and so in most cases it will not be necessary to teach the concept, but the subject-specific ways in which terminology and phraseology are employed. Atomistic separation of 'the elements' in listening tasks is probably not very helpful either, but assessment of this at KS3 can still regularly be encountered, even though inventing separated listening examples where the elements of music appear in isolation is problematic:

> You cannot give students a test of their pitch discrimination, for example, without presenting them with tones that have duration, loudness, and timbre, and it is difficult to be certain that students have homed in on pitch, rather than the other features of the music that are inevitably present. (Mills 2005: 109).

So, using the National Curriculum terminology of 'the elements' will normally require assessment of terminological understanding and usage, rather than assessment of conceptual grasp.

Assessment using oral questioning

Having considered Bloom's taxonomy in developmental listening terms, one area where it is does have the potential to be helpful is in the area of assessing pupil learning via the use of questioning. Questioning is a good formative assessment strategy, and is one of the commonest forms of teacher interaction with pupils. Asking good questions is a skill, and using Bloom's taxonomy is a helpful way of developing progressive questions which help take learning forward. Oral questioning differs from written questions in one obvious but important way, and that is that the immediacy of the oral question means that teachers can be both reactive and iterative, and can ask questions which help the learner in clarifying their own thinking, and not just providing simple recall-based answers. We saw earlier that Bloom's original taxonomy hierarchically listed six aspects of thinking, with knowledge, comprehension, and application forming lower-order thinking, and analysis, synthesis, and evaluation forming higher-order thinking. Moving towards higher-order thinking is a desideratum, and questioning concerning music listening can help with this. For example:

> . . . activities based around 'audience' listening (e.g. discussing or writing about a piece of recorded music) will require the higher-level thinking skills that are a prominent feature of creativity. For example: recognising and identifying a style of music because of similarities to music heard previously ('application'); identifying specific features within the music ('analysis'); using different pieces of information to come to a decision about the music ('synthesis'); and giving a considered and supported opinion about the music, particularly when recognising the value or success of a piece of work, relative to its intention ('evaluation').[1] (DfES 2006a: 5)

This extract from the DfES secondary strategy shows the terminologies of Bloom's taxonomy being applied to music-specific thinking.

Finding out what pupils know, and challenging their thinking by the use of questioning, can be achieved by working through Bloom's taxonomy. Formative assessment involving questioning can be planned for, and one way in which this can be achieved is via the use of ascending orders of questions built upon the layers of the taxonomy. One way for this to be undertaken is by the use pre-prepared question stems (Fautley & Savage 2007; Fautley 2009). This allows the teacher to work with pupils in developing their thinking about music, and probes them to engage with the music. Table 12.1 gives some possible examples of questions built upon the taxonomy.

These questions become formative assessment when the teacher and pupils jointly take responsibility for what happens next. The purpose of them is not simply to find out what the pupils know, but for the teacher to engage in an assessment dialogue with the pupils, with a view to both challenging their thinking, and planning what can be done in future listening and learning encounters.

---

[1] Parentheses in original.

Table 12.1 Question stems built upon Bloom's taxonomy

Knowledge	What instruments are playing here?
	What is the name of this ensemble?
	What style of music is . . .?
Comprehension	What is going on in this piece when . . .?
	What do you understand by . . .?
Application	Can you think of another example of . . .?
	Can you show me an instance where . . .?
	How could you . . .?
Analysis	Is there a regular beat?
	How might this be similar to . . .
	Can you compare . . .?
	Can you tell the difference between . . .?
	What happens when the . . . (e.g. key changes)?
Synthesis	How could you do this differently . . .?
	Could you put those ideas into your own music . . .?
	What would happen if they were to use a sample from . . .?
Evaluation	What was successful about . . .?
	What was less successful . . .?
	Can you justify why you think . . .?
	Does this music make you think of anything in particular?
	Why do you think that . . .?
	Would it be a good thing if . . .?

Assessment of structural awareness

'Through passive or active exposure, listeners internalize regularities in the music of their own culture, forming long-term knowledge schemata into which novel music stimuli are assimilated' (Thompson & Schellenberg 2006: 75).

Simply having a passive exposure to music means that at least a nodding acquaintance with aspects of structural awareness of music is likely to have been formed in most children at a fairly early stage in their development. What the music teacher will want to do is to develop specific knowledge of common ways in which pieces of music can be assembled and structured. Cook's observation earlier in this chapter about listeners being surprised by '. . . how little distinct material there is in a great deal of familiar music' (Cook 1990: 45) is precisely this point. Music teachers want to try to unpick aspects of form and structure with their pupils, and help them towards aural recognition of the essential building blocks by which music can be assembled. We know, for example, that some of this assembling takes place during mental processing of musical stimuli: 'The listener appreciates the organization of a musical work by assigning significance to the sounded elements according to their roles in the musical context, and by integrating them into the broader pattern' (Krumhansl 1990: 3). So, what the teacher will do is to introduce the pupils to different structural elements in music, starting with simple ones, and then building up towards the more complex. In many units of work taught in schools this produces a hierarchy of musical form-knowledge which can be readily observed, with an ascending order of perceived difficulties. This common ordering tends to go:

Binary—Ternary—Rondo—Verse and Chorus—Theme and Variations—Twelve bar blues

Assessment for aural awareness of these can be undertaken using obvious examples drawn from a variety of sources, and, possibly more importantly, these will then be evidenced in music which the pupils compose themselves, and structural knowledge will also be evidenced. As has been observed a number of times already, 'Procedural knowledge (knowing how) is more important in music than formal declarative knowledge (knowing about)' (Gruhn & Rauscher 2006: 62). In which case it is not simply 'knowing about' that we want the pupils to evidence, but to be able to put their knowledge of structural elements into practice too.

Teaching and concomitant assessment decisions need to be made in a developmental fashion, depending on the level of complexity of structural knowledge required. At its most basic, ternary form, for example, can be thought of as essentially tripartite, with the outer parts being identical. More complex understandings of ternary form, for example involving modulation and cadential progressions, are likely to be employed at later stages in the learner's development. This can be thought of as being oversimplistic, but serves to illustrate the point being made.

We know that aural awareness of structural elements is a complex process (Lerdahl & Jackendoff 1983; Sloboda 1985), and that music teachers involved in teaching aspects of structure worry about how to make this apparent to their students. We know too that extrapolation of this sort of information from listening to music is difficult.

If we assume that harmony, metrical structure, and the like are real and important factors in music listening, then listening must involve extracting this information from the incoming notes. How, then, is this done; by what processes are these structures inferred? At present, this is very much an open question. It is fair to say that no full satisfactory answer has been offered for any of the kinds of structure listed above; in some areas, answers have hardly even been proposed. (Temperley 2001: 1)

If this is the case in terms of cognitive research, then how can music teachers deal with this? For many teachers, it would seem obvious at first glance to use staff

notation to help with this. After all, music teachers are competent in staff notation, and use it as a tool themselves, so why not use it with the pupils? But to get
to a level where notation can be used as an analytical aid takes time. Indeed, '...
although literacy is hard to acquire, its acquisition can profoundly alter cognitive
functioning' (Sloboda 1985: 19). This being the case, music teachers, whose
cognitive functionings have been significantly altered, need to think about ways
in which those of their pupils with unaltered functions can gain access to understandings which would be helpful to them! Understanding musical structure is a
complex undertaking, and whether or not musical notation helps with this is
going to be a matter for the individual teacher, with a knowledge of the needs of
their classes, to make an informed decision in this regard (Terry 1994). However,
this is not the only way in which notation is employed in music listening, and it is
to a consideration of these other areas that we now turn.

Assessment of aural awareness using staff notation

Assessment of developing staff notation was considered in Chapter 10 in
relation to skill acquisition on instruments. We know that notation taught in
isolation from other musical skills is a factor which might make teaching
(and learning) less than effective (Bray 2000b: 74), so how might developing
awareness of notation be used and assessed with regard to music listening?
One problem with such an approach is that knowledge of staff notation is not
of itself sufficient to grasp tonal and metrical structures without a great deal of
intermediary explanation. It may be apparent to a competent analyst from the
score that the second subject of a piece of music in sonata form is in the tonic
key when it returns in the recapitulation; but if this information is known
already, then the score is probably not needed, if it is not known, then the
score may not be helpful, and, what does it mean (or matter?) to those for
whom it is entirely a foreign language?

Assessment of understanding of musical features involving staff notation
occurs in a number of examination situations, such as GCSE and A level. To
prepare pupils for this teachers will often begin teaching it to younger pupils.
We know that typically less than 10% of pupils opt for GCSE music at age 14+,
and that there are a variety of reasons for this. (Bray 2000a; Lamont & Maton
2008). Music teachers are well aware that they do not want to put pupils off the
subject, but equally they want to stretch the most able. Finding ways to do this
will need to be a matter which teachers choose in the light of personalization of
curricular materials. Assessment of notation learning is obviously most appropriately undertaken through a practical modality, where there is a purpose to it.
Assessment in isolation of aspects of notation will probably be best undertaken

in a formative fashion, until learners are in a strong enough position to be able to deal with the more intricate complexities of it.

Assessment problems abound in some of the ways in which aspects of music notation theory are taught, however. Clapping a semibreve or a semiquaver results in a sound of the same length in either case; it is the 'silence' after it which alters. Saying a crotchet is 'worth one beat' is nonsense in 6/8 time, or any compound time signature. Establishing understanding of beat patterns aurally needs to precede the codified learning and assessment thereof. What is important to bear in mind is that assessment of developing knowledge of staff notation is not an assessment of emerging musicality or understanding, '. . . the idea that true understanding of music is reserved exclusively for those who can read notation is preposterous' (Priest 2002: 98). Assessment of notation skills should be a means to an end, not an end in itself.

Aural tests

Often linked with development and assessment of listening through staff notation is the use of aural tests. Often these are constructed without referencing 'real' music in ways which allow students to form connections. I remember an A level student becoming deeply angry at having to listen to, and write down, a rhythm dictation played on a snare drum, from a poor quality cassette. What did this have to do with real music? 'A . . . student, recalling her first experience of an ABRSM aural test for a grade exam, said "it didn't sound like any other music I knew" ' (Priest 2002: 99). But this is the whole point! These tests are taken out of a musical context in order to focus on the elements of music, in the way that we have seen 'real' music does not do. Why we want people to have these skills is an entirely different question, however, and ultimately depends more upon the philosophy of the examination system than on the view of the teacher, or, most probably, the pupils! But they exist, and teachers want to prepare pupils for them, so how to use assessment?

One of the important aspects of this is in developmental learning. To do this teachers need to start with small manageable chunks of musical listening, maybe reproduced orally, or using an instrument. Informal learning relies heavily on repetition of phrases, so for those who have not had the experience of learning more formally, this might be an appropriate place to start. One of the problems with aural tests is that the pupils are 'thrown in at the deep end', often at a level beyond their comfortable competence. Simply because they are doing, say, Grade 4, does not mean their listening skills are at this level yet. They need to be given tasks at which they can succeed, and then *pace* Mrs Curwen, be taken to the related unknown. Assessment can help in this, as the emotional impact of assessment can be detrimental to success. Aural tests invade the personal space of the learner, they have to sing, clap, and undertake embodied responses. These can be private spaces, and so assessment needs to take this into account.

Assessment of listening through evaluation

Listening to music, and being guided through the structure, is, of course, only a part of what is going on. Knowing that Mendelssohn's *Hebrides Overture* is in Sonata form, or that Yes's *Tales from Topographic Oceans* is through-composed but with strophic elements, is only a part of the picture. What about knowing that Eric Clapton wrote 'Tears in Heaven' in memory of his son? Or that Shostakovich's seventh symphony was first performed during the harrowing time of the siege of Leningrad? These are layers of meaning which are overlaid on the music, in the sense that they are difficult to deduce from hearing alone. Certainly their affective response may generate feelings of sadness, the Clapton song having words which help convey literal meaning. But how can assessment be used to undertake music appreciation? Indeed, should it? Is it related to how people listen to music?

... despite being avid listeners to popular music, and despite the fact that popular music has been a part of the school curriculum for many years, school pupils of this age do not tend to listen to it with a great deal of perceptiveness, awareness, or even appreciation. (Green 2008: 87)

Engagement with musico-emotional content is a contentious issue. How do we assess a person's affective response? Should we? Can we? At the moment such matters do not figure as part of listening assessments, maybe rightly so; after all, a pupil saying 'I'm a level 4 in emotional response' probably does not tell us very much!

What can also be of concern is the notion of equality of opportunity in music appreciation:

The problem with the conventional approach lies in its implicit assumptions about the social network that exists between the musics and the students in a classroom. That is, the traditional approach assumes that the aim of music listening instruction is the fostering of conservative/Western/male connoisseur value-stance. In stark contrast, the students in my classroom automatically conceived Western classical music as music for 'rich people' and 'white people' who 'live in mansions.' In fact, the students' 'labeling' highlighted set [*sic*] of social/political assumptions that were not entirely wrong. (Silverman 2009: 18)

The sociological overtones of music choice present difficult choices for the music teacher!

Listening to each other's music

So far this chapter has concentrated upon listening to music by others. A large part of music lessons will be taken up by listening to music that the pupils have produced themselves. The role of listening to each others' music is an important one in the development of critical faculties, and in a similar way to performing, listening is being done in the service of another aspect of music education. It is a truism that for music to be listened to is its *raison d'etre*, but nonetheless there are different sorts of listening, and critical listening to improve pupil work is high on the agenda for many music teachers.

What teachers will want their pupils to do is to move from a position where pupils offer a 'knee-jerk' reaction to music, to one where a more informed opinion can emerge. As Angela Major observes, 'Evaluative comments can occur without real engagement with the music . . .' (Major 2008: 315), and it is real engagement that teachers are often hoping for. Listening to, evaluating, and appraising the work done in class has one significant feature that listening to recordings of extant works lacks, namely the opportunity to influence its future development. This is potentially a novel concept for pupils. Much music listening is predicated on non-involvement, and so for the learners to have a voice in production is significant. Developing pupil skills in this area requires the teacher to structure opportunities, and to do so in the spirit of a community of practice. The whole class are engaged in a similar pursuit, and so conjoint critical thinking is a cement which binds the community together. Major (Major 2007, 2008) writes of a typology of pupil talk with regard to composing, where pupils move from description, via the stages of opinion, affective response, and evaluation, to problem solving. However, as she observes, '. . . talk for the purposes of developing critical appraisal skills needs a sensitive context, and the lack of ability to articulate in whole class settings cannot be used as the sole indicator of the level of maturity of thinking or conceptual understanding' (Major 2007: 176). One implication of this is that, as we saw in Chapter 4, Polanyi's observation that 'we can know more than we can tell' (Polanyi 1966: 4) holds true here too!

A key aspect of formative assessment is the use of peer assessment. In making evaluative comments about their own work, and the work of their classmates, pupils will be engaging with peer assessment. This does not need to include giving grades or levels, but does involve carefully considered reflective observations, which have the potential for having a significant impact upon attainment. One objective for this is to enable and facilitate self-criticality in the pupils. If their own internal critical faculties can be developed then they will become more self-aware in terms of the music they produce, and the ways in which they can develop and extend it.

Although much of the above discussion has been about composing, critical listening to performing is also an important skill to develop, and again involves peer and self-assessment protocols. Instrumental learning too benefits from this, with instrument-specific listening being promoted amongst groups of learners. In both composing and performing, the role of the teacher-as-questioner is paramount. Good questions, as we have already seen, are important. Whilst experienced teachers have a range of questions upon which they can draw, it is worthwhile to think through what good questions for developing critical listening might entail.

Chapter 13

Developing classroom improvising by the use of assessment

Improvising is not the same activity as composing; although the two activities may share many of their cognitive competencies, nonetheless in terms of professional music practice, and in terms of what goes in the classroom, there are important distinctions between them. Differences between adult and novice conceptions of improvisation are, however, not altogether clear (Burnard 2002). In educational discourse the boundary between improvising and composing is blurred (Koutsoupidou 2005). In general terms, and for the purposes of this chapter, differences between the two will centre around the idea that composing involves revisiting ideas in order to bring them to fruition, whereas improvising involves spontaneous, or seemingly spontaneous, musical utterances made and realized in real time.

The role of improvising as a generalist activity often takes second place to composing,

The very idea of improvisation is a Western construct that has arisen from a presumed detachment between pre-composition and performance . . . This detachment, which has become evident in music and music education practices, has tended to distract unsuspecting musicians and music learners from what improvisation offers as a mode of musical action. (Lines 2005: 66)

In the deconstruction of the process of composing proposed in Chapter 11, generation of ideas occupied a privileged position in the first stages of creating pieces of music. Like composing, improvising also involves the generation of ideas, but in a much more immediate context. In England the National Curriculum states that, 'Pupils should be taught how to . . . improvise, developing rhythmic and melodic material when performing' (DfEE/QCA 1999: 18). This is a surprisingly difficult task though. Is it possible to teach people how to improvise? After all, '. . . the improviser's task is that of making choices—choosing to play one thing instead of another, taking one path instead of all the others that beckon. Such an ability seems not only difficult to define but also not the sort of thing one could "learn" ' (Benson 2003: 141). If it is difficult to learn, then how can it be taught? One possible answer lies in planning and structuring appropriate improvisatory learning experiences. Developmental learning of improvising can be done by the teacher constructing situations where limitations of choice are deliberately put into place to help scaffold the learning. Improvising happens in real time, and so the key to success is to build up confidence in spontaneous music making over a series of supportive stages. Advanced improvisers have at their disposal a repertoire of gestures which they can access in order to put the right thing into play at the right time. Over time the pupils build up these gestures into what Paterson and Odam refer to as a personal 'Dynamic Library', this being a collection of '. . . information, a library of sounds, gestures, styles and other craft skills and techniques which they [the pupils] have accumulated in their heads' (Paterson & Odam 2000: 9).

Pedagogies of developmental improvising rely heavily on appropriate formative assessment judgements being made by the music teacher and shared with the learner. Often pedagogies of improvising also involve a purposeful delimiting of available musical resources, too much choice being considered a barrier to success. For example, for some pupils it may be appropriate to set boundaries for early improvisations by using mainly unpitched percussion instruments. Many teachers then go on to introduce melodic improvising by the use of the pentatonic scale over an ostinato figure. The results can sound a bit like 'cod Chinese music', as one teacher put it, but the confidence that is built up in a situation where mistakes do not sound bad can help pave the way for more complex forms of improvising at a later date. This also helps with meeting the requirement of trying to ensure that '. . . the starting points for improvising and composing are based on children's existing knowledge and experience' (Burnard 2000: 22).

Pressing (1984) hypothesizes that any improvisation can be partitioned into a sequence of non-overlapping sections. These sections can contain a number of musical events. Of these musical events three are of particular significance to educational improvising. These are the acoustic, appertaining to sounds; the musical, which are cognitive representations of sounds; and the movement aspect, including muscular actions. The ways in which pupils generate sounds when working at the initial stages of composing can be seen to be related to some of the Pressing criteria. In particular the notion that particular events may be generated by finger movements. This relates to Gibson's notion of affordances (Gibson 1979), where the shape and structure of an instrument can have an effect on the way that it is played. We saw in discussing composing how certain patterns of notes can often be seen when a pupil uses a tuned percussion instrument such as a xylophone, and plays it by starting at one end and working note-by-note to the other. Whilst this may be inappropriate in a developed composition, it might not be inappropriate in novice classroom improvising. What this means is that in improvisation, the notion of affordances-as-gestures can be an important part of the developmental learning process.

Cognition and skill

We know that cognition of music involves a complex series of mental processes, some of which are handled simultaneously, and some sequentially (Bharucha et al. 2006). We are aware too that the development of cognitive understandings of tonal music are complex (Krumhansl 1990; Lerdahl & Jackendoff 1983; Sloboda 1985). We also know that affordances and gestures play a large part in the development of improvising. What this means is that skill development in improvising involves a complex set of mental and physical attributes that operate simultaneously. The implications of this for the classroom teacher are that pupil understandings are intrinsically linked to skill development in this area of music learning. Unlike composing, where we saw that the opportunity for revision is an important aspect of the process, improvising happens in real time, and cognitive and sensory-motor skills need to be sufficiently developed to be able to both process and execute the requirements of the task.

Improvising within a group

'. . . creativity researchers now believe that creativity cannot always be defined as a property of individuals; creativity can also be a property of groups' (Sawyer 2003: 25).

Making up a piece of music as you go along seems to be a difficult task for some expert musicians trained in Western Classical genres, and it may also be the case that thinking 'outside the box' of this mindset is problematic for some teachers who have been trained in this tradition. However, setting improvisation tasks for pupils has the potential for being less restrictive than it might seem. Novice perceptions of what creativity researchers call 'the domain' (Csikszentmihalyi 1999) are far less fixed, and so pupils do not necessarily need to find this task any more difficult or unusual than other things they are asked to do in school! To facilitate this though, the requirements of the instrument of choice for this task would patently be one where technical demands are not so high as to prevent meaningful participation. Classroom instruments would be a logical place to begin, for example.

Improvising within a group setting also involves aspects of individual contributions too. Teachers may decide to structure such work so that turn-taking forms a part of what is being done, so that individual pupils improvise within a group sequentially, or it can involve whole-group responses where the individual contribution is contained and located within the structure of the group. Call-and-response techniques are also appropriate, with the teacher able to hand over responsibility for the 'call' as pupil confidence develops.

Assessment of improvising

As expertise in solo instrumental competence increases, then some musical traditions privilege a move towards the development of individualized improvising skills. Jazz would be a prime example. Here again we can see that expert jazz performers seldom improvise *ex nihilo*, out of nothing, as it were, but use their dynamic library and developed aural skills to fit what they are doing into the context of the music being performed. Examination syllabi for ABRSM Jazz syllabus, for example, talk about assessment of the choice of musical resources, which, '. . . encompasses the need to decide in the moment which of a number of pitch, rhythm and harmonic options to use. Manipulation of those resources involves the creation of coherent structures by, for example, repeating ideas, varying the spaces between them and developing them motivically or rhythmically' (ABRSM 2007: 41). This developed and advanced property of individual or group improvising is amenable to assessment using the notion established elsewhere in this book of connoisseurship, the person doing the assessing will be proficient in their field.

For instrumental teachers, the development of improvising skills in their pupils can proceed hand-in-hand with more general development. This does not need to take place at the expense of instrumental learning, but can be an important part of it, 'In a teaching approach that regularly incorporates improvisation, each new step, whether in note-learning, scales, dynamic devices, and so on, can be developed and consolidated. The technical and expressive aspects of playing can be brought together . . .' (Glover & Scaife 2004: 82).

The idea that technique and expressivity can be linked in improvising is obviously a useful one, and this can clearly take place in group lessons as well as in individual instrumental tuition. Indeed, group lesson are probably better suited to this, because, as Janet Mills observes, '. . . group lessons are ideal for creative work, because of the larger number of instrumentalists present to originate, try out, evaluate, and develop ideas (Mills 2007: 157). The notion of evaluation is important here. Charles Byrne has observed that some teachers are uncomfortable with '. . . talking with children about their compositions and improvisations' (Byrne 2005: 301), but in improvising, whether in the instrumental lesson or the classroom, this will be an important part of the assessment process. Indeed, formative assessment involving careful questioning is likely to be highly appropriate here:

Teacher intervention should most often arise through effective and direct questioning about the fortuitous discoveries in the pupils' previous performances. I am suggesting that what is important is the issues to think about and ways of thinking about them, rather than specific answers. As listeners and enablers asking how interaction occurs, teachers can begin to formulate goals concerning aesthetic effect, the ethics of music-making, roles and relationships, focus, sound ideals, musical processes, cues and communicative gestures. (Burnard 2002: 168)

What Pamela Burnard is describing here is formative assessment in action: the teacher discusses what has happened with the pupils, and provides useful feedback on the improvisation that has taken place, and feed-forward on what the pupils can do next time they undertake work of this nature.

Improvising has a much closer process-product relationship than does composing. Indeed, it could be argued that improvising is all about process, with the product arising as a direct result of the process. This raises questions about teacher interventions whilst the process is actually taking place. We know that improvising unfolds over time, so how does this affect the way in which teachers can intervene? There is a fine balance of judgements which need to be made here. Sometimes it may be appropriate to intervene orally whilst the process is taking place, it can also be appropriate for teachers to intervene musically, for example by modelling processes of improvising during the course of a group improvisation with learners. On the other hand, there can also be times when the best role for the teacher to adopt is one of non-intervention, and use formative assessment strategies such as feedback and questioning after the improvising has finished. There is clearly a role here for audio (and/or video) recording, and, as we have seen before, employing recording facilities means that the learners are able to take a step back from the immediacy of being involved with the process, and critically evaluate their own contributions to the improvisation.

Criteria for summative assessment of improvising

The role of summative assessment of improvising in generalist music education is largely underdeveloped at present. To employ summative assessment of improvising in generalist music classes would involve a clear distinction between criteria-led assessment, and holistic assessment. If criteria are to be used, the teacher will need to decide on what the appropriate criteria are going to be. Keith Swanwick is critical of some published grade criteria, and observes that, '. . . to be useful, criteria statements should indicate qualitative differences rather than quantitative shifts' (Swanwick 1988: 151). The implications of this for summative assessment criteria of improvising are that they should be developmental, rather than introducing new areas for the accumulation of marks. As improvising involves developing technical proficiency on instruments, then assessment criteria will need to involve some aspect of developmental instrumental proficiency too. Assessment of composing, it was suggested, could have assessment criteria which included intentionality and effectiveness. These assessment criteria from composing are appropriate for improvising too, but where teachers may wish to diverge from this is with regard to emergent instrumental proficiency. Assessment of performing is not the same as assessment of improvising, and relevance of assessment constructs is as important here as elsewhere in the curriculum. What this might mean is that teachers themselves can decide to make their own version of 'double-duty' assessments, and assess performing skills via the use of an improvisation. The difficulty will be in disentangling the criteria for improvising, which is itself performance based, with the criteria for performing, which are skill-specific in terms of instrumental attainment.

Chapter 14

Assessment and ICT in music education

There are two distinct roles for assessment and ICT in music education, these are:

- The use ICT as a musical tool
- The use of ICT as an assessment tool

Each of these are separate activities, and although assessment of ICT use can itself use ICT, there are clearly significant differences between them. This chapter investigates general principles concerning ICT in music education, and considers broad concepts and ways in which it can be used for assessment purposes in the classroom, rather than focusing on specific items of hardware and software.

The use of ICT as a musical tool

ICT in music education has the power to significantly transform pupil learning (Wright 2002). At the same time it posses the potential to change the very nature of music teaching and learning, 'These practical changes are very considerable, and, what is perhaps even more important, they have brought into question some of the most basic conceptual frameworks that have under-pinned music teaching' (Cain 2004: 217). Composing can now be undertaken using little more than 'drag and drop' computer techniques, where the main proficiency required is that of mouse usage. Music software programmes exist which allow pupils to create compositions that they cannot play. Step-time entry into sequencing programmes allows pupils to create performances not in real time. Music exists which has been created and manipulated electronically before emerging as sound. But does this differ significantly from the work of musicians such as Varèse or Kraftwerk? This is an ongoing philosophical debate which is likely to impact increasingly on music education as the means of production in music become more and more democratized (Woodford 2005). The implications of this are that the ways in which musical learning is conceived (Kwami 2001), and, possibly, the way in which music itself is thought of as an art form are brought into question.

... the relationship between music and ICT is not one of servant and master, but rather a subtle, reciprocal and perhaps empathetic one in which the very nature of what constitutes musical practice is challenged, mediated and redefined through performers' and composers' uses of ICT. Ultimately, given a conceptual grasp of this alternative perspective, it could lead pupils and teachers to engage with and organise sounds in new ways, challenging the very nature of music itself at a fundamental level. (Savage 2005: 168)

This creates a series of issues for the music teacher in terms of assessment of musical learning using ICT. There is a potential problem that ICT will come to be seen as an end in itself, rather than as a part of musical learning (Hodges 2001: 179). There is another potential issue in that music ICT itself will be seen to favour boys, adding '... another layer of symbolic masculinity ...' (Armstrong 2008: 377) to the music classroom.

Yet another layer of complexity is added by considering the interface between the personal worlds of the pupils, and the educational world of the school. Here the pupils may have different notions as to what constitutes music, such as mobile phone ring-tones (Baxter 2007; Finney 2007b). Pupils will be engaged in informal learning of their choice of music, possibly in bedrooms and garages (Green 2002), and will be exploring the potential of music software programmes by themselves and with others, including people they have never met in person via the use of the internet (Seddon 2006, 2007). All of these impinge on the skills, knowledge, and attitudes that the learners bring to the music classroom or instrumental lesson.

Assessment of musical work created using ICT

Assessment using the notion of intentionality becomes complex when considering the use of ICT, as the possibility exists of serendipitous outcomes which the pupils could not possibly have foreseen. Indeed, exploring the potential of sound manipulation could well be one of the learning outcomes that teachers have planned for in lessons using ICT. This is an assessment problem where intentionality might need to be subsumed within the notion of effectiveness, with assessment judgements appropriate to the means of production having to be made, 'It is important for an assessor to sort out the differences between the musical affordances provided by the software and the creative use of the leverage provided by the software. To assist in sorting out tool from technique, it can help to have students provide an explanation of their work' (Brown 2007: 250). What this means is that in using ICT in the music classroom as a means of production, intentionality will need to be teased out in ways which non-ICT composed or produced music might evidence intrinsically. This is where formative assessment clearly plays a role, and where teacher involvement in the process of composing will be central in making assessment judgements. Indeed, in the quotation from Andrew Brown above, the essence of having students provide explanations can probably best be drawn out using appropriate questioning techniques, themselves a component of formative assessment. In a similar fashion Jonathan Savage (2002; 2007b) advocates assessment of work using ICT in music to be elicited through discussion with pupils.

We are currently at a crossroads in the use of ICT and music education, with existing schemes of external summative assessment being grafted onto new ways of working in music espoused by a number of teachers, with variable degrees of success resulting from this uneven marriage. It can be the case that music teachers' own backgrounds and skills conspire against them using ICT in learning effectively. Prensky (2001a, 2001b) writes of 'digital natives' and 'digital immigrants', most pupils are the former, and a number of music teachers are the latter. What this means for music education is that ICT in music will continue, in the short term at least, to be treated by some teachers as an outsider, to be wholeheartedly embraced by others, and for there to be a range of in-between positions. The implications of this for assessment of musical production using ICT are that it needs to take into account very particularly the role of ICT, and, specifically, to differentiate between the agency of the pupils, and the affordances of the technology. It is also appropriate to permit the pupils a voice in the assessment of work they produce using ICT, with regard to both means of production and outcome.

The use of ICT as an assessment tool

There are two primary ways in which ICT can be used as an assessment tool. These are collecting and storing assessment data, and interpreting and analysing assessment data (Fautley & Savage 2008).

Throughout the course of this book, the use of audio or video recording of pupils' work has been championed as one of the best ways in which formative assessment can take place, and one that provides a primary source of evidence for summative assessment too. Audio recording does not need to be expensive, or involve costly equipment. Most computers have a microphone input on them, and a line-out or headphone socket. With the provision of an inexpensive microphone and free or built-in recording software, the computer can become a high-quality digital recorder. If separate items of recording equipment are wanted, then a range of hardware is available, from inexpensive dictation machines, via portable stereos of varying complexity and cost, to sophisticated hand-held digital audio recorders, and fully installed recording studios, all of which will do the job of capturing the music which pupils create, make, and play. Likewise with video, from webcams that plug into computers, via inexpensive hand-held video cameras, through to camcorders, a range of equipment is available here too. Many mobile phones will record audio and video too, and the 'digitally native' pupils are well used to this aspect, and it figures daily in their lives.

The immediacy of playing back a recording of musical work done by pupils enables reflection and, given time, for a considered response to be made. Where ICT can be helpful is in the storing of these recordings. The days are gone when teachers had to sort through boxes of cassettes or CDs to find the recording they wanted, music is now available on demand on an iPod or computer. Recordings of pupil work can be made available in the same fashion. But this plethora of storage opportunity brings with it its own problem, which is that of cataloguing and accessing data. Whilst computer software can be purchased which will help with this aspect of the music teacher's role, many teachers also manage to use links directly from pupil name-lists to recordings of work the pupils have done. Some schools and instrumental teachers have encouraged pupils to take responsibility for this aspect of their own learning themselves, and have developed the use of e-portfolios, often housed on school secure intranet facilities, but sometimes available to outside listeners too. The use of e-portfolios allows pupils to build up evidence over time of their own personal progress in music. This can be a powerful incentive in externally validating their creative work in music. Whilst proud mums can display emergent art work on the fridge, the musical equivalent is harder to deal with. By allowing home access to pupil work created at school the music made by pupils at school does not disappear once it has been made (Savage 2007a).

One of the purposes of formative assessment is to improve learning and attainment in the future, and the generation of effective and meaningful targets is predicated upon having this sort of information available to the teacher. By building up evidence over time, and storing musical work evidenced in musical outputs, the teacher is able to achieve this. What this also means is that there is a recognition that audio recording is central to music as an evidentiary requirement of the subject. This is similar to the way that art teachers build up photographic portfolios of pupil work, the photographs are not the work, but they provide evidence to show outcomes.

The teacher's markbook is still an important tool in the storage of assessment data. From recording marks gained in summative assessments, through to making formative comments, there is a lot to be said for the immediacy and simplicity of the pen-and-paper approach that a markbook brings. The use of

ICT as an e-markbook can simply replicate this, but the possibility of linking to media files means that an electronic markbook can be a much more versatile tool than the paper version. Formative assessment comments, for example, can be codified and added, 'to do' notes can be inserted, and reminders programmed.

Interpreting and analysing assessment data

Having collected assessment data, and devised suitable ways in which the data can be retrieved, the next stage is to do something with the data. There is a problem in this technological age of information overload, and the same can be true of e-assessment data. Whilst the use of ICT can vastly simplify the storage and retrieval of musical evidence, it cannot replace the teacher in deciding what the best course of action should be next. True, there are self-marking computer-based testing regimes available, based on the inputting of correct answers. These can be used for theory and right/wrong answers of knowledge about music. What they cannot do is make informed decisions about what to do about it. Teachers still need to use their own professional judgement in deciding what are the most appropriate courses of action to take for the learning of the pupils in their care.

Chapter 15

The role of baseline assessment

There are a number of occasions in music education when a teacher meets learners for the first time. This can be in the classroom, the studio, the instrumental lesson, the learning ensemble, or any combination of these. What the teacher needs to know, and probably needs to know fairly quickly, is what the pupils already know and can do. To do this, some form of baseline assessment is needed. If a 'magic bullet' were to be hypothecated for music education, then a reliable way of assessing pupils' current performance and attainment levels under these circumstances, through the use of a straightforward assessment test, would be near the top of the list. Sadly such a thing does not exist at present. Indeed, some would say that just as magic lies mainly in the realm of fiction, so does this sort of baseline assessment!

In order to investigate what baseline assessment is, and what it can do for teaching and learning, this chapter look into conceptions of baseline assessment, and discusses ways in which teachers can use it to obtain meaningful information about their pupils which will be helpful in planning for future learning.

Baseline tests of musical ability

The psychometrics movement of the twentieth century produced a range of tests which were designed to test for latent musical ability. One such test, the Bentley test (Bentley 1966), was discussed in Chapter 12, but many others exist too. We know that tests of musical aptitude that focus on listening are problematic (Vispoel 1999), and we also know that the cognitive foundations upon which the brain organizes music perception are not yet clear (Peretz & Zatorre 2005). Janet Mills writes about the use of aural tests designed to weed out students for instrumental music lessons, rather than encouraging them to take up an instrument (Mills 2005: 121). Using such ability tests with generalist music classes is not that common in the UK, but it is still to be found. Graham Welch writes of musical aptitude tests being used to divide pupils into 'musical sheep and non-musical goats', and questions their rationale (Welch 2001a: 2–3). Twenty-first-century children are musically sophisticated—they have been surrounded by music since before birth, they will have been subject to many hours of listening to it by the time they start school—so testing for detection of musical primitives might seem somewhat questionable. Indeed, many other factors can be relevant in determining the scores which are achieved including experience in taking tests of musical ability (Good et al. 1997)!

What is baseline assessment?

The notion of baseline assessment does not at present have a consensual basis in music education. Different teachers mean a range of things when they talk about it. However, a number of common themes emerge from talking to teachers about what it might mean, and what would be useful for them. These include:

1. Where the pupils are now in terms of attainment
2. Predictions of where they could be in *N* years/months/terms/lessons
3. What the pupils currently know/can do
4. What the pupils currently do not know/cannot do
5. What National Curriculum or other attainment level the pupils are now
6. What their predicted National Curriculum or attainment level will be (see item 2 above!)
7. What musical experiences the pupils have had in the past
8. What the music teacher needs to do now in terms of developmental lesson planning

To do all this would be to ask a lot of a single assessment instrument! What these themes have in common is that they are required to summarize past attainment, and to provide evidence which can be used in a formative fashion, to develop future learning and plan for forthcoming units of work. Some would also like baseline assessment to have a predictive component too, and be able to predict future attainment, preferably in terms of grades or levels. This means that conceptions of baseline assessment can be diagrammatically represented as in Fig. 15.1.

In terms of assessment, what Fig. 15.1 shows is that there is a range of different uses to which baseline assessment is being put. These include formative, for planning units of work and for organising future musical experiences for the learners; and summative, in that they are summarizing attainment to date. A further use is also shown, which is a predictive one. Many teachers want something that will predict what attainment level a pupil will achieve at some point in the future. Let us start by looking at this last issue.

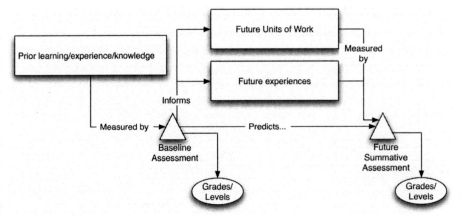

Fig. 15.1 Baseline assessment

Predictive assessment

Predictive assessment is where an assessment taken at one point in time is used to estimate what attainment will be at some point in the future. What predictive assessment does is to extrapolate forwards using statistical techniques to predict what the likelihood of such future attainment will be. This type of system, it has to be remembered, is statistical, in that it is working with groups of numbers, not with people. What it is saying is that common results can be calculated from a range of pupils who have scored grade X in the past, will score grade $X+1$ in the future, and $X+2$, at some point beyond that, or whatever the system says. This is, in many ways analogous to how car insurance companies work. Based on your address, the type of car you drive, your age, gender, and occupation, amongst other variables, the insurance companies calculate the risk you offer, and base their car insurance estimates on this. They cannot tell that in eight months time you'll be sideswiped by a lorry on the M6, for example, as this is down to circumstance! The same is true of statistical achievement predictions (and, in some cases, is based on much the same data as the car insurance example, with postcode and free school meals being key variables), they are statistical averages. Some commercial packages offer to do this for schools. Just as the insurance company cannot foresee having an accident on the M6, then these commercial packages can only deal with statistical averages. Indeed, commercially produced predictive assessment figures for music are only about 70% accurate to one grade level at GCSE. For statistical purposes these packages are good enough to give a general indication, but they probably should not be seen as a basis upon which accurate statistics of future attainment of a specific cohort of named pupils should be set, for example. Nor should they be used for modern versions of 'payment by results', or performance management targets (Mansell 2008), in that they do not provide accurate information for any given named child, in that what is being dealt with are statistics for cohort averages.

Predictive assessment using data produced by music teachers can have similar problems. We know that some pupils flourish, musically speaking, and others do not. What we do not always know is why this is. Why does getting involved with music 'tick the box' for many young people, but not for others? Predicting what can happen in grade terms three years forwards can, again, only be a matter for statistics. This is important to remember when dealing with what grades Darren and Jatinder in class 9Z will achieve. Darren and Jatinder are people, with specific attributes and needs, not just statistics in a spreadsheet showing their arithmetical likelihood of progression. Darren may have to deal with being bullied, Jatinder may really enjoy playing the guitar in class, both of which can affect their attainment in their music lessons. Statistics don't have emotional responses like real people do! It is important to remember that music teachers teach people, not numbers.

Using baseline assessment to plan learning

Whilst the notion of a one-shot baseline assessment test in music is problematic, what baseline assessment can do is to reveal information about pupils which can be helpful in planning learning programmes and units of work for the future. This cannot, as has been seen, be done easily via a single test, but can be achieved by the use of assessment tasks and by the interpretation of data such tasks reveal. We already know there can be a problem of discontinuity between phases in music education, and that pupils are demotivated when, upon transfer, a new teacher decides that it is easiest to start from first principles to ensure every one is at the same position (Glover & Young 1999: 212). This is the same as the assumption made that upon entry to secondary schools, some music teachers appear to believe that the pupils '. . . know nothing about music' (Coll 2002: 100), and that the teacher needs to begin the teaching programme from a position of assuming total ignorance in their pupils. We have seen in earlier chapters how this is going to be demotivating for pupils. We also saw in earlier chapters how errors creep in when teachers misinterpret assessment evidence. The same can be true of baseline assessment. For example, the teacher asks a new class if they have done any composing. 'No' answers the class, 'we haven't done any composing'. And so the teacher plans for them to make up this deficit by composing some music to go with a picture or a story. However, had the teacher inquired if they had done this, by asking, 'have you made up music to go with a picture or a story', the answer could well have been very different! What the music teacher called 'composing' sounded very grand to the pupils; no, they hadn't done that, but they had worked in groups making up sound sequences to go with texts and images. Asking the right questions is clearly important. Equally important is to seek musical evidence in a musical fashion. A straightforward way to find out what pupils can do musically is to give them a range of tasks, then see how they get on whilst they are actually doing them. Using baseline assessment to plan for learning thus becomes a medium term process.

This sort of baseline assessment uses assessment tasks to achieve its ends, and the purpose of them is to find out what the pupils are able to do (Fautley 2005b). This means that open-ended tasks are going to be the most useful, as they will reveal how pupils treat the work in question. Many teachers have found that setting composing tasks is a good way to do this, as it enables the pupils to display both creating and performing skills in the music they produce. What this requires from the teacher is a view that interpretation of the data that arises will affect future teaching. There is, after all, little point in setting a baseline assessment task if the teacher then teaches what they were going to anyway! The purpose of the baseline assessment is to reveal the shading of units of work that will need to be employed. Clearly teachers are not going to start with an entirely blank canvas, but employing baseline assessment in this way gives a steer to future work.

So, what will this sort of baseline assessment look like in practice? A series of open-ended composing tasks will inform the teacher about composing and performing abilities. Asking the pupils to compose from a series of starting points is possibly the most helpful here. For example, over a series of lessons, the pupils are given three composing tasks to undertake:

Composing task 1:
Make up a piece of music to go with a pictorial stimulus (this can be anything provided by the teacher, from a haunted house image to a seascape).

Composing task 2:
Make up a piece of music which includes all of the following:
a) the notes C, F sharp, G, D, B flat (or whatever the teacher chooses!)
b) a repeating note pattern
c) the number 5 (this allows for creative or divergent responses!)
d) a regular and an irregular beat
e) changes in volume

Composing task 3:

You have been asked to compose music for a school play. Short pieces of music are needed for the following three scenes:

a) The entry of the King and Queen to the court

b) A scene where the Princess has been poisoned and falls senseless

c) A magical scene where a wizard casts a spell to revive the Princess.

These give a range of possible responses, and allow the teacher to see what the pupils are capable of doing. They can be interspersed with performing opportunities, singing, and listening examples too. Clearly this will take time, and it may well be a matter of weeks before the teacher is able to arrive at preliminary judgements as to what the pupils can do. These sorts of assessment tasks allow for a range of responses, though. As we have seen, musical knowledge is not amenable to a 'one-hit' test, and so although school assessment managers may want this information quickly, for assessment to be meaningful, time has to be taken to ensure that information is reliable and relevant.

Looking to the future, the landscape of music education is shifting in many countries. From a local perspective, England will see major changes in coming years as the 'wider opportunities' programme of whole class instrumental and vocal tuition (WCIVT) comes on stream, providing access to music learning for a broad range of primary school pupils. Similar projects are in place in other areas too. What this will mean is that the range of musical experiences which pupils have had before transfer to secondary school is likely to broaden considerably, and that 'starting again' will not be a viable option for pupils who have spent some months learning to sing and play instruments.

Baseline assessment and linear progression

We saw in Chapter 7 that there are problems assuming a linear progression of musical development. This has links to the notion of baseline assessment, in that its purpose is not that of trying to 'flatten out' differences between pupils. There are bound to be some pupils who are more advanced instrumental learners than others, and some who have more divergent responses to creative tasks. The purpose of baselining is for the teacher to get to know the pupils. This means that although group work may well be employed, the teacher will be looking for individual achievements being evidenced through the conjoint format, not just for collectivized grades. What this can also mean is that baseline assessment of this sort can reveal problems with the data which is already available for these new cohorts of pupils. In England and Wales, transfer information from Primary to secondary schools often involves the assigning of

National Curriculum levels for music. We have already seen how this is an unmoderated system, so for schools to base their estimates of future progression upon unreliable data will cause problems. As a result of work which the pupils undertake in their first term of music lessons at secondary school, teachers will need to monitor how National Curriculum levels awarded elsewhere are translated into actual classroom assessment. The assumption of linear progression can easily break down when unreliable judgements are made. If you tell a painter that you live on the first floor, and want your outside windows painted, the painter would be perturbed if when he arrives he finds you live on the tenth floor! The same is true of music levels. The information needs to be accurate for appropriate action to be taken. The painter can still do the job, but will need to revise his estimate—exactly the same applies to level information!

What this means is that baseline assessment is best suited to providing a general overview of work that needs to be done with the pupils. It is assessment for formative purposes, and will inform the future direction that teacher and pupils will take. In the same way that that summative grades can be a shorthand way of summarizing achievement, then baseline assessment can also reveal whether there is a disparity in the assessment information provided from other sources. Assessment is again doing 'double duty', but in this case it is in the interests of the learners and teachers that appropriate action is taken.

Endnote

This chapter has considered the role of baseline assessment in music education, from musical ability tests to more open-ended assessment tasks. One of the problems with testing for musical ability harks back to material from earlier in this book, in that if there is no clear notion as to what musical ability is, then it is hard to devise a way of testing for it! What this means for the classroom teacher is that it is probably better to adopt a system of formative baseline assessment based on observed responses of what pupils can actually do, and then structure teaching around this, rather than try to test for something when it is not clear what that something is that is being tested for in the first place!

Chapter 16

Putting it together: holistic approaches to learning and assessment in music

Having explored the various components of learning and assessment in the school music curriculum separately, this chapter turns to exploring ways in which they can be put together and used holistically. As we have seen throughout this book, the nature of what is being assessed involves a series of decisions, often difficult, for the teacher to make, and, as we have seen in earlier chapters, there are always political overtones to assessment. Gary Spruce reminds us of this with regard to music education, when he observes that, '. . . the manner in which musical achievement is defined and assessed inevitably articulates a set of philosophical and political principles about the nature and purpose of learning, the subject being assessed, and the relationship between school and society . . .' (Spruce 2001a: 118).

What summative assessment inevitably does is to prioritize what someone else feels to be important. That could be the music teacher, a local authority music service, an examination board, a government committee, or a host of other interested parties. What it probably will not do is to take account of what the pupils say, 'what is important to *us* about *our* music'. This is where formative assessment and sensitively designed summative assessment criteria can be employed by the music teacher, in designing *with* the pupils what some appropriate assessment criteria might be.

Although what musical progression is perceived to be will vary from one context to another, and the associated role of assessment will be inextricably linked to this, there are some principles which can be seen to emerge from the various sections of this book. Key amongst these is the notion that musical learning needs to involve a variety of facets to be truly considered musical, these are the knowledge types we have discussed—'knowing about', 'knowing of', and 'knowing how'. Assessing any one of these alone will not give a rounded view of the pupil. So, for example, assessment of musical understanding based on written answers, whether in text or staff notation, will not be a valid way of assessing *musical* understanding. But there is also a perspective which swings too far the other way, and makes all music education predicated on 'doing' music, with little by way of conceptual or theoretical engagement, in the mistaken belief that developing practical skills alone will be sufficient of itself for understanding to somehow emerge unaided.

What emerges from these discussions is that we can consider approaches to summative assessment as coming from one of two perspectives, that of either top-down, or bottom-up. Top-down assessment begins from an overview of musical attainment, and grades are awarded based on the subjective understanding of the expert connoisseur, with little by way of criteria. Bottom-up assessment involves atomistically dividing musical attainment into a series of competencies or concepts. Both of these approaches are problematic. Top-down is too reliant on connoisseurship, and can be questioned as being little more than informed value judgement; bottom-up can be so piecemeal that, as Swanwick observes, '... we lose the sense of the whole in making explicit what was once tacitly apprehended' (Swanwick 1988: 147).

To address the problems caused by these extremes a middle way will be necessary, with teachers moving between the extremes as circumstances and musical learning dictate. Gathering a range of evidence is key to knowing pupils and what they can do. This might involve some top-down summative assessment, and some bottom-up. But in between these extremes will be the day-to-day use of formative assessment as music teachers engage in conversation with their pupils, and help them to develop. The role of assessment in developing musical learning means that the teacher has to pay attention to, and take regard of assessment information. A school I knew of contained a teacher, not of music, whose lessons were all held in a filing cabinet. When a class arrived the teacher simply took out lesson number 54 (or whatever) from the cabinet, taught it, then put it back for next year. This involves no formative assessment at all! It pays no attention to the developmental role of lessons, of reacting to understandings and misunderstandings, and of personalizing the learning for the specific pupils in the class.

But what does this mean in practice? If the role of assessment is to develop learning, rather than simply audit it, then how can this be achieved?

Holistic approaches

The oft-cited idea that 'the whole is greater than the sum of its parts' can be turned on its head in assessment terms. The sum of the parts do not make up the whole, something is missing. This is an important concept when dealing with assessment. The best that can be hoped for is that the wider the range of assessment data that can be accrued, the nearer we will get to understanding the whole, but, and this is crucial, the sum of the assessment-parts will never equal the pupil-whole! What this means for the music teacher is that assessment data should be collected from a range of sources and types, but that this data then needs to be interpreted. Keith Swanwick suggested that the elements of music education can be characterized by the mnemonic C(L)A(S)P: composition, literature studies (of and about music), audition (responsive listening), skill acquisition, and performance (Swanwick 1979: 45). In the UK the National Curriculum has codified these into the three areas of performing, listening, and composing. Whatever the local or national context, these elements together will form the basis of a rounded education in music, and so assessment needs to reflect this.

Whilst it is clear that listening will play a central role in music education (Bresler 1995), the development of listening can be undertaken alongside that of performing and composing. Indeed, composing with pupils offers a key methodology for tapping into all aspects of musical learning, and some music teachers are able to construct their entire music curriculum for pupils aged 11–14 years old with a wide range of musical learning stemming from composing-based activities. Doing this is an holistic approach which enables progression in listening and performing to be employed in the service of composing. How this will appear in practice is likely to involve a combination of bottom-up and top-down assessments being employed simultaneously. The three dimensions of assessment which were discussed in Chapter 9 come into play here for bottom-up criteria, and at the same time a top-down overview can be employed for an impression of musicality.

As an instance of how this can work in practice, let us consider an example of summative assessment of a group composing project being undertaken in a Year 7 KS3 music class. The class are composing music in response to a visual stimulus, a picture of a ruined house in a rural setting. The pupils will work in groups composing their piece of music, and will then perform their resultant compositions to the rest of the class. The assessment criteria for this work need to involve a range of competencies and attainments. A short, but not exclusive, list of assessment areas which the teacher and pupils will be concerned with in this composing project are shown in Table 16.1.

There is a distinction to be made here between those aspects of musical attainment which can be summatively assessed during the process of composing, i.e. those which appertain to the final product, and those for which a combination of process and product would be the most suitable assessment methodology. At this stage we need to make a clear distinction between formative and summative purposes of assessment. In this example the focus of attention, although focused on summative assessment, also needs to take into account an element of formative assessment, in that the teacher will have been

Table 16.1 Assessment areas in composing project

Composing:	Generation
	Organization
	Revision
	Transformation and development
Performing:	Work-in-progress performances
	Instrumental skills
	Control
	Final performance
Listening:	Reviewing
	Evaluating
	Audiation
Group Work:	Awareness
	Responding
	Ensemble-ness
Musicality:	Expressive-ness (in context)
	Feelingful-ness

making formative assessments throughout the composing process. These formative judgements are likely to inform some aspects of the final summative assessment decisions. This therefore becomes an assessment which takes into account the *process* of composing, it is not (possibly erroneously) based solely on the final performance of the piece.

In a similar fashion, there are divisions which can be made between assessments made by the teacher, and peer and self-assessments which can be undertaken by the pupils themselves. Looking back to the model of composing discussed in Chapter 11, Fig. 16.1 shows where these assessment opportunities occur during the process of composing.

It should be noted that although some areas have been labelled as being amenable to peer or self-assessment, the key word here is *straightforward*, and these are aspects of the composing process, and of the finished compositional product where such assessments are least problematic. In the centre of the diagram are those aspects of the composing process where the teacher can be involved. In Chapter 11 this was discussed with relation to formative assessment of the composing process, here these are examples of assessments doing not 'double-duty', but 'treble-duty', in that they take the form of being formative and summative, and also allow for the formative use of summative assessment.

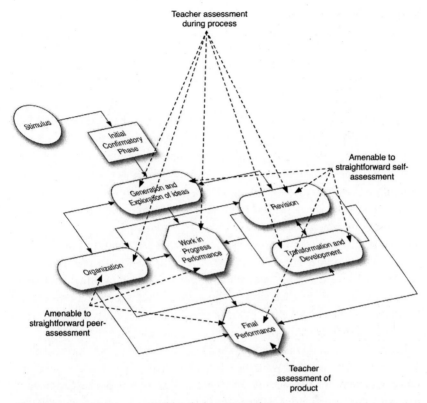

Fig. 16.1 Assessment opportunities during composing

Figure 16.1 uses the model of composing previously investigated in Chapter 11, but in an holistic approach the teacher also needs to consider the roles of performing and listening, and make assessment judgements concerning these too. Listening, as discussed earlier in this chapter, is going to be central to practical music-making activities; this is allied to the way in which the pupils create their own music, which will be via performing their compositions. In this sense listening and performing are integral to the group-composing process, and assessing them separately on an atomistically formulated criterion basis is unlikely to prove helpful. But what can be done is that judgements can be made, by both teacher and pupils, on specific aspects of the work in question. For example:

◆ Are the pupils listening to their work, and making evaluative judgements?

◆ Are they reviewing their work and revising it appropriately?

◆ Are they listening critically?

These may seem like value judgements, and in that case lack closely defined criteria, but this is assessment in response to a complex and multi-faceted task, where listening is but one element amongst many. The same thing is true of performing. Here, as discussed in Chapter 10, assessment of performing will take the form of performing in the service of composing. To this end assessment will be focused on a broad notion of instrumental skill, in that the pupils will be evidencing achievement of their ideas. Important here again will be the notion of intentionality—a pupil may only play one triangle note, but it is the way they do that that matters. Although this can be thought of in terms of the dimensions of *technique* and *intentionality* (which were discussed in the chapter on performing), what can also be assessed is the efficacy of the work in progress performances, and of the final performances, and these are both likely to be top-down assessments

What is missing from Fig. 16.1 is the notion of assessment of musicality. This provides another layer of assessment opportunity to an already complex picture. We have seen that assessment of musicality can be considered as a multidimensional construct, where although it feels as if a value judgement is being made, the resultant effect of the teachers connoisseurship, and the emergent understandings of the pupils, are likely to prove sufficient.

This multiple simultaneous complexity of assessment opportunities needs thinking about in terms of what the teacher will actually do in order to undertake assessment in a manageable fashion, and this is probably best addressed in terms of recording judgements made.

Recording assessments

Having made this complex set of decisions concerning assessment uses and purposes, what will follow are yet more difficult decisions about how these assessment judgements will be recorded. This act, that of recording assessment decisions, is what teachers often mean when they talk about 'doing assessment'; it is the recording of the assessment judgement which can be in many cases the most problematic area. For the purposes of this example, the simplistic threefold grading criteria which has already been explored, of –/=/+, or 'working towards', 'working at', and 'working beyond' will be employed as the basis of recording and grading. This is not to decry the use of five-point or other schemes, the three-point scale has been chosen to simplify illustration of the process. An example of how this can be accomplished in paper or e-markbook format using the parameters discussed so far in this chapter is shown in Fig. 16.2.

This markbook extract has been designed for the group working at their composing task, and has columns for the three areas of assessment judgement,

	Process			Product		
	-	=	+	-	=	+
Composing						
Generation				▓	▓	▓
Organization						
Revision						
Transformation and Development						
Performing						
Work in progress performances				▓	▓	▓
Instrumental Skills						
Control						
Final performance	▓	▓	▓			
Listening						
Reviewing						
Evaluating						
Critical Listening						
Group Work						
Awareness						
Responding						
Ensemble-ness						
Musicality						

Fig. 16.2 Recording holistic assessments

where the minus column indicates that the pupils have not yet achieved expectation in that criterion, the equals column is where they have achieved it, and the plus column shows they have exceeded expectation. The columns are duplicated for both process and product, with some inapplicable areas greyed out, so that the teacher can undertake assessment judgements 'on the hoof', and simply put a tick in the appropriate place. Combining the top-down assessment of musicality, and the bottom-up assessment criteria of the three sub-elements of composing, performing, and listening, gives a holistic view of assessment which combines the two approaches. This reductive approach inevitably loses something between task and assessment, but for the busy teacher, there have to be compromises between reliability, validity, and manageability.

Manageability

Manageability is clearly going to be an issue, with so many assessment criteria involved. Swanwick posits the notion of the 'good-enough' music teacher, observing that, 'Consistent evaluation of music teaching and learning under so many varied conditions becomes problematic and is not susceptible to standardised itemised check-lists' (Swanwick 2008: 12). This is certainly the case for the teacher in this assessment example. We have already seen that assessment is not an exact science (Gipps 1994), and so what we are looking for here is, to use Swanwick's terminology, 'good-enough' assessment. There have been stories of teachers having to deal with an enormous number of assessment criteria simultaneously, and so in the example here, for the teacher to have to manage fewer criteria, but aiming for meaning within the criteria selected, is likely to be of benefit. This can be helped by the notion of *selective assessment*. The teacher should be in command of the assessment process, and so if some aspects of pupil performance have not been observed, this does not of itself mean that the pupils cannot do something, but simply that the teacher has not seen the evidence required. To this end it is entirely legitimate to leave blanks in the assessment grid.

A further aspect of manageability occurs in considering the role of the individual within a group. In this example the assessment made is that of the group, and there is a need to individuate some aspects of this assessment to take account of the performance of an individual pupil. Here, teachers anecdotally report that they often feel that there can be real issues of validity and equanimity in terms of allotment of marks and grades. It would patently be far too labour-intensive to duplicate the assessment grid for each pupil in the class, so what the teacher might want to do here is to employ formative and summative assessment evidence. In order to do this, three sources of evidence can be used: the teacher's own, that of the group in which the pupils were working, and self-assessment of the individual pupil. Recording of formative assessment evidence can take the form of brief comments made by the teacher recorded by the pupils themselves. This places the onus of collection onto the learner. The teacher can jot brief observation notes as they work with the pupils, and use these. Some teachers allocate a separate criterion for the contributory role of each of the pupils in a group, which the pupils themselves decide.

Even with all of these sources of evidence, the use of selective assessment techniques, and getting pupils to record formative comments, there is still the potential for assessment data overload! One way in which this can be addressed is to not assess everyone in the class in the same depth on this composing project. This is not as neglectful as it sounds! What assessments made in this way will do over time is to build up into a series of assessment profiles from which judgements against broader criteria, such as National Curriculum levels, can be made.

The example given for discussion here focuses solely on one composing project, and the assessment judgements made relate to that. It is expected that a project of this nature takes place over a number of lessons, and therefore a number of weeks, so by building in time to obtain a range of assessment evidence, rather than relying solely on final performances, which, as we have seen elsewhere are problematic in many ways, the teacher is in a stronger position to develop assessment profiling which builds up over time.

Differential attainment

A different aspect of the notion of holistic approaches to assessment in music education is that of various areas of pupil attainment, and their relative strengths in each. Music education involves a broad range of topics, of learning and of doing, and encompasses a variety of philosophies. Within this breadth though, a number of commonalities are clear. These have been addressed in this book through chapters on composing, performing, and listening. The balance between weightings of these different aspects will be a matter for regional, local, and individual preferences. Whatever the balance is which is adopted, then any individual pupil is likely to show different levels of attainment in each. Figure 16.3 shows a simplistic rendition of this, using the three principle areas of composing, performing, and listening.

For this pupil, attainment is highest in performing, and lowest in composing. This is an assessment snapshot, taken of a particular pupil at a specific point in a project. It is likely to be the case that each pupil in a class will be at a different level of attainment at any given moment. Knowing this, devising specific focuses for assessment means that the teacher can concentrate on assessing within these main areas. So, having considered a composing example

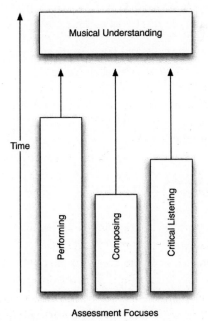

Fig. 16.3 Differing attainment of an individual

previously, let us return to the aspects of assessment which this raised, and consider summatively assessing them from a different perspective.

In Fig. 16.4 a graphical recording method for summative assessment is shown.

What happens here is that the teacher simply marks with a cross where they feel that the pupil is in relation to a notional average expectation. Having decided that summative assessment is not scientific, this assessment recording scheme relies on forming an holistic impression of the work of an individual pupil, and marking where they think the pupil is in relation to this with a cross. To use this over time, teachers use the same grid for each pupil, but use different coloured pens, or put the date by the cross. Some teachers have used overlaying transparencies, such as those from an overhead projector, for the same thing. E-assessment can be readily undertaken in this fashion, using appropriate software. Over time, this will again build up into a graphical representation of a pupil's attainment, and from this the teacher can again extrapolate into wider assessment schemes so as to report on progression.

Assessing understanding

The assessment of composing, listening, and performing as separate activities, and then assembling them together creates a tension in thinking about holistic assessment processes. Another way in which attainment in music can be

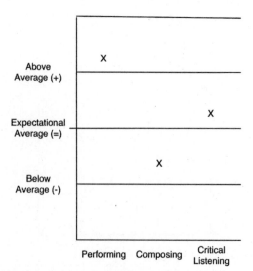

Fig. 16.4 Graphical recording of summative assessment

assessed is by assessing musical understanding. Understanding, according to Bennett Reimer, '. . . is best conceived not as a fixed entity but as a process in ongoing development' (Reimer 2003: 213). Assessing understanding, then, involves making judgements along a continuum. Getting at an individual's personal understanding is difficult, and much music learning in the school is most likely to be evidenced through practical music making. Assessment in this fashion is not concerned with the demonstration of skills in the ways discussed above, but in the learner showing through their music making that they understand something about the music they are playing. To investigate this, let us revisit Fig. 10.1 from Chapter 10, and concentrate specifically on the lower portion of it, adding evidentiary requirements. This revised version is shown in Fig. 16.5.

The right-hand side of Fig. 16.5 shows interlinked outcomes of evidencing musical understanding. These include music making, writing about music, writing music (although this is genre-specific, and includes, but is not solely restricted to, staff notation), and, importantly for pupils, talking about music. Many music teachers have anecdotal evidence of pupils who struggle to write sentences, but have developed insights into music which they are able to evidence orally. The four evidentiary areas will not always apply, as for some classroom work there may be little by way of written evidence, for example, but those which do will feed into assessment judgements. Making a gradation in these judgements is concerned with the extent to which understandings are revealed. This means that a hierarchy of understandings need to be developed. A range of commentators have discussed this issue. Many official publications recommend

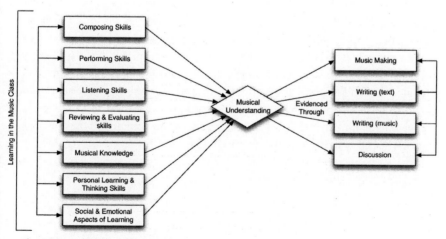

Fig. 16.5 Assessing understanding

Bloom's taxonomy for this, but Bloom places creativity at the top of his taxonomy, and in music we are likely to want pupils to learn through being creative. Swanwick suggests criteria based on sound materials, expressive form, musical form, and valuing (Swanwick 1999: 81), whilst Reese (2003) describes a continuum of directive responses, labelled as being from heuristic to didactic. In England, teachers will want to have some acknowledgement of the model of development adopted by the National Curriculum levels, but avoiding the pitfalls of over-prescription we have discussed before. Taking the first statements from each NC level statement (see Table 7.1 in Chapter 7) would give:

◆ recognize and explore
◆ identify and explore
◆ discriminate between and explore
◆ discriminate between and exploit
◆ discriminate between and develop

Using these as a basic response to emergent understanding accords with statutory requirements, and allows shaded responses to be made. The danger is, as we have seen, that understanding is equated with complexity, whereas the converse may be true, in the fashion of Occam's razor, and that simplicity may be best! Assessment in this fashion becomes a matter of using the evidentiary requirements of Fig. 16.5, and then deciding into which of the five broad headings the work evidenced by the pupil/s work can be placed.

The formative use of summative assessment

So far this chapter has concentrated upon summative assessment. Formative assessment will be taking place all the time, but with regard to the types of assessment being discussed here, teachers are likely to want to make use of their summative assessments in a formative fashion. Tunstall and Gipps (1996) distinguish between formative assessment feedback which specifies attainment, and that which specifies improvement. In the case of the summative assessments we have considered in this chapter, the emphasis has clearly been on attainment, as that is a use of summative assessment. But these assessments are likely to be used in formative fashion too, for target setting, and for focusing pupil attention onto areas which need improvement. This gives a range of four ways in which summative assessment can be used:

◆ Not sharing grades, but providing formative feedback (comment-only assessment)
◆ Sharing grades, but not providing formative feedback

- ◆ Sharing grades and providing formative feedback
  - o Focused on attainment
  - o Focused on improvement
  - o Focused on attainment and improvement (target setting)
- ◆ Not sharing grades or feedback

This list is quite closely linked to the idea of tangible and intangible assessment data which was discussed in Chapter 2. Whichever of these will be chosen is a matter for the teacher to decide, and may vary between projects, pupils, and assessment opportunities. What is useful for the teacher is to think about the information that is produced from the assessment chosen in terms of its informative potential. If it is to help learning, has it been constructed in that way, if it is to audit achievement it may be of limited value in helping improve learning. These decisions impact upon the type of assessment chosen.

Endnote

This chapter has looked at assessment modalities which are very much in the present, and in the complex ontology of the current assessment climate. To end with, the next chapter looks at ways in which assessment could be used in other ways, and at new ways of thinking about assessment in music education.

Chapter 17

The way forward: new developments in assessment

Having looked at a range of ways in which assessment is currently being used, the final chapter of this book turns its attention to ways in which assessment in music education could potentially be used, and how these ways might be of benefit to pupils and teachers.

Assessment and performativity

The drive to improve educational practice has resulted in what has come to be known as the 'standards agenda'. This places performativity at the heart of what schools and teachers do, and finds its most public outworking in league tables of school results. There are tensions between creativity and the standards agenda (Troman et al. 2007), and many teachers have had to find their own ways of working to include creative learning within a culture of performativity (Fautley & Hatcher 2008). In music education, in the UK at least, this has resulted in a variety of approaches to music learning that take assessment as their starting point, and then plan teaching and learning to fit. This pejorative viewpoint may seem a surprising stance in a book championing assessment! However, what has happened is that the servant has taken control of the master, or, as many commentators have observed, the tail of assessment now wags the dog of learning! This is patently wrong, and assessment should be used to fulfil its primary role of helping learning, and, later, of auditing it. Stephen Ball describes how teachers '. . . find their values challenged or displaced by the terrors of performativity' (Ball 2003: 216), and Stronach et al (2002) describe how education is governed in an 'outside-in' fashion, causing issues for professionalism. Teachers, however, cannot move away from this reality by classroom practice alone, and so have to find ways of dealing with it. Bob Jeffrey describes how the performativity agenda is seductive, '. . . because it is possible to be properly passionate about excellence, about achieving peak performance . . .' (Jeffrey 2002: 545), but goes on to warn how it also can dehumanize interpersonal relationships. Music teachers have long worked with assessment, and results have been valorized in, for example public performances and practical instrumental examinations. But the talented few are now measured alongside the many, the general population. This is a new departure in assessment terms, and has brought with it tensions of its own. Performativity cannot be ignored, and so changes to this way of thinking about educational assessment, and allowing the dog to start wagging the tail again, would be warmly welcomed in many areas. However, this lies beyond the remit of music teachers alone, and lies chiefly in the province of legislators and other decision makers. So it is to a discussion of new ways of assessing which music teachers themselves are able to enact that we now turn.

New pedagogy, new assessment

During the late twentieth and early twenty-first centuries, pedagogies of music education have expanded to include a number of areas heretofore excluded from consideration, or not valued in school or assessment settings. These include informal learning, group learning, and personalization of provision. Developments in assessment have followed to some extent these new ways of working, but in many cases have been treated rather in the way of 'bolt-on' accessories, instead of being reconfigured afresh. The example of informal learning provides a case in point. In the UK, the 'Musical Futures'[1] approach is concerned with applying informal learning strategies in classroom settings. Lucy Green, writing from direct involvement with Musical Futures, writes of how although assessment did not form a central focus for research, that teachers '. . . found that they could apply their usual assessment methods to the project' (Green 2008: 184). However, from an evaluative perspective, Hallam et al (2008) reported that there were challenges for assessment in this way of working. Looking at informal learning in music more widely, it can be seen to be the case that a shift has occurred, from teacher to learner, and from teaching to learning (Folkestad 2006). This privileges learning over teaching, and so assessment has to reflect this. What this means is a shift in approach from assessing how much of programme of study learners have absorbed, to how much progress they have made on their own terms. This means that variants of ipsative assessment need to be employed, with pupil progress being self-referentially evaluated against their attainment. What this means for teachers and learners is that personalization of learning assessment is a necessity. In teacher-centred pedagogy, assessment is of how close the learner has come to the expert knowledge imparted by the teacher. In informal learning the learner

---

[1] www.musicalfutures.org.uk

decides what is to be learned. This has the potential for taking some music teachers beyond their comfort zone, especially when some forms of pop and rock music are used. An effect of this is to prioritize self-assessment and peer assessment, with the consequence that formal external valorizations will need to move away from a concern with attainment, and toward one of progress and development. This will involve a significant shift in the way summative assessment is recorded and reported.

Group learning has developed considerably in music in recent years, from group instrumental tuition, via informal learning in groups, to group composing in the classroom. Assessment of group learning and attainment is sometimes built on a model of individual assessment, and endeavours to account for the learning of an individual within a group, often without a consideration of the nature of the group itself. In the real world, as Sawyer observes, '. . . employers are increasingly interested in educational strategies that train students in collaborative group work' (Sawyer 2003: 185). This places music very firmly at the centre of developments in education, and so a challenge for music education is to devise new ways of group assessment which take into account the distinctive nature of corporate endeavour. New pedagogies for collaborative work will therefore need to focus on the ways in which learners interact with each other, as well as the historically important assessed interactions with the teacher, 'A model of pedagogy which reduces analysis to pupil-teacher interaction alone results in a very partial view of processes of social formation in schooling' (Daniels 2001: 175).

The emergence of pupil-pupil interactions is clear in group work in music education, and to help with assessment of this one promising methodology is that of *activity theory*.

Activity theory

One of the problems with looking at conjoint endeavour is that of disentangling the various elements at work within an activity. Activity theory arises from the work of the Russian psychologists Vygotsky, Luria, and Leont'ev (M. Cole 1996), and places the activity itself at the heart of analysis, and looks at the interplay of object, actions, and operations (Nardi 1996). Activity theory involves an interaction between tools, which are referred to as mediating artefacts, the subject, and the object. Tools can be real, such as a flute, or involve cognitive aspects, such as talk. The subject can be an individual, or a group of individuals, and the object in a music lesson will often be the music itself. As Jennie Henley observes:

In its most basic form, the subject is the student, the object is to play a piece of music and this is done through the use of tools such as instruments, musical notation, physical gestures etc. The individual cannot play the music without the instrument, and the instrument cannot play without the student, therefore it is the mediation between the two that fulfils the object of producing the music. (Henley 2008)

Overlaid on these basic interactions, are three further constructs: *rules*, which determine the nature of the activity; *division of labour*; and a notion of *community*. The structure of an activity system, as presented by Yrjö Engeström (1999) is usually represented in the form of a series of interlocking triangles, as shown in Fig. 17.1.

What arises from the activity is the outcome, which is shown in Fig. 17.1 as emerging from the object. What this means for assessment is that each of the areas in the activity triangle can be considered from the perspective of a musical task. Burnard and Younker do this in relation to classroom composing and arranging activities (Burnard & Younker 2008), finding that discourse with regard agreement and solving disagreement was a key informant. For classroom assessment activity theory offers the possibility of teacher and pupil assessments of the various stages undertaken during the course of groupwork task, in other words this can facilitate assessment of process. Taking the various stages of the activity, teachers can think about assessment in the terms shown in Table 17.1.

The *outcome* stage can be assessed by the ways covered in earlier sections of this book; what is new here is the notion of assessing interactions in specific ways

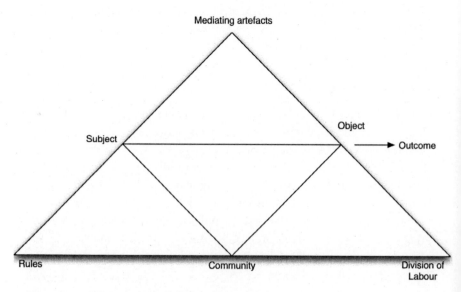

Fig. 17.1 Activity theory (Engeström 1999: 31)

Table 17.1 Activity theory and assessment

Artefacts:	Use of instruments; use of musical constructs (such as 'the elements of music'); use of talk; use of gesture (e.g. starting/ending together)
Subject:	Ways in which learners evidence knowledge
Object:	The music-specific aspects of the task (e.g. composing process)
Rules:	Both emergent ('we'll do it like this') and imposed ('it has to be in ternary form')
Community:	How interactions worked (or didn't) during the creation of the music
Division of labour:	Who played what instrument; who did what in the composing process
Outcome:	The piece of music which emerges form the activity

using the activity theory framework. Assessment is most readily undertaken on a formative basis here, but can also be summative, in the sense that the activity itself can be deconstructed and assessed according to criteria for each component, or holistically as an overview of the process. Self- and peer assessment can also be used here, and assessment judgements can be formulated as a combination of teacher assessment and pupil assessment.

The role of talk is an important one here, as it is in many group learning situations, and as Burnard and Younker found, many aspects of pupil talk reveal important insights into the processes involved in the activity. Foregrounding talk means that, 'Assessment is seen then as an intersubjective accomplishment, brought forward and collaboratively constituted through dialogue, where metasocial and metalinguistic aspects are central to the way it is played out as a social practice . . .' (Crossouard et al. 2004: 4). Assessment as a social practice is a new direction, but in terms of music education is one which is timely. One of the advantages of using activity theory for assessment purposes is that the teacher can concentrate on the group processes involved in the task, and make judgements about each of these separately from judgments concerning the product, the outcome of the process. Assessment can then more neatly be divided between assessment of group process, and that of group product. This fulfils a need in music education to distinguish one from the other.

In music education, activity theory is currently underutilized, but is emerging as an analytical tool, notably in Welch's account of female choristers entering an hitherto all male choir (Welch 2007), Burnard and Younker's account of composing and arranging (Burnard & Younker 2008), and Henley's account of adult instrument learners (Henley 2008).

Privileging formative assessment

A simple way in which assessment can be taken forwards for twenty-first-century pedagogies is by the active promotion and widespread adoption of formative assessment strategies. There is currently a confusion in the minds of many teachers concerning the true nature of formative assessment. For these teachers, the performativity agenda has either downplayed formative assessment, or caused confusion such that they feel they need to provide summative assessment data rather than formative comments. Despite a considerable investment in formative assessment training for teachers, in the UK at least, there are still misconceptions concerning what formative assessment is, and how it can be employed. As Andrew Fowler observes, 'The problem, then, is that we are often required, as professional music teachers, to make comments in summative form more frequently than we would like . . .' (Fowler 2008). Reducing the expectation that music teachers provide summative assessment data from the current situation of over-prescription would make a considerable difference.

Portfolio assessment

The notion of portfolio assessment was introduced in Chapter 14 with regard to e-portfolios. However, it also has a role to play in assessment more generally, when considered alongside the notion of differential attainment as discussed in the previous chapter. Musical understanding involves attainment across a range of competencies, including, as a minimum, composing, listening, and performing. In the UK portfolio assessment is to some extent subsumed within the notion of 'best fit' for ascribing a National Curriculum level to an individual pupil. This involves building up a range of evidence of attainment over time, and in a number of different areas, then deciding how the various strengths in composing, listening, and performing can be tallied and balanced to reach a judgement concerning an appropriate NC level. What portfolio assessment does is to place a range of key pieces of evidence together so that the overall picture of progression can emerge. In music the issue is that many of these pieces of assessment evidence could be intangible, they might be performances, conversations, recordings, composing work, and so on. They can also include work done outside the classroom, playing instruments in garages, composing using computer software, even karaoke singing! All of these are achievements, and all are musical. This makes music a very different subject from many others in school. Pupils are unlikely to have an iPod with their favourite equations on it; they may take part in civil war re-enactments, but are probably more likely to go to a gig; they may go geo-caching, but are more likely to strum at a guitar. Keeping track of pupil attainments is a full-time job, but it will inform assessment, especially assessment of progression.

Assessing progression

The issue of progression in music education is another area where developments in assessment could take place. At present it is not entirely clear what progression in music learning entails. In England there is only one major model, that of National Curriculum levels. As we have seen, this is itself problematic. What reliance on a single model does is to shoehorn every possible aspect of progression into fitting this single pattern. It does not allow for alternative patterns of progression to be explored, does not differentiate clearly and simply between breadth and depth, and treats assessment as unproblematic if the espoused model is followed. The fact that this model is backed by inspection for compliance serves to close down discussion of alternative views of what progression might entail, as such discussions are deemed illegitimate, or worse, never entered into, as the territory has become so forbidden as to be proscribed.

Alternative models of progression which take into account the multifaceted nature of music education would be helpful in opening up the area for discussion. These would include models which allow for aesthetic development, personal interests being followed, mastery of specific genres and styles encouraged, and skill development being unpicked. The possibility of multiple simultaneous models of progression would also be helpful in facilitating teachers to decide what is best for the pupils in their school. Personalization of learning is seen as a key issue in teaching and learning at the moment, and assessment needs to be broad enough to follow this.

Progression is akin to making a journey, and what assessment in music education is not yet proficient at is making evaluative judgements concerning the process of journeying. In my car I have an odometer which records how far I have driven. It does not, of course, evaluate where I have driven to. For example, the odometer could show that I have travelled one hundred miles. This could be a journey in a more-or-less straight line which takes me from, say, Birmingham towards Wales, or it could mean that I have driven round the suburbs, and never left the city. The National Curriculum would seem to value the former, in that distance has been covered, whereas getting to know the immediate locality can be rewarding and important knowledge too. This means that those pupils who undertake journeys in a number of different directions, and do the equivalent of lots of one hundred mile journeys to impressive stately homes, are seen as having made more progress than those pupils who prefer to travel in detail, on foot possibly, around areas of specific local interest. What this means in music is that teachers feel a disparate range of significant musical landmarks have to be covered, and curricula are constructed which read like a 'Grand Tour' of world heritage sites, racing from Gamelan, to Samba, to Waltzes, to film music, and ending up at the Blues. Breathless from this exertion, it is small wonder that progression is hard to define, let alone to measure! For some pupils this might well be appropriate, but for others their knowledge and interests will take them deeper into a smaller number of areas. Of course, part of the role of music education is to show the pupils places that they might not have realized exist, but there may well be points at which it is appropriate to stop and take stock.

For assessment to follow teaching and learning, what this means is that breadth and depth need to be treated as separate items in developmental terms. Again, there is a natural tendency to assume one follows the other, but the key issue here is surely *quality*. What is good about the pupils' music making, and what is distinctive about it? Key Stage 3 in the UK is three years long, how is the pupils' music noticeably different after three years of learning? What makes year 9 music different from year 7 music? This is what a discussion about progression should entail. Once this has been sorted out, then assessment can follow suit. At present this is another area where the tail is firmly in control of the dog!

Endnote

This book began by observing that assessment is a key issue in the current educational climate. The succeeding chapters have discussed and deconstructed a range of approaches to assessment in music education which cover a wide gamut of learning situations. Ultimately the potential power of assessment rests with the key stakeholders, the teachers and learners themselves. It is important that this is where power remains, and that diversions of external data-collection, statistical sampling, and pseudo-scientific demonstrations of progression are not allowed to compromise the fundamental relationship between the teacher and the learner. Music is too important for that!

References

ABRSM (2007), 'The Basis of Jazz Assessment'. <www.abrsm.org/resources/jazz_assess_criteria.pdf>

Adams, P. (2000), 'Assessment in the Music Classroom', in C. Philpott (ed.), *Learning to Teach Music in the Secondary School*; London: RoutledgeFalmer.

Allen, P. (2003), 'Finding the Perfect Song: A Look at Classroom Repertoire', in A. Paterson & E. Bentley (eds.), *Bluebirds and Crows: Developing a Singing Culture In and Out of School*; Matlock: National Association of Music Educators (NAME).

Amabile, T. (1996), *Creativity in Context*; Boulder, CO: Westview Press.

Armstrong, V. (2008), 'Hard Bargaining on the Hard Drive: Gender Bias in the Music Technology Classroom', *Gender and Education*, 20 (4), 375–86.

Asmus, E. P. (1999), 'Music Assessment Concepts', *Music Educators Journal*, 86 (2), 19–24.

Assessment Reform Group (1999), 'Assessment for Learning: Beyond the Black Box', Cambridge: University of Cambridge School of Education.

—— (2002), 'Assessment for Learning: 10 Principles'. <http://k1.ioe.ac.uk/tlrp/arg/publications.html>

Ausubel, D. P. (1961), 'In Defense of Verbal Learning', *Educational Theory*, 11 (1), 15–25.

Ball, S. J. (2003), 'The Teacher's Soul and the Terrors of Performativity', Journal of Education Policy, 18 (2), 215–28.

Bamberger, J. (2006), 'What Develops in Musical Development?', in G. McPherson (ed.), *The Child as Musician: A Handbook of Musical Development*; Oxford: Oxford University Press.

Baxter, A. (2007), 'The Mobile Phone and Class Music: A Teacher's Perspective', in J. Finney & P. Burnard (eds.), *Music Education with Digital Technology*; London: Continuum Press.

Benson, B. E. (2003), *The Improvisation of Musical Dialogue: A Phenomenology of Music Making*; Cambridge: Cambridge University Press.

Bentley, A. (1966), *Musical Ability in Children and its Measurement*; London: Harrap.

Berkley, R. (2001), 'Why is Teaching Composing so Challenging? A Survey of Classroom Observation and Teachers' Opinions', *British Journal of Music Education*, 18 (2), 119–38.

Bernstein, B. (1971a), 'On the Classification and Framing of Educational Knowledge', in M. Young (ed.), *Knowledge and Control*; London: Collier-Macmillan.

—— (1971b), *Class, Codes and Control Vol. 1*; St. Albans: Paladin.

—— (1971/2003), 'On the Classification and Framing of Educational Knowledge', in D. Scott (ed.), *Curriculum Studies Vol. 2: Curriculum Forms*; London: RoutledgeFalmer.

Bharucha, J., Curtis, M., & Paroo, K. (2006), 'Varieties of Musical Experience', *Cognition*, 100 (1), 131–72.

Black, P. & Wiliam, D. (1998a), 'Assessment and Classroom Learning', *Assessment in Education*, 5 (1), 68.

—— (1998b), *Inside the Black Box: Raising Standards through Classroom Assessment*; London: School of Education, King's College.

Black, P., et al. (2003), *Assessment for Learning: Putting it into Practice*; Maidenhead: Open University Press.

—— (2004), 'Working inside the Black Box', *Phi Delta Kappan*, 86 (1), 8–21.

—— (2006), 'Learning How to Learn and Assessment for Learning: A Theoretical Inquiry', *Research Papers in Education*, 21 (2), 119–32.

Blakemore, S.-J. & Frith, U. (2008), 'The Literate Brain', *The Jossey-Bass Reader on the Brain and Learning*; San Francisco: Jossey-Bass.

Bloom, B. S. (1956), *Taxonomy of Educational Objectives, Handbook I: The Cognitive Domain*; New York: David McKay Co. Inc.

Bloom, B. S., Krathwohl, D., & Masia, B. (1964), *Taxonomy of Educational Objectives, Book 2: Affective Domain*, New York: David McKay & Co.

Boden, M. A. (1990), *The Creative Mind: Myths and Mechanisms* (2nd edn); London: Routledge.

Boltz, M. G. (1999), 'The Processing of Melodic and Temporal Information: Independent or Unified Dimensions?', *Journal of New Music Research*, 28 (1), 67–79.

Boud, D. (2000), 'Sustainable Assessment: Rethinking Assessment for the Learning Society', *Studies in Continuing Education*, 22 (2), 151–67.

Bray, D. (2000a), 'An Examination of GCSE Music Uptake Rates', *British Journal of Music Education*, 17 (1), 78–89.

—— (2000b), *Teaching Music in the Secondary School*, Oxford: Heinemann Educational.

—— (2002), 'Assessment in Music Education', in G. Spruce (ed.), *Aspects of Teaching Secondary Music*, London: RoutledgeFalmer.

Bresler, L. (1995), 'Ethnography, Phenomenology and Action Research in Music Education', *Quarterly Journal of Music Teaching and Learning*, 6, 4–17.

Broadfoot, P. (1999), 'Assessment and the Emergence of Modern Society', in B. Moon & P. Murphy (eds.), *Curriculum in Context*; London: Paul Chapman/Open University.

Brocklehurst, J. B. (1962), *Music in Schools*; London: Routledge.

Brophy, T. S. (2000), *Assessing the Developing Child Musician: A Guide for General Music Teachers*, Chicago: GIA Publications.

Brown, A. R. (2007), *Computers in Music Education: Amplifying Musicality*, New York & London: Routledge.

Bruner, J. (1966), *Toward a Theory of Instruction*; Cambridge, MA: Harvard University Press.

—— (1971), *The Relevance of Education*; New York: Norton.

Bunting, R. (2006), *Muslim Music and Culture*; Birmingham: BASS.

Bunting, T. (2002), 'The Place of Composing in the Music Curriculum', in G. Spruce (ed.), *Teaching Music in Secondary Schools: A Reader*; London: RoutledgeFarmer.

Burnard, P. (2000), 'How Children Ascribe Meaning to Improvisation and Composition', *Music Education Research*, 2 (1), 7–23.

—— (2002), 'Investigating Children's Meaning-Making and the Emergence of Musical Interaction in Group Improvisation', *British Journal of Music Education*, 19 (2), 157–72.

—— (2006), 'The Individual and Social Worlds of Children's Musical Creativity', in C. McPherson (ed.), *The Child as Musician: A Handbook of Musical Development*; Oxford: Oxford University Press.

Burnard, P. & Younker, B. A. (2002), 'Mapping Pathways: Fostering Creativity in Composition', *Music Education Research*, 4 (2), 245–61.

—— (2004), 'Problem-Solving and Creativity: Insights from Students' Individual Composing Pathways', *International Journal of Music Education*, 22 (1), 59–76.

—— (2008), 'Investigating Children's Musical Interactions within the Activities Systems of Group Composing and Arranging: An Application of Engeström's Activity Theory', *International Journal of Educational Research*, 47 (1), 60–74.

Byrne, C. (2005), 'Pedagogical Communication in the Music Classroom', in D. Miell, R. MacDonald, & D. Hargreaves (eds.), *Musical Communication*; Oxford: Oxford University Press.

Byrne, C. & Sheridan, M. (1998), 'Music: a Source of Deep Imaginative Satisfaction?', *British Journal of Music Education*, 15 (3), 295–302.

Cain, T. (2004), 'Theory, Technology and the Music Curriculum', *British Journal of Music Education*, 21 (2), 215–21.

Cantwell, R. H. & Jeanneret, N. (2004), 'Developing a Framework for the Assessment of Musical Learning: Resolving the Dilemma of the "Parts" and the "Whole" ', *Research Studies in Music Education*, 22 (2), 2–12.

Chaiklin, S. (2003), 'The Zone of Proximal Development in Vygotsky's Analysis of Learning and Instruction', in A. Kozulin, et al. (eds.), *Vygotsky's Educational Theory in Cultural Context*; Cambridge: Cambridge University Press.

Chandler, D. (2002), *Semiotics: The Basics*; London: Routledge.

Cohen, L., Manion, L., & Morrison, K. (2000), *Research Methods in Education* (5th edn), London & New York: RoutledgeFalmer.

Cole, M. (1996), *Cultural Psychology: A Once and Future Discipline*; Cambridge, MA: Belknap Press of Harvard University.

Cole, M. & Engeström, Y. (1993), 'A Cultural-Historical Approach to Distributed Cognition', in G. Salomon (ed.), *Distributed Cognitions*; Cambridge: Cambridge University Press.

Coll, H. (2002), 'Planning for Transfer and Transition in Music Education', in G. Spruce (ed.), *Teaching Music in Secondary Schools*; London: Routledge/Open University.

Colwell, R. (2002), 'Assessment's Potential in Music Education', in R. Colwell & C. Richardson (eds.), *The New Handbook of Research on Music Teaching and Learning: A Project of the Music Educators National Conference*; Oxford & New York: Oxford University Press.

Cook, N. (1990), *Music, Imagination, and Culture*; Oxford: Clarendon Press.

Cox, G. (2001), 'Teaching Music in Schools: Some Historical Reflections', in C. Philpott & C. Plummeridge (eds.), *Issues in Music Teaching*; London: RoutledgeFalmer.

Craft, A. (2003), 'The Limits to Creativity in Education: Dilemmas for the Educator', *British Journal of Educational Studies*, 51 (2), 113–27.

Cramer, R. (1997), 'What Materials are you Going to Teach "About Music" "Through Music" While "Performing Music"?', in R. Miles (ed.), *Teaching Music through Performance in Band, vol.1*; Chicago: GIA Publications.

Cross, I. (2003), 'Music and Biocultural Evolution', in M. Clayton, T. Herbert, & R. Middleton (eds.), *The Cultural Study of Music: A Critical Introduction*; London: Routledge.

Crossouard, B., Pryor, J., & Torrance, H. (2004), 'Creating an Alternative Assessment Regime with Online Formative Assessment: Developing a Researcher Identity', paper presented at European Conference on Education Research, Crete.

Csikszentmihalyi, M. (1997), 'Assessing Aesthetic Education: Measuring the Ability To "Ward off Chaos" ', *Arts Education Policy Review*, 99 (1), 33–8.

—— (1999), 'Implications of a Systems Perspective for the Study of Creativity', in R. J. Sternberg (ed.), *Handbook of Creativity*; Cambridge: Cambridge University Press.

Curwen, A. J. (1886), *The Teacher's Guide to Mrs. Curwen's Pianoforte Method (The Child Pianist). Being a Practical Course in the Elements of Music*; London: Curwen's Edition.

Daniels, H. (2001), *Vygotsky and Pedagogy*; London: RoutledgeFalmer.

—— (2004), 'Activity Theory, Discourse and Bernstein', *Educational Review*, 56 (2), 121–32.

Davidson, L. & Scripp, L. (1988), 'Young Children's Musical Representations: Windows on Music Cognition', in J. Sloboda (ed.), *Generative Processes in Music*; Oxford: Clarendon Press.

—— (1992), 'Surveying the Coordinates of Cognitive Skills in Music', in R. Colwell (ed.), *Handbook of Research on Music Teaching and Learning*, New York: Oxford University Press.

Deliege, I. & Sloboda, J. (eds.) (1996), *Musical Beginnings*; Oxford: Oxford University Press.

Desforges, C. (2000), 'Learning', in B. Moon, S. Brown, and M. Ben-Peretz (eds.), *Routledge International Companion to Education*; London: Routledge.

DfEE/QCA (1999), *The National Curriculum: Music*; London: HMSO.

DfES (2002), *Training Materials for the Foundation Subjects*; London: DfES.

—— (2004a), *Assessment for Learning: Whole School Training Materials*; Norwich: HMSO.

—— (2004b), *Excellence and Enjoyment: Creating a Learning Culture—Conditions for Learning*; London: DfES.

—— (2006a), 'Secondary National Strategy: Foundation Subjects—KS3 Music. Unit 3: Creative Teaching and Learning in Music', in DfES (ed.), Department for Education and Skills.

—— (2006b), 'Secondary National Strategy: Foundation Subjects—KS3 Music. Unit 1: Structuring Learning for Musical Understanding', in DfES (ed.), Department for Education and Skills.

Dixon, S. (2000), 'Assessing the Performer'. <http://www.palatine.ac.uk/events/viewdoc/207/>, accessed August 2008.

Durrant, C. & Welch, G. (1995), *Making Sense of Music*; London: Cassell.

Edexcel (2006), *Edexcel GCSE in Music*, UG017100: Edexcel.

Elliott, D. (1995), *Music Matters: A New Philosophy of Music Education*; New York: Oxford University Press.

—— (2006), 'Music Education and Assessment: Issues and Suggestions', in P. Taylor (ed.), *Assessment in Arts Education*; Portsmouth, NH: Heinemann.

Engeström, Y. (1999), 'Activity Theory and Individual and Social Transformation', in Y. Engeström, R. Miettenen, & R. L. Punamaki (eds.), *Perspectives on Activity Theory*; Cambridge: Cambridge University Press.

Engeström, Y., Miettenen, R., & Punamaki, R. L. (eds.) (1999), *Perspectives on Activity Theory*, (Cambridge: Cambridge University Press.

Fautley, M. (2004), 'Teacher Intervention Strategies in the Composing Processes of Lower Secondary School Students', *International Journal of Music Education*, 22 (3), 201–18.

—— (2005a), 'A New Model of the Group Composing Process of Lower Secondary School Students', *Music Education Research*, 7 (1), 39–57.

—— (2005b), 'Baseline Assessment of Pupil Composing Competencies on Entry to Secondary School: A Pilot Study', *British Journal of Music Education*, 22 (2), 155–66.

—— (2006), 'Composing at KS3 as Developmental Activity', *NAME (National Association of Music Educators) Journal*, (19).

—— (2007), 'Lost in Translation: The Changed Language of Assessment in Music Education', *NAME (National Association of Music Educators) Journal*, 2–4.

—— (2009), 'Assessment for Learning in Music', in J. Evans & C. Philpott (eds.), *A Practical Guide to Teaching Music in the Secondary School*; Abingdon: Routledge.

Fautley, M. & Hatcher, R. (2008), 'Dissemination of Creative Partnerships Projects'; Birmingham: Birmingham City University.

Fautley, M. & Savage, J. (2007), *Creativity in Secondary Education*, Achieving QTS; Exeter: Learning Matters.

—— (2008), *Assessment for Learning and Teaching in Secondary Schools*, Achieving QTS; Exeter: Learning Matters.

Finney, J. (2000), 'Curriculum Stagnation: The Case of Singing in the English National Curriculum', *Music Education Research*, 2 (2), 203–11.

—— (2006), 'The Possibility of Richer Learning, Poetic Thinking and Musical Understanding', *National Association of Music Educators (NAME) Magazine*, 18 (June).

—— (2007a), 'The Place of Music in the Secondary School', in C. Philpott & G. Spruce (eds.), *Learning to Teach Music in the Secondary School* (2nd edn); Abingdon: RoutledgeFalmer.

—— (2007b), 'Music Education as Identity Project in the Age of Electronic Desire', in J. Finney & P. Burnard (eds.), *Music Education with Digital Technology*; London: Continuum Press.

Fodor, J. (1983), *The Modularity of Mind*; Harvard: MIT Press.

Folkestad, G. (2006), 'Formal and Informal Learning Situations or Practices vs Formal and Informal Ways of Learning', *British Journal of Music Education*, 23 (2), 135–45.

Fowler, A. (2008), 'Assessment—A View from the Classroom', *NAME (National Association of Music Educators) Journal*, 23, 10–12.

Fox, R. (2005), *Teaching and Learning*; Oxford: Blackwell.

Freeman, R. & Lewis, R. (1998), *Planning and Implementing Assessment*; London: Kogan Page.

Frith, S. (1996), 'Music and Identity', in P. Du Gay & S. Hall (eds.), *Questions of Cultural Identity*; London: Sage.

Fritz, C., et al. (2006), 'Perceptual Correlates of Violin Acoustics: Preliminary Studies.', in M. Baroni, et al. (eds.), *9th International Conference on Music Perception & Cognition (ICMPC9)* (Proceedings of the 9th International Conference on Music Perception & Cognition (ICMPC9)), Bologna, Italy: ICMP, 1864–71.

Gardner, H. (1973), *The Arts and Human Development*; New York: John Wiley.

Gardner, H. & Boix-Mansilla, V. (1999), 'Teaching for Understanding in the Disciplines—and Beyond', in J. Leach & B. Moon (eds.), *Learners and Pedagogy*; London: Paul Chapman.

Gardner, J. (2006), *Assessment and Learning*; London: SAGE.

Gibson, J. (1979), *The Ecological Approach to Visual Perception*; Boston, MA: Houghton Mifflin.

Gipps, C. (1994), *Beyond Testing: Towards a Theory of Educational Assessment*, London: Falmer Press.

Glover, J. (2000), *Children Composing 4–14*, London: Routledge Farmer.

Glover, J. & Young, S. (1999), *Primary Music: Later Years*, London: Falmer.

Glover, J. & Scaife, N. (2004), 'All together!: Teaching Music in Groups', in ABRSM (ed.), *All Together!: Teaching Music in Groups*, London: The Associated Board of the Royal Schools of Music.

Goehr, L. (1992), *The Imaginary Museum of Musical Works*, Oxford: Clarendon Press.

Good, J., et al. (1997), 'Measuring Musical Aptitude in Children: On the Role of Age, Handedness, Scholastic Achievement, and Socioeconomic Status', *Psychology of Music*, 25 (1), 57–69.

Gordon, E. (2003), *A Music Learning Theory for Newborn and Young Children*, Chicago: GIA Publications.

Graue, M. (1993), 'Integrating Theory and Practice through Instructional Assessment', *Educational Assessment*, 1 (4), 283–309.

Green, L. (2000), 'Music as Media Art', in J. Sefton-Green (ed.), *Evaluating Creativity*, London: RoutledgeFalmer.

—— (2002), *How Popular Musicians Learn: A Way Ahead for Music Education*, London & New York: Ashgate.

—— (2006), 'Popular Music Education in and for Itself, and for "Other" Music: Current Research in the Classroom', *International Journal of Music Education*, 24 (2), 101.

—— (2008), *Music, Informal Learning and the School: A New Classroom Pedagogy*, Aldershot: Ashgate.

Gruhn, W. & Rauscher, F. (2002), 'The Neurobiology of Music Cognition and Learning', in R. Colwell & C. Richardson (eds.), *The New Handbook of Research on Music Teaching and Learning*, Oxford: Oxford University Press.

—— (2006), 'The Neurobiology of Music Cognition and Learning', in R. Colwell (ed.), *MENC Handbook of Musical Cognition and Development*, New York: Oxford University Press.

Hallam, S. (2001), 'Learning in Music: Complexity and Diversity', in C. Philpott & C. Plummeridge (eds.), *Issues in Music Teaching*, London: RoutledgeFalmer.

—— (2006), *Music Psychology in Education*, London: Institute of Education.

Hallam, S., et al. (2008), 'Survey of Musical Futures for the Paul Hamlyn Foundation'; London: Institute of Education.

Handy, C. B. (1994), *The Empty Raincoat*, London: Hutchinson.

Hargreaves, D. (1986), *The Developmental Psychology of Music*, Cambridge: Cambridge University Press.

Hargreaves, D. & Zimmerman, M. (1992), 'Developmental Theories of Music Learning', in R. Colwell (ed.), *Handbook of Research on Music Teaching and Learning*; New York: Schirmer.

Hargreaves, E. (2005), 'Assessment for Learning? Thinking Outside the (Black) Box', *Cambridge Journal of Education*, 35 (2), 213–24.

Harlen, W. (2005a), 'Teachers' Summative Practices and Assessment for Learning: Tensions and Synergies', *The Curriculum Journal*, 16 (2), 207–23.

—— (2005b), 'Trusting Teachers' Judgement: Research Evidence of the Reliability and Validity of Teachers' Assessment used for Summative Purposes', *Research Papers in Education*, 20 (3), 245–70.

—— (2007), *Assessment of Learning*, London: Sage.

Harlen, W. & James, M. (1997), 'Assessment and Learning: Differences and Relationships between Formative and Summative Assessments', *Assessment in Education*, 4 (3), 365–79.

Harris, D. (2006), *Music Education and Muslims*; Stoke-on-Trent: Trentham Books.

Henley, J. (2008), 'Learn As You Play: Gloucestershire's Adult Ensembles from Scratch', *National Association of Music Educators (NAME) Magazine* (25), 31–5.

Hewitt, A. (2003), 'Levels of Significance Attributed to Musical and Non-Musical Factors of Individual Difference by Classroom Music Teachers', *Research Studies in Music Education*, 20 (1), 48.

—— (2006), 'A Q Study of Music Teachers' Attitudes towards the Significance of Individual Differences for Teaching and Learning in Music', *Psychology of Music*, 34 (1), 63.

Hickey, M. (2003), 'Creative Thinking in the Context of Music Education', in M. Hickey (ed.), *Why and How to Teach Music Composition: A New Horizon for Music Education*; Reston, VA: MENC.

Hickman, R. (2007), '(In Defence of) Whippet-Fancying and Other Vices: Re-evaluating Assessment in Art and Design', in T. Rayment (ed.), *The Problem of Assessment in Art and Design*; Bristol: Intellect Books.

Hirst, P. (1981), 'The Forms of Knowledge Revisited', in S. Brown, J. Fauvel, & R. Finnegan (eds.), *Conceptions of Inquiry*; London: Methuen.

Hodges, R. (2001), 'Using ICT in Music Teaching', in C. Philpott & C. Plummeridge (eds.), *Issues in Music Teaching*; London: RoutledgeFalmer.

James, M. (1998), *Using Assessment for School Improvement*; Oxford: Heinemann Educational.

—— (2006), 'Assessment, Teaching and Theories of Learning', in J. Gardner (ed.), *Assessment and Learning*; London: SAGE.

James, M. & Brown, S. (2005), 'Grasping the TLRP Nettle: Preliminary Analysis and some Enduring Issues Surrounding the Improvement of Learning Outcomes', *Curriculum Journal*, 16 (1), 7–30.

Jeffrey, B. (2002), 'Performativity and Primary Teacher Relations', *Journal of Education Policy*, 17 (5), 531–46.

Johnson, P. (1997), 'Performance as Experience: The Problem of Assessment', *British Journal of Music Education*, 14 (3), 271–82.

Jonassen, D. H., Tessmer, M., & Hannum, W. H. (1999), *Task Analysis Methods for Instructional Design*, Mahwah, NJ & London: Erlbaum Associates.

Juslin, P. N. & Sloboda, J. A. (2001), *Music and Emotion: Theory and Research*, Series in Affective Science; Oxford: Oxford University Press.

Karmiloff-Smith, A. (1992), *Beyond Modularity*; Cambridge, MA: Massachusetts Institute of Technology Press.

Kennell, R. (2002), 'Systematic Research in Studio Instruction in Music', in R. Colwell & C. Richardson (eds.), *The New Handbook of Research on Music Teaching and Learning*; Oxford: Oxford University Press.

Koutsoupidou, T. (2005), 'Improvisation in the English Primary Music Classroom: Teachers', *Music Education Research*, 7 (3), 19.

Krumhansl, C. L. (1990), *Cognitive Foundations of Musical Pitch*; New York: Oxford University Press.

Kutnick, P. & Rogers, C. (1984), 'Groups in Classrooms', in P. Kutnick & C. Rogers (eds.), *Groups in Schools*; London: Cassell.

Kwami, R. M. (2001), 'Music Education in a New Millennium', in A. Loveless & V. Ellis (eds.), *ICT, Pedagogy and the Curriculum: Subject to Change*; London: RoutledgeFalmer.

Lamont, A. (2001), 'Music Psychology and the Secondary Music Teacher', in G. Spruce (ed.), *Teaching Music in Secondary Schools: A Reader*; London: RoutledgeFalmer.

Lamont, A. & Maton, K. (2008), 'Choosing Music: Exploratory Studies into the Low Uptake of Music GCSE', *British Journal of Music Education*, 25 (3), 267–82.

Lave, J. & Wenger, E. (1991), *Situated Learning: Legitimate Peripheral Participation*; Cambridge: Cambridge University Press.

Lehmann, A. C. & Davidson, J. (2002), 'Taking an Acquired Skills Perspective on Music Performance', in R. Colwell & C. Richardson (eds.), *The New Handbook of Research on Music Teaching and Learning*; Oxford: Oxford University Press.

Lerdahl, F. & Jackendoff, R. (1983), *A Generative Theory of Tonal Music*; Cambridge, MA: Massachusetts Institute of Technology Press.

Lines, D. K. (2005), 'Improvisation and Cultural Work in Music and Music Education', in D. K. Lines (ed.), *Music Education for the New Millennium: Theory and Practice Futures for Music Teaching and Learning*, Malden, MA & Oxford: Blackwell Publishing.

Ludlow, L. (1996), 'Psychometrics Lectures'; Boston, MA: Boston College.

MacDonald, R., Hargreaves, D., & Miell, D. (2002), *Musical Identities*; Oxford: Oxford University Press.

Major, A. (2007), 'Talking about Composing in Secondary School Music Lessons', *British Journal of Music Education*, 24 (2), 165–78.

—— (2008), 'Appraising Composing in Secondary-School Music Lessons', *Music Education Research*, 10 (2), 307–19.

MANA—Music Advisers National Association (1986), 'Assessment and Progression in Music Education', MANA.

Mansell, W. (2008), 'Fischer data under growing scrutiny', *Times Educational Supplement* (12/12/08).

Mason, R. & Steers, J. (2007), 'The Impact of Formal Assessment Procedures on Teaching and Learning in Art and Design', in T. Rayment (ed.), *The Problem of Assessment in Art and Design*; Bristol: Intellect Books.

Maugars, C. (2007), 'Formative Assessment in Music Education', *Visions of Research in Music Education*, 9 (1). <http://www-usr.rider.edu/~vrme/v9n1/index.htm>, accessed August 2008.

McCormick, R. & James, M. (1983), *Curriculum Evaluation in Schools*; Beckenham: Croom Helm.

McCormick, R. & Paechter, C. (1999), 'Introduction: Learning and Knowledge Construction', in R. McCormick & C. Paechter (eds.), *Learning and Knowledge*; London: Paul Chapman.

McPherson, G. (2005), 'From Child to Musician: Skill Development during the Beginning Stages of Learning an Instrument', *Psychology of Music*, 33 (1), 5–35.

McPherson, G. & Gabrielsson, A. (2002), 'From Sound to Sign', in R. Parncutt & G. McPherson (eds.), *The Science and Psychology of Music Performance: Creative Strategies for Teaching and Learning*; New York: Oxford University Press.

McPherson, G. & Schubert, E. (2004), 'Measuring Performance Enhancement in Music', in A. Williamon (ed.), *Musical Excellence: Strategies and Techniques to Enhance Performance*; Oxford: Oxford University Press.

McPherson, G. & Davidson, J. (2006), 'Playing an Instrument', in G. McPherson (ed.), *The Child as Musician*; Oxford: Oxford University Press.

Mills, J. (1991a), 'Assessing Musical Performance Musically', *Educational Studies*, 17 (2), 173–81.

—— (1991b), *Music in the Primary School*; Cambridge: Cambridge University Press.

—— (2005), *Music in the School*; Oxford: Oxford University Press.

—— (2007), *Instrumental Teaching*, Oxford Music Education Series; Oxford: Oxford University Press.

MMCP (1970), *Manhattanville Music Curriculum Programme*; New York: Media Materials.

Moon, J. (2004), *A Handbook of Reflective and Experiential Learning: Theory and Practice*; Abingdon: RoutledgeFalmer.

Morrison, R. (1991), 'A Generation Drummed Out', *The Times*, 13/02/1991.

Murphy, R. (2007), 'Harmonizing Assessment and Music in the Classroom', in W. Bresler (ed.), *International Handbook of Research in Arts Education*; Dordrecht, NL: Springer.

Nardi, B. (1996), 'Studying Context: A Comparison of Activity Theory, Situated Action Models, and Distributed Cognition', in B. Nardi (ed.), *Context and Consciousness: Activity Theory and Human-Computer Interaction*; Harvard: MIT Press.

Neesom, A. (2000), *Report on Teachers' Perceptions of Formative Assessment*; London: QCA.

Newton, D. P. (2000), *Teaching for Understanding: What It Is and How To Do It*; London: Routledge.

Ofsted (2003), 'Good Assessment Practice in Music (HMI Document 1479)'; London: Ofsted.

—— (2009), 'Making More of Music'; London: Ofsted.

Paley, W. (1820), *A View of the Evidences of Christianity*; Edinburgh: Edinburgh.

Panaiotidi, E. (2003), 'What is Music? Aesthetic Experience Versus Musical Practice', *Philosophy of Music Education Review*, 11 (1), 71–89.

Paterson, A. & Odam, G. (2000), *The Creative Dream*; High Wycombe: National Association of Music Educators.

Paynter, J. (1982), *Music in the Secondary School Curriculum*; Cambridge: Cambridge University Press.

—— (2002), 'Music in the School Curriculum: Why Bother?', *British Journal of Music Education*, 19 (3), 215–26.

—— (2008), 'Music in the School Curriculum: Why Bother?', in J. Mills & J. Paynter (eds.), *Thinking and Making*; Oxford: Oxford University Press.

Pellegrino, J. W. & Goldman, S. R. (2008), 'Beyond Rhetoric: Realities and Complexities of Integrating Assessment into Classroom Teaching and Learning', in C. A. Dwyer (ed.), *The Future of Assessment: Shaping Teaching and Learning*; New York: Lawrence Erlbaum Associates.

Peretz, I. & Zatorre, R. (2005), 'Brain Organization for Music Processing', *Annual Review of Psychology*, 56 (1), 89–114.

Philpott, C. (2000), 'Musical Learning', in C. Philpott (ed.), *Learning to Teach Music in the Secondary School*; London: RoutledgeFalmer.

—— (2007), 'Assessment in Music Education', in C. Philpott & G. Spruce (eds.), *Learning to Teach Music in the Secondary School* (2nd edn); London: RoutledgeFalmer.

Piaget, J. (1952), *The Origin of Intelligence in the Child*, trans. M. Cook; London: Routledge & Kegan Paul.

Pirsig, R. (1974), *Zen and the Art of Motorcycle Maintenance*; London: Vintage.

Pitts, S. (2000a), 'Reasons to Teach Music: Establishing a Place in the Contemporary Curriculum', *British Journal of Music Education*, 17 (1), 32–42.

—— (2000b), *A Century of Change in Music Education*; Aldershot: Ashgate.

Plummeridge, C. (1999), 'Aesthetic Education and the Practice of Music Teaching', *British Journal of Music Education*, 16 (02), 115–22.

Polanyi, M. (1966), *The Tacit Dimension*; New York: Anchor.

Prensky, M. (2001a), 'Digital Natives, Digital Immigrants', *On the Horizon*, 9 (5), 1–6.

—— (2001b), 'Digital Natives, Digital Immigrants (Part 2): Do They Really Think Differently', *On the Horizon*, 9 (6), 1–6.

Pressing, J. (1984), 'Cognitive Processes in Improvisation', in W. Crozier & A. Chapman (eds.), *Cognitive Processes in the Perception of Art*, Amsterdam, Oxford: North-Holland.

Price, D. (2006), 'Redefining Music Training: Shaping Music Education, an Emerging Vision. Pamphlet 5, Musical Futures Project. The Paul Hamlyn Foundation'.

Priest, P. (2002), 'Putting Listening First: A Case of Priorities', in G. Spruce (ed.), *Aspects of Teaching Secondary Music*; London: RoutledgeFalmer.

Proctor, C. (1965), *The Class Music Teacher*; London: Herbert Jenkins.

QCA (2007), 'Music—Programme of Study: Key Stage 3'. <www.qca.org.uk/curriculum>, accessed 26/7/07.

—— (2008a), 'Music Key Stage 3'. <http://curriculum.qca.org.uk/key-stages-3-and-4/subjects/music/index.aspx>

—— (2008b), 'Assessing Pupils' Progress—Assessment at the Heart of Learning'. <www.qca.org.uk/assessment>

Raney, K. & Hollands, H. (2000), 'Art education and talk—From modernist silence to postmodern chatter.' In Sefton-Green, J. (ed.) *Evaluating Creativity*, London, Routledge.

Reay, D. & Wiliam, D. (1999), ' "I'll Be a Nothing": Structure, Agency and the Construction of Identity Through Assessment', *British Educational Research Journal*, 25 (3), 343–54.

Reese, S. (2003), 'Responding to Student Compositions', in M. Hickey (ed.), *Why and How to Teach Music Composition: A New Horizon for Music Education*; Reston, VA: MENC.

Regelski, T. A. (2005), 'Curriculum: Implications of Aesthetic versus Praxial Philosophies', in D. J. Elliott (ed.), *Praxial Music Education. Reflections and Dialogues*, 219–48.

Reimer, B. (1970), *A Philosophy of Music Education*; New Jersey: Prentice Hall.

—— (1986), 'David Elliott's "New" Philosophy of Music Education: Music for Performers Only', *Bulletin of the Council for Research in Music Education*, 128, 59–89.

—— (2003), *A Philosophy of Music Education: Advancing the Vision* (3rd edn); New Jersey: Pearson Education.

Roth, W.-M. (1999), 'Authentic School Science', in R. McCormick & C. Paechter (eds.), *Learning & Knowledge*; London: Paul Chapman.

Ryle, G. (1949), *The Concept of Mind*; Harmondsworth: Penguin Books.

Sadler, D. (1989), 'Formative Assessment and the Design of Instructional Systems', *Instructional Science*, 18, 119–44.

Salaman, W. (1983), *Living School Music*; Cambridge: Cambridge University Press.

Salomon, G. (1993a), 'No Distribution Without Individuals' Cognition: A Dynamic Interactional View', in G. Salomon (ed.), *Distributed Cognitions*; Cambridge: Cambridge University Press.

—— (ed.), (1993b), *Distributed Cognitions*; Cambridge: Cambridge University Press.

Savage, J. (2002), 'New Models for Creative Practice with Music Technologies', in D. Harris & A. Paterson (eds.), *How Are You Doing? Learning and Assessment in Music*; Matlock: National Association of Music Educators.

—— (2003), 'Informal Approaches to the Development of Young People's Composition Skills', *Music Education Research*, 5 (1), 81–5.

—— (2005), 'Working Towards a Theory for Music Technologies in the Classroom: How Pupils Engage with and Organise Sounds with New Technologies', *British Journal of Music Education*, 22 (2), 167–80.

—— (2006), *Meeting the Needs of your Most Able Students in Music*; London: David Fulton.

—— (2007a), 'Is Musical Performance Worth Saving? The Importance of Musical Performance in Teaching and Learning', in G. Spruce & C. Philpott (eds.), *Learning to Teach Music in the Secondary School* (2nd edn); London: Routledge.

—— (2007b), 'Pedagogical Strategies for Change', in J. Finney & P. Burnard (eds.), *Music Education with Digital Technology*; London: Continuum Press.

Sawyer, R. K. (2003), *Group Creativity. Music, Theater, Collaboration*; Mahwah, NJ: Lawrence Erlbaum.

Schools Council (1968), *Enquiry 1: Young School Leavers*; London: HMSO.

Scruton, R. (1996), 'Review of Simon Frith: *Performing Rites: On the Value of Popular Music*', *The Times* (24/10/96).

Seddon, F. (2006), 'Collaborative Computer-Mediated Music Composition in Cyberspace', *British Journal of Music Education*, 23 (3), 273.

—— (2007), 'Music E-Learning Environments: Young People, Composing and the Internet', in J. Finney & P. Burnard (eds.), *Music Education with Digital Technology*; London: Continuum.

Sefton-Green, J. (2000), *Evaluating Creativity*; London: Routledge.

Sfard, A. (1998), 'On Two Metaphors for Learning and the Dangers of Choosing Just One', *Educational Researcher*, 27 (2), 4–13.

Shepard, L. (1997), 'The Centrality of Test Use and Consequences for Test Validity', *Educational Measurement: Issues and Practice*, 16 (2), 5–13.

—— (2000), 'The Role of Classroom Assessment in Teaching and Learning'; Los Angeles, CA: Center for the Study of Evaluation, National Center for Research on Evaluation, Standards, and Student Testing Graduate School of Education & Information Studies. University of California, Los Angeles.

Shepherd, J., et al. (1977), *Whose Music? A Sociology of Musical Languages*; London: Transaction Books.

Shulman, L. (1986), 'Those Who Understand: Knowledge Growth in Teaching', *Educational Research Review*, 57 (1), 4–14.

—— (1993), 'Those Who Understand: Knowledge Growth in Teaching', in A. Pollard & J. Bourne (eds.), *Teaching and Learning in the Primary School*; London: Routledge.

Shuter-Dyson, R. & Gabriel, C. (1981), *The Psychology of Musical Ability* (2nd edn); London: Methuen.

Silverman, M. (2009), 'Rethinking Music "Appreciation" ', *Visions of Research in Music Education*, 14. <www-usr.rider.edu/~vrme/>, accessed February 2009.

Sink, P. (2002), 'Behavioral Research on Direct Music Instruction', in R. Colwell & C. Richardson (eds.), *The New Handbook of Research on Music Teaching and Learning*; Oxford: Oxford University Press.

Sloboda, J. (1985), *The Musical Mind*; Oxford: Oxford University Press.

—— (2005), *Exploring the Musical Mind*; Oxford: Oxford University Press.

Small, C. (1998), *Musicking: The Meanings of Performing and Listening*; Hanover NH: University Press of New England.

Spruce, G. (2001a), 'Music Assessment and the Hegemony of Musical Heritage', in C. Philpott & C. Plummeridge (eds.), *Issues in Music Teaching*; London: RoutledgeFalmer.

—— (2001b), 'Planning for Music Teaching and Learning', in G. Spruce (ed.), *Aspects of Teaching Secondary Music: Perspectives on Practice*; London: RoutledgeFalmer.

—— (2002), 'Assessment in the Arts: Issues of Objectivity', in G. Spruce (ed.), *Teaching Music in Secondary Schools: A Reader*; London: RoutledgeFalmer.

—— (2008), 'The Implications of the KS2 Music CPD Programme and Whole Class Instrumental and Vocal Teaching, for Teacher Educators', Trinity Guildhall/The Open University.

Stanley, M., Brooker, R., & Gilbert, R. (2002), 'Examiner Perceptions of Using Criteria in Music Performance Assessment', *Research Studies in Music Education*, 18 (1), 46–56.

Stephens, J. (2003), 'Imagination in Education: Strategies and Models in the Teaching and Assessment of Composition', in M. Hickey (ed.), *Why and How to Teach Music Composition: A New Horizon for Music Education*; Reston, VA: MENC.

Stobart, G. (2008), *Testing Times: The Uses and Abuses of Assessment*; Abingdon: Routledge.

Stronach, I., et al. (2002), 'Towards an Uncertain Politics of Professionalism: Teacher and Nurse Identities in Flux', *Journal of Education Policy*, 17 (1), 109–38.

Swanwick, K. (1979), *A Basis for Music Education*; Windsor: NFER-Nelson.

—— (1988), *Music, Mind, and Education*; London: Routledge.

—— (1994), *Musical Knowledge: Intuition, Analysis and Music Education*; London: Routledge.

—— (1996), 'Music Education: Is There Life Beyond Schools?', *Finnish Journal of Music Education*, 1 (1), 41–5.

—— (1997), 'Assessing Musical Quality in the National Curriculum', *British Journal of Music Education*, 14 (3), 205–15.

—— (1998), 'The Perils and Possibilities of Assessment', *Research Studies in Music Education*, 10 (1), 1–11.

—— (1999), *Teaching Music Musically*; London: Routledge.

—— (2008), 'The "Good-Enough" Music Teacher', *British Journal of Music Education*, 25 (1), 9–22.

Swanwick, K. & Taylor, D. (1982), *Discovering Music*; London: Batsford.

Swanwick, K. & Tillman, J. (1986), 'The Sequence of Musical Development: A Study of Children's Compositions', *British Journal of Music Education*, 3 (3), 305–9.

Taetle, L. & Cutietta, R. (2002), 'Learning Theories as Roots of Current Musical Practice and Research', in R. Colwell & C. Richardson (eds.), *The New Handbook of Research on Music Teaching and Learning*; New York: Oxford University Press.

Tan, S.-L., Wakefield, E. M., & Jeffries, P. W. (2009), 'Musically Untrained College Students' Interpretations of Musical Notation: Sound, Silence, Loudness, Duration, and Temporal Order', *Psychology of Music*, 37 (1), 5–24.

Temperley, D. (2001), *The Cognition of Basic Musical Structures*; Harvard: MIT Press.

Terry, P. (1994), 'Musical Notation in Secondary Education: Some Aspects of Theory and Practice', *British Journal of Music Education*, 11 (2), 99–111.

TGAT (1988), *Task Group on Assessment and Testing: A Report*; London: DES.

Thomas, R. B. (1970), *MMCP Synthesis: A Structure for Music Education*; Bardonia, NY: Media Materials Inc.

Thompson, W. F. & Schellenberg, E. G. (2006), 'Listening to Music', in R. Colwell (ed.), *MENC Handbook of Musical Cognition and Development*; New York: Oxford University Press.

Thorndike, E. L. (1921), 'Measurement in Education', *Teachers College Record*, 22, 371–79.

Troman, G., Jeffrey, B., & Raggl, A. (2007), 'Creativity and Performativity Policies in Primary School Cultures', *Journal of Education Policy*, 22 (5), 549–72

Tunstall, P. & Gipps, C. (1996), 'Teacher Feedback to Young Children in Formative Assessment', *British Educational Research Journal*, 22 (4).

Vispoel, W. (1999), 'Creating Computerized Adaptive Tests of Music Aptitude: Problems, Solutions, and Future Directions', in F. Drasgow & J. Olson-Buchanan (eds.), *Innovations in Computerized Assessment*; Mahwah, NJ: Lawrence Erlbaum Associates.

von Glasersfeld, E. (1989), 'Cognition, Construction of Knowledge, and Teaching', *Synthese*, 80 (1), 121–40.

Vygotsky, L. (1978), *Mind in Society*; Cambridge, MA: Harvard University Press.

—— (1987), 'Thinking and Speech', in R. W. Rieber & A. S. Carton (eds.), *The Collected works of L. S. Vygotsky*; New York & London: Plenum.

Wallas, G. (1926), *The Art of Thought*; London: Watts.

Watkins, C. (2001), 'Learning about Learning Enhances Performance', *Research Matters*, 13 (2).

Webster, P. (2003), ' "What Do You Mean, Make My Music Different?" Encouraging Revision and Extensions in Children's Music', in M. Hickey (ed.), *Why and How to Teach Music Composition: A New Horizon for Music Education*; Reston, VA: MENC.

Weeden, P., Winter, J., & Broadfoot, P. (2002), *Assessment: What's in it for Schools?*, What's in it for Schools?; London & New York: RoutledgeFalmer.

Weisberg, R. (1999), 'Creativity and Knowledge: A Challenge to Theories', in R. Sternberg (ed.), *Handbook of Creativity*; Cambridge: Cambridge University Press.

Welch, G. (1994), 'The Assessment of Singing', *Psychology of Music*, 22 (1), 3–19.

—— (2001a), *The Misunderstanding of Music*; London: Institute of Education.

—— (2001b), 'United Kingdom', in D. Hargreaves & A. North (eds.), *Musical Development and Learning: The International Perspective*; London: Continuum.

—— (2006), 'Singing and Vocal Development', in G. McPherson (ed.), *The Child as Musician*; Oxford: Oxford University Press.

—— (2007), 'Addressing the Multifaceted Nature of Music Education: An Activity Theory Research Perspective', *Research Studies in Music Education*, 28 (1), 23.

Welch, G. & Howard, D.M. (2002), 'Gendered Voice in the Cathedral Choir', *Psychology of Music*, 30 (1), 102–20.

Wiliam, D. (2000a), 'The Meanings and Consequences of Educational Assessments', *Critical Quarterly*, 42 (1), 105–27.

—— (2000b), 'Integrating Summative and Formative Functions of Assessment', *Keynote Address to the European Association for Educational Assessment*, Prague, Czech Republic.

—— (2001), 'What is Wrong with our Educational Assessment and What Can be Done About it?', *Education Review*, 15 (1), 57–62.

Wiliam, D. & Black, P. (1996), 'Meanings and Consequences: A Basis for Distinguishing Formative and Summative Functions of Assessment?', *British Educational Research Journal*, 22 (5), 537–48.

Wiliam, D. & Thompson, M. (2008), 'Integrating Assessment with Learning: What Will It Take to Make It Work', in C.A. Dwyer (ed.), *The Future of Assessment: Shaping Teaching and Learning*; New York: Lawrence Erlbaum Associates.

Wilkinson, H. (1996), 'You Can't Separate Blur from Schubert', *The Independent* (9/2/96).

Wood, D., Bruner, J., & Ross, G. (1976), 'The Role of Tutoring in Problem Solving', *Journal of Child Psychology and Psychiatry*, 17, 89–100.

Woodford, P. (2005), *Democracy and Music Education: Liberalism, Ethics, and the Politics of Practice*; Bloomington, IN: Indiana University Press.

Wright, P. (2002), 'ICT in the Music Curriculum', in G. Spruce (ed.), *Teaching Music in Secondary Schools*; London: RoutledgeFalmer.

Young, M. (ed.), (1971), *Knowledge and Control*; London: Collier-Macmillan.

Younker, B. (2000), 'Thought Processes and Strategies of Students Engaged in Music Composition 1', *Research Studies in Music Education*, 14 (1), 24.

Index

This index is in letter-by-letter order. Page numbers in *italics* indicate figures and diagrams; those in **bold** indicate tables.